OFFICIAL SQA PAST PAPERS WITH ANSWERS

STANDARD GRADE | GENERAL | CREDIT

MODERN STUDIES
2006-2009

SQA

BrightRED PUBLISHING

First exam published in 2006.
Published by Bright Red Publishing Ltd, 6 Stafford Street, Edinburgh EH3 7AU
tel: 0131 220 5804 fax: 0131 220 6710 info@brightredpublishing.co.uk www.brightredpublishing.co.uk

ISBN 978-1-84948-022-2

A CIP Catalogue record for this book is available from the British Library.

Bright Red Publishing is grateful to the copyright holders, as credited on the final page of the book, for permission to use their material. Every effort has been made to trace the copyright holders and to obtain their permission for the use of copyright material. Bright Red Publishing will be happy to receive information allowing us to rectify any error or omission in future editions.

STANDARD GRADE | GENERAL

2006

[BLANK PAGE]

G

2640/402

NATIONAL QUALIFICATIONS 2006

MONDAY, 22 MAY
10.20 AM–11.50 AM

MODERN STUDIES STANDARD GRADE
General Level

1 Read every question carefully.

2 Answer all questions as fully as you can.

3 If you cannot do a question, go on to the next one. Try again later.

4 In question 3, answer **one** section only; Section (A) The USA **or** Section (B) Russia **or** Section (C) China.

5 Write your answers in the answer book provided. Indicate clearly, in the left hand margin, the question and section of question being answered. Do not write in the right hand margin.

SCOTTISH QUALIFICATIONS AUTHORITY

SYLLABUS AREA 1—LIVING IN A DEMOCRACY

QUESTION 1

(*a*) *Trade union members have rights and responsibilities.*

Describe **one** right and **one** responsibility that a trade union member has.

(Knowledge & Understanding, **4** marks)

(*b*) Study Sources 1 and 2 below, then answer the question which follows.

SOURCE 1

Workers who are Trade Union Members (%)		
Year	***Male***	***Female***
1999	27·3	27·1
2001	26·6	27·1
2003	25·5	27·2

SOURCE 2

Trade Union Membership in Different Jobs (%)				
Type of Job	***1998***		***2002***	
	Males	***Females***	***Males***	***Females***
Managers and Administrators	18	21	16	22
Secretarial	30	22	31	23
Sales and Customer Services	18	12	13	13

Write down **two** conclusions about the membership of trade unions.

You must **only** use the information above.

You should write **one** conclusion about **each** of the following.

- Changes in male **or** female trade union membership between 1999 and 2003
- Changes in male **and** female trade union membership **in one of the jobs** between 1998 and 2002

(Enquiry Skills, **4** marks)

QUESTION 1 (CONTINUED)

(*c*) Study the information below, then answer the question which follows.

TRADE UNIONS AND THE SCOTTISH LABOUR PARTY

- Labour has the largest number of MSPs in the Scottish Parliament.
- A committee of the Labour Party in Scotland, which has trade union representatives on it, writes policies on which the Labour Party fights elections.
- Some trade unions give money to and campaign for Labour Party candidates in elections.
- Many MSPs who were elected at the 2003 election were not members of trade unions.
- A quarter of a million Scottish voters are members of trade unions.
- Trade unionists do not need to vote for the Labour Party in Scotland.

Trade unions play an important part in the election of Labour MSPs. Trade unions also play a part in policy making for the Labour Party.

View of Anne Hall

Give **two** reasons to **support** the view of Anne Hall.

(Enquiry Skills, **4** marks)

(*d*) *Local councillors and MSPs are representatives who work on behalf of people in their area.*

Choose **ONE** of the following representatives:

- local councillors
- MSPs.

Describe **two** ways in which *the representative you have chosen works on behalf of people in their area.*

(Knowledge & Understanding, **4** marks)

[Turn over

SYLLABUS AREA 2—CHANGING SOCIETY

QUESTION 2

(*a*) Many elderly people live in their own homes. Some of these homes have been adapted to meet their needs.

Give **two ways** in which homes can be adapted to meet the needs of some elderly people.

For **each** way, explain how it meets their needs.

(Knowledge & Understanding, **4** marks)

(*b*) Study Sources 1 and 2 below, then answer the question which follows.

SOURCE 1

Goodbye Geriatrics – Hello Geri-actives

Older people today have decided to become "Geri-actives" in their retirement. They want to enjoy new experiences. What these "Geri-actives" plan to do in retirement varies greatly. Their top six plans for "life after work" are gardening (60%), meeting friends (58%), travelling (57%), painting (14%), golf (11%) and writing novels (9%). Paying for these new activities may cost a lot of money. Arranging to have a good pension and saving as much as possible are essential for people nearing retirement.

SOURCE 2

The Percentage of Grandmothers who . . .

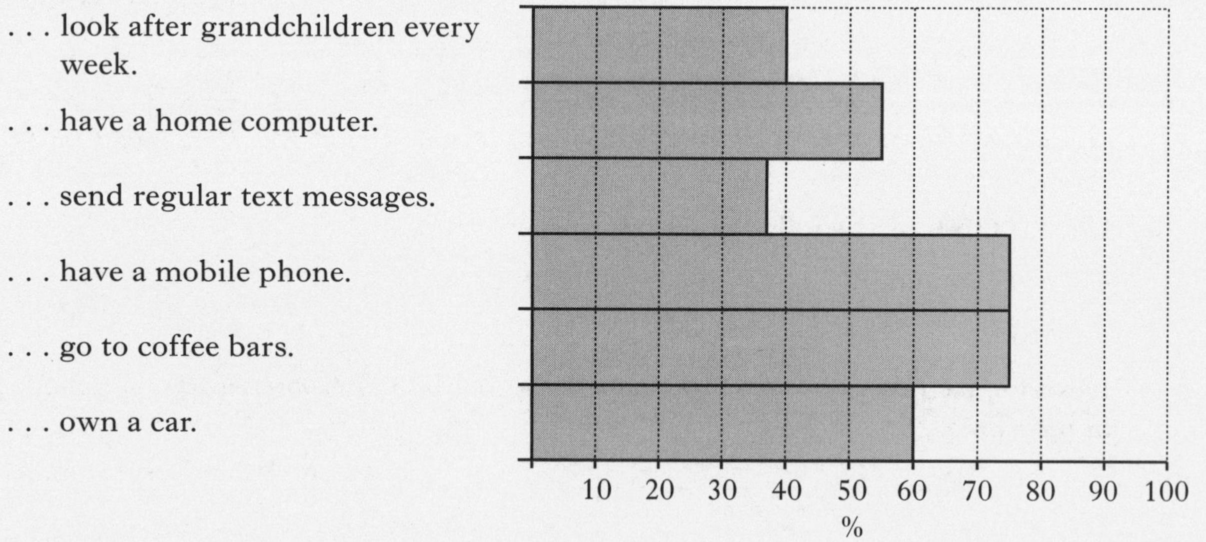

There are more elderly people today than ever before. Most grandmothers use very little technology. When most people retire, they just want to meet friends, travel and play golf. Elderly people should have a good pension.

View of Dennis Baxter

Using **only** Sources 1 and 2 above, write down **two** statements made by Dennis Baxter that are **exaggerated**.

Using the information in the Sources, give **one** reason why **each** of the statements you have chosen is **exaggerated**.

(Enquiry Skills, **4** marks)

QUESTION 2 (CONTINUED)

You are investigating the topic in the box below.

Local groups that help the elderly.

Answer questions (*c*), (*d*), (*e*) and (*f*) which follow.

(*c*) As part of the **Planning Stage**, give **two** relevant aims for your investigation.

(Enquiry Skills, 2 marks)

You decide to collect information about **local groups that help the elderly**.

(*d*) Give **two** relevant **ways** to gather information to help in your investigation.

(Enquiry Skills, 2 marks)

(*e*) For **one** of these ways, explain why it is a **good** way to get information to help in your investigation.

(Enquiry Skills, 2 marks)

You have been asked to develop your investigation. You decide to find out about a **national organisation** which helps the elderly.

You see the following advert in a newspaper.

Study the advert carefully, then answer the question which follows.

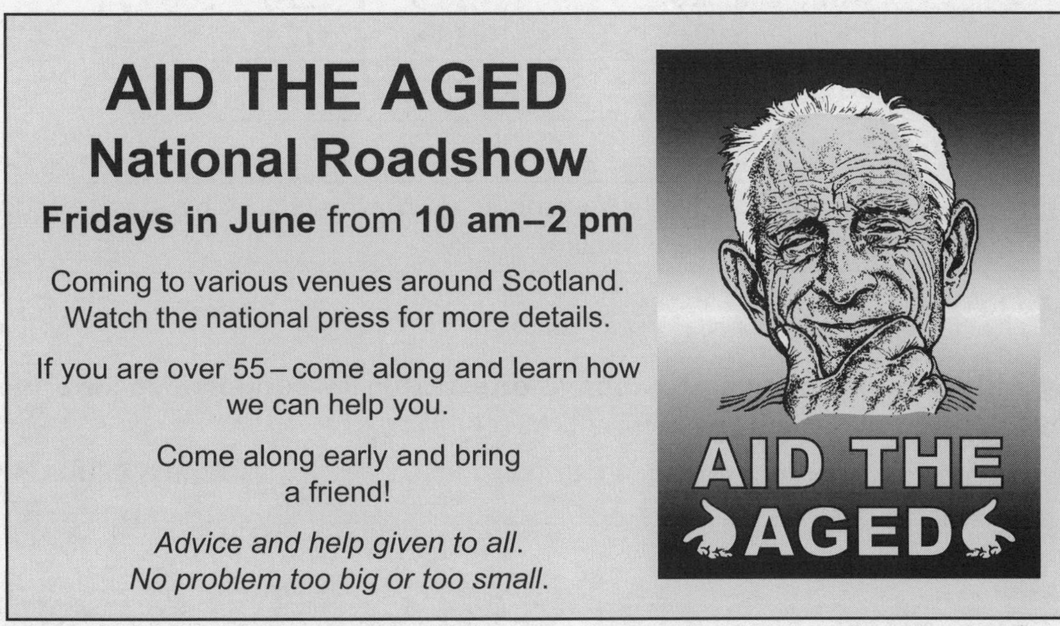

(*f*) You decide to visit the Aid The Aged National Roadshow to collect more information to help in your investigation.

Using **only** the information in the advert above, give **one difficulty** you might have in visiting this roadshow.

(Enquiry Skills, 2 marks)

SYLLABUS AREA 3—IDEOLOGIES

QUESTION 3

Answer **ONE** section only: Section (A)—The USA on pages *six* to *eight*
OR Section (B)—Russia on pages *nine* to *eleven*
OR Section (C)—China on pages *twelve* to *fourteen*

(A) **THE USA**

(*a*) *The American people can use the media to criticise the government.*

Describe **two** ways that *the American people can use the media to criticise the government.* In your answer you **must** use American examples.

(Knowledge & Understanding, **4** marks)

(*b*) Study the information below, then answer the question which follows.

Cigarette Smoking amongst selected Groups in the USA (%)

	1990	**2001**
All Males	28·0	24·7
White Males	27·6	24·9
Black Males	32·8	27·6
All Females	22·9	20·8
White Females	23·5	22·1
Black Females	20·8	17·9
US Average	25·3	22·7

In the USA, men are less likely to smoke than women. The smallest drop in smoking has been amongst white females.

View of Nancy Holstein

Using **only** the information above, give **one** reason to **support** and **one** reason to **oppose** the view of Nancy Holstein.

(Enquiry Skills, **4** marks)

QUESTION 3 (A) (CONTINUED)

(*c*)

In recent years, many members of ethnic minority groups in the USA have seen an improvement in their standards of living.

Give **two** reasons to explain why *many members of ethnic minority groups in the USA have seen an improvement in their standards of living.*

In your answer you **must** use American examples.

(Knowledge & Understanding, **4** marks)

[Turn over

QUESTION 3 (A) (CONTINUED)

(*d*) Study the Timeline below, then answer the question which follows.

TIMELINE – WAR ON TERROR

KEY EVENTS 2001–2005

Date	Event
September 11 2001	Nearly 3000 people are killed when 2 airliners are hijacked by Al Qaeda terrorists and are crashed into the World Trade Centre in New York.
October 2001	American and allied troops invade Afghanistan to remove the Taliban government and destroy Al Qaeda forces in that country.
February 2003	Khalid Mohammed, a suspected terrorist and chief planner of the September 11 attacks, is captured in Pakistan.
March 2003	Thousands of US troops and their allies invade Iraq to remove the government of Saddam Hussein. He is accused of helping terrorist groups and of making weapons of mass destruction.
December 2003	Saddam Hussein is captured near Baghdad. It is expected that he will be charged with many crimes.
July 2005	Terrorist bombs explode on a bus and on a number of underground passenger trains in the city of London. Many people are killed and injured.

Since September 11 2001, US troops have only invaded one country. In that time terrorists have killed more innocent people. America is the only country to suffer from terrorist attacks. Some important people have been captured in the war against terror.

Statements by an American Journalist

Using **only** the information above, write down **two** statements made by the American Journalist which are **exaggerated**.

Using the Timeline, give **one** reason why **each** of the statements you have chosen is **exaggerated**.

(Enquiry Skills, **4** marks)

NOW GO TO QUESTION 4 ON PAGE FIFTEEN

QUESTION 3 (CONTINUED)

(B) **RUSSIA**

(*a*) *The Russian people can use the media to criticise the government.*

Describe **two** ways that *the Russian people can use the media to criticise the government.*

In your answer you **must** use Russian examples.

(Knowledge & Understanding, **4** marks)

(*b*) Study the information below, then answer the question which follows.

Salaries of People in selected Occupations in Russia

Average Salary (US Dollars)			
Occupation	***2002***	***2003***	***% Change***
Financial Controller	500	650	+30
IT Company Director	3000	4500	+50
Lawyer	1750	2100	+20
Personnel Director	1250	2000	+60
Sales Manager	400	900	+125
Secretary	300	325	+8
Training Manager	750	1050	+40

Jobs in IT and the Law have the highest salaries. These jobs have also seen the biggest change in salaries between 2002 and 2003.

View of Natalia Medvedev

Using **only** the information above, give **one** reason to **support** and **one** reason to **oppose** the view of Natalia Medvedev.

(Enquiry Skills, **4** marks)

[Turn over

QUESTION 3 (B) (CONTINUED)

(*c*)

People living in the major cities tend to have a better standard of living than those living in other parts of Russia.

Give **two** reasons why *people living in the major cities tend to have a better standard of living than those living in other parts of Russia.*

In your answer you **must** use Russian examples.

(Knowledge & Understanding, **4** marks)

QUESTION 3 (B) (CONTINUED)

(*d*) Study the Timeline below, then answer the question which follows.

TIMELINE – CHECHNYA

KEY EVENTS 2000–2004

Date	Event
May 2000	President Putin of Russia declares that Chechnya will be ruled directly from Moscow. He is determined to defeat the Chechen rebels by all means available to him.
November 2001	Official talks take place between Russian authorities and Chechen rebels on a possible peace settlement. Talks break up without agreement.
December 2001	A captured rebel Chechen army commander is sentenced to life imprisonment by a court in Moscow.
October 2002	Chechen rebels seize a theatre in Moscow, the Russian capital, and hold 800 people hostage. 120 hostages are killed by the rebels when Russian forces storm the building. Most of the rebels are then killed by the Russian troops in the battle which follows.
March 2003	Russian people are pleased with the result of the ballot in Chechnya which shows a majority of Chechens in favour of remaining part of Russia.
May 2004	Recently elected President of Chechnya, Akhmad Kadyrov, killed in a bomb blast carried out by Chechen rebels.

It is the Chechen rebels who have carried out all the killings. Elections have taken place in Chechnya. Important politicians on both sides have been directly involved in the war. A settlement between the two sides is within reach.

Statements by a Russian Journalist

Using **only** the information above, write down **two** statements made by the Russian Journalist, which are **exaggerated**.

Using the Timeline, give **one** reason why **each** of the statements you have chosen is **exaggerated**.

(Enquiry Skills, **4** marks)

NOW GO TO QUESTION 4 ON PAGE FIFTEEN

QUESTION 3 (CONTINUED)

(C) **CHINA**

(*a*) *The Chinese people are not allowed to criticise the government.*

Describe **two** actions which the Chinese Government might take to deal with those who do criticise the government.

In your answer you **must** use Chinese examples.

(Knowledge & Understanding, **4** marks)

(*b*) Study the information below, then answer the question which follows.

Population with Internet Access in selected Countries (%)

Country	*2003*	*2004*	*2005*
China	8	10	25
USA	43	47	54
Russia	15	17	24
Japan	48	51	53
UK	40	42	46

China has always had the lowest Internet access of all the world's major countries. However, it is showing the fastest growth.

View of Li Tie

Using **only** the information above, give **one** reason to **support** and **one** reason to **oppose** the view of Li Tie.

(Enquiry Skills, **4** marks)

QUESTION 3 (C) (CONTINUED)

(*c*)

People living in the major cities tend to have a better standard of living than those living in other parts of China.

Give **two** reasons why *people living in the major cities tend to have a better standard of living than those living in other parts of China.*
In your answer you **must** use Chinese examples.

(Knowledge & Understanding, **4** marks)

[Turn over

QUESTION 3 (C) (CONTINUED)

(*d*) Study the Timeline below, then answer the question which follows.

TIMELINE–THE THREE GORGES DAM PROJECT

KEY EVENTS 1992–2009

Date	Event
1992	Work starts on the dam. The project is expected to take 17 years to complete and will open in 2009.
February 1993	20 000 people start work around the clock on the dam. 250 000 people will have had jobs building the dam by the time it is finished.
July 1993	Journalist Dai Qing is jailed for ten months for criticising the project. Over the next year, hundreds of others are also jailed by the Chinese government.
1999	The government begins an inquiry into safety at the site after 40 workers are killed in an accident.
2003	The Chinese government claims that only 1·2 million people will lose their homes when the valley is flooded. Some people claim it will be 2 million.
2009	Over 100 million people will have electricity for the first time when the dam is finished.

The Three Gorges Dam is a huge building project. Every Chinese person will benefit when the project is finished. Electricity will improve the lives of many Chinese people. Everyone in China supports the project.

Statements by a Chinese Journalist

Using **only** the information above, write down **two** statements made by the Chinese Journalist which are **exaggerated**.

Using the Timeline, give **one** reason why **each** of the statements you have chosen is **exaggerated**.

(Enquiry Skills, **4** marks)

NOW GO TO QUESTION 4 ON PAGE FIFTEEN

SYLLABUS AREA 4—INTERNATIONAL RELATIONS

QUESTION 4

(*a*) **United Nations Specialised Agencies**

Food and Agricultural Organisation

United Nations Children's Fund

World Health Organisation

Choose **one** of the UN Specialised Agencies above.

Describe **two** ways in which the agency you have chosen tries to meet the **needs** of people in Africa.

(Knowledge & Understanding, **4** marks)

(*b*) Study Sources 1 and 2 below, then answer the question which follows.

SOURCE 1

United Nations Press Release
A large number of people have been forced to leave their homes and over 50 000 have been killed in the Darfur region of Sudan since 2003. Darfur itself is a very dry area in the west of Sudan, the largest country in Africa. There has been conflict between black Africans and Arabs in the region for many years. Due to this there is a lack of aid and children are now dying of hunger.

SOURCE 2

Sudanese Government Press Release
Darfur is a desert area in the west of the largest country in Africa, Sudan. It is well known that there is fighting between the Arabs and black Africans in Darfur which has caused many deaths. Our country needs more money to be able to develop. However, everybody has enough to eat. A large number of people have chosen to leave their homes in Darfur and move to other countries such as Chad.

Sources 1 and 2 give different views about **what has been happening in the Darfur region of Sudan**.

Write down **two** differences between these views.

You **must** only use information from the Sources above.

(Enquiry Skills, **4** marks)

[Turn over for Questions 4(*c*) and 4(*d*) on *Page sixteen*

QUESTION 4 (CONTINUED)

(*c*)

TIED AID – SOME FACTS

- Tied aid cuts the value of aid by 25–40%.
- The United Kingdom is one of only four countries stopping tied aid.
- 60–75% of Canadian aid is tied.
- The USA, Germany, Japan and France still insist on most of their aid being "tied".
- The USA makes sure that 80c in every dollar is returned to the USA.
- The USA insists that anti-AIDS drugs are bought from the USA instead of cheaper products from South Africa, India or Brazil.

Give **two** reasons why some rich countries give tied aid to countries in Africa.

(Knowledge & Understanding, **4** marks)

(*d*) Study the information below, then answer the question which follows.

Selected Statistics for three African Countries in 2004			
	Benin 	Kenya 	Nigeria 
Infant deaths (per 1000 live births)	85	62	70
Life expectancy (years)	51	45	50
HIV/AIDS in adult population (%)	1·9	6·7	5·4
Population below poverty line (%)	37	50	60
Literacy rate (%)	41	85	68
Voting age (years)	18	18	18

Statements made by Alison Grey, Aid Worker

- Benin has a smaller percentage of its population living in poverty than either Kenya or Nigeria.
- Nigeria has the highest rate of HIV/AIDS amongst adults.
- Infant deaths are lowest in Benin.
- The literacy rate in all three countries is very similar.
- Life expectancy is lowest in Kenya.

Using **only** the information above, write down **two** statements made by Alison Grey which are **correct**.

Using the information, give **one** reason why **each** of the statements you have chosen is **correct**.

(Enquiry Skills, **4** marks)

[*END OF QUESTION PAPER*]

STANDARD GRADE | CREDIT

2006

[BLANK PAGE]

C

2640/403

NATIONAL QUALIFICATIONS 2006

MONDAY, 22 MAY
1.00 PM – 3.00 PM

MODERN STUDIES STANDARD GRADE
Credit Level

1 Read every question carefully.

2 Answer all questions as fully as you can.

3 If you cannot do a question, go on to the next one. Try again later.

4 In question 3, answer **one** section only: Section (A) The USA **or** Section (B) Russia **or** Section (C) China.

5 Write your answers in the answer book provided. Indicate clearly, in the left hand margin, the question and section of question being answered. Do not write in the right hand margin.

SCOTTISH QUALIFICATIONS AUTHORITY

SYLLABUS AREA 1—LIVING IN A DEMOCRACY

QUESTION 1

(*a*) *Candidates rely on help from party workers and volunteers during election campaigns.*

Describe, **in detail**, the ways in which party workers and volunteers can help during election campaigns.

(Knowledge & Understanding, **6** marks)

(*b*) *In a democracy, it is important that people use their right to vote.*

Explain, **in detail,** why it is important for people to use their **right** to vote.

(Knowledge & Understanding, **4** marks)

You have been asked to carry out **two** investigations.

The first investigation is on the topic in the box below.

Voting systems used in elections in Scotland.

Now answer questions (*c*) and (*d*) which follow.

(*c*) State a relevant **hypothesis** for your investigation.

(Enquiry Skills, **2** marks)

(*d*) Give **two** relevant **aims** to help you prove or disprove your hypothesis.

(Enquiry Skills, **2** marks)

QUESTION 1 (CONTINUED)

The second investigation is on the topic in the box below.

Peoples' attitude towards voting.

Now answer questions (*e*) and (*f*) which follow.

(*e*) While collecting information for your investigation, you find the following survey result.

Question: Can people influence political decisions by voting?	
Age	**% saying yes**
16–19	17
20–29	26
30–39	25
40–49	27
50–64	25
65+	22
Source: Home Office Citizenship Survey: (Statistics Directorate), September 2004 [based on 9600 replies, UK wide]	

Give **two** detailed reasons why the above survey is a **good** source of information to use in your investigation.

(Enquiry Skills, **4** marks)

(*f*) You then decide to collect more information by carrying out your own survey about peoples' attitude to voting in your local area.

Give **one other relevant** question which you could include in your survey.

(Enquiry Skills, **2** marks)

[Turn over

SYLLABUS AREA 2—CHANGING SOCIETY

QUESTION 2

(*a*) **Recent Government Policies to improve Employment Opportunities**

new deal

Skillseekers

jobcentreplus

ema Education Maintenance Allowance

MODERN APPRENTICESHIPS

Choose **two** policies from the list above.

Describe, **in detail**, the ways in which each policy has tried to improve employment opportunities.

(Knowledge & Understanding, **6** marks)

QUESTION 2 (CONTINUED)

(*b*) Study Sources 1 and 2 below, then answer the question which follows.

SOURCE 1

Households by type in Scotland, 1981–2003 (%)			
	1981	**1991**	**2003**
Single Adult	7·2	12·9	15·9
Pensioner (single or couple)	28·9	29·8	30·8
Couple no children	28·4	27·1	26·7
Single Parent with children	2·3	4·9	5·8
Couple with children	33·2	25·3	20·8

SOURCE 2

Selected Scottish households living in poverty (%)

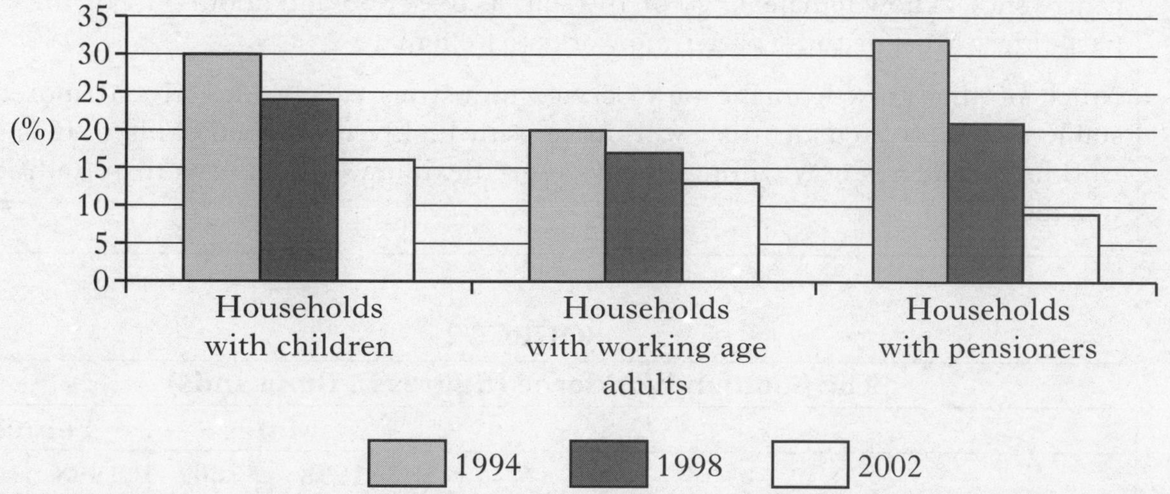

> Households consisting of pensioners have grown the most in percentage terms. However, they have experienced less of an improvement in the quality of their lives than other groups.

View of Sandy Mathieson

Give **two** reasons to **oppose** the view of Sandy Mathieson.

(Enquiry Skills, **4** marks)

[Turn over

QUESTION 2 (CONTINUED)

(*c*) Study Sources 1, 2, 3 and 4 below and opposite, then answer the question which follows.

SOURCE 1

Scotland – a country in industrial change

The traditional male dominated production and construction industries in Scotland are all in decline. In 2000, Scotland only had 35 000 working in oil, gas and fishing, traditionally some of Scotland's key industries. The new growth industries in Scotland are all service industries such as call centres, Biotechnology, Software and e-Business.

A new service industry which has grown in Scotland is call centres. In 1998, Scotland's call centre industry employed 16 000 workers, of which 42% were women. By 2000, this figure had grown to 37 000. Five years on, there are 60 000 people employed in them. Considerable growth is predicted in the industry and of the 290 call centres, 92 predict increased employment by 2007. Around 67% of Scottish call centre staff is now female. 75% of the staff is under 35 and about 33% of the staff is part-time. Most of these part-time workers are female.

Much of this growth in the new service industries can be directly attributed to a stable and motivated Scottish workforce with highly developed skills. It is also a workforce which is now willing to have more flexible work patterns than traditionally was the case.

SOURCE 2

The Scottish Workforce (figures in thousands)

	Males		Females	
	1998	**2002**	**1998**	**2002**
Agriculture, Forestry and Fishing	31	29	8	8
Production and Construction Industries				
Construction	113	108	24	14
Energy and Water	37	32	9	9
Manufacturing	227	189	99	74
Service Industries				
Banking, Finance and Insurance	156	187	170	191
Distribution, Hotels and Catering, Repairs	214	238	289	308
Public Administration, Education and Health	163	176	394	458
Transport and Communication	86	93	28	32
Other Services	52	62	54	63
Total employed	**1079**	**1114**	**1075**	**1157**

QUESTION 2(*c*) (CONTINUED)

SOURCE 3

Working conditions – Number of part-time workers in Scotland (000s)

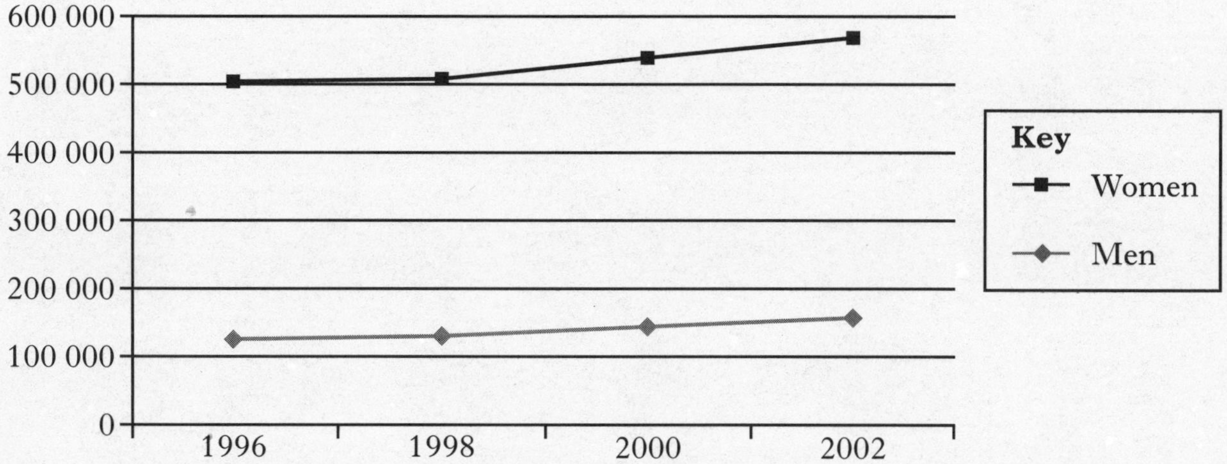

SOURCE 4

Working conditions – Female earnings as a percentage (%) of male earnings

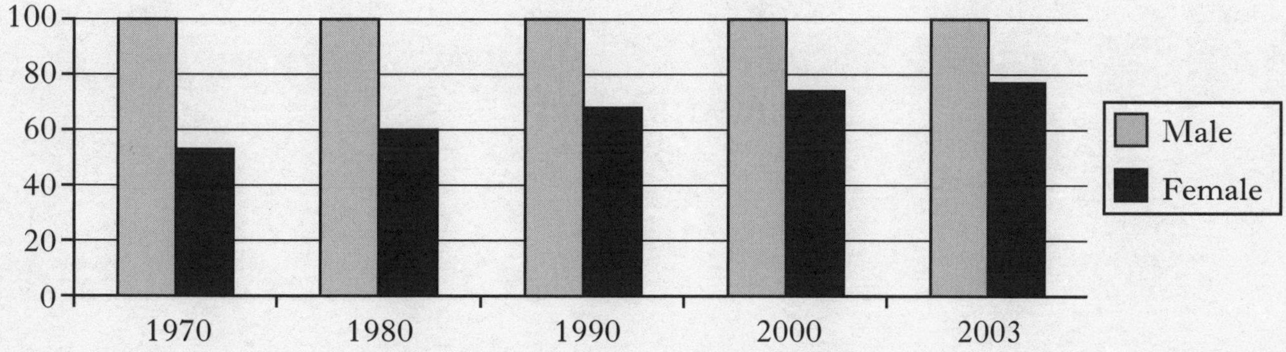

Women are becoming more important to the Scottish economy in the 21st century. Furthermore, this is reflected in the changes in their pay and conditions.

View of Tom Anderson

Using **only** Sources 1, 2, 3 and 4, explain **the extent to which** Tom Anderson could be accused of being **selective in the use of facts**.

(Enquiry Skills, **8** marks)

[Turn over

[BLANK PAGE]

SYLLABUS AREA 3—IDEOLOGIES

QUESTION 3

Answer **one** section only: Section (A)—The USA on pages *nine* to *eleven*
OR Section (B)—Russia on pages *thirteen* to *fifteen*
OR Section (C)—China on pages *seventeen* to *nineteen*

(A) **THE USA**

(*a*) *In the USA, citizens have both political rights and the responsibilities that go with them.*

Describe, **in detail**, the ***political rights*** *of American citizens and the* ***responsibilities*** *that go with them.*

In your answer you **must** use American examples.

(Knowledge and Understanding, **8** marks)

[Turn over

QUESTION 3 (A) (CONTINUED)

(*b*) Study Sources 1, 2, 3 and 4 and the information on New York City, then answer the question which follows.

Information about New York City

Population of the 5 New York Boroughs

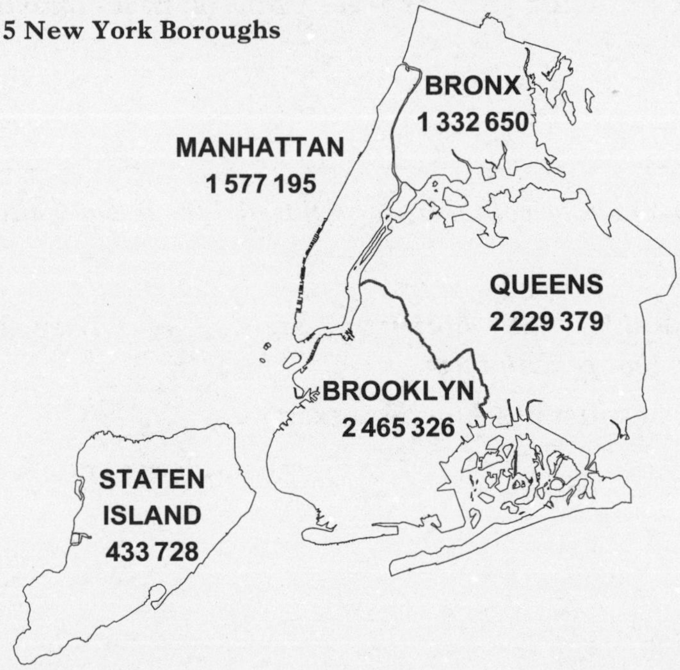

New York has a population of 8 008 278, which makes it America's largest city.
It has experienced a 10% increase in its population since 1990.
It is a city with a great mix of different races, nationalities and cultures.
The city is itself divided into five Boroughs: The Bronx, Brooklyn, Manhattan, Queens and Staten Island.

Racial Composition of Population in New York City		
White	2 801 267	35·0%
Hispanic	2 160 554	27·0%
Black	1 962 154	24·5%
Asian/Pacific Islanders	783 058	9·8%
Native Americans	17 321	0·2%
Other	283 924	3·5%

SOURCE 1

New York Boroughs: Population in 2000 by Race (%)

	Bronx	Brooklyn	Manhattan	Queens	Staten Island
White	14·5	34·6	45·8	32·9	71·3
Hispanic	48·4	19·8	27·2	25·0	12·1
Black	31·2	34·4	15·3	19·0	8·9
Asian/Pacific Islanders	2·9	7·5	9·4	17·5	5·6
Native Americans	0·3	0·2	0·2	0·3	0·1
Others	2·7	3·5	2·1	5·3	2·0

QUESTION 3 (A) (*b*) (CONTINUED)

SOURCE 2

New York Boroughs: Educational Attainment in 2000 by those aged 25+ (%)

	Did not complete High School	College Graduate
Bronx	38	15
Brooklyn	31	22
Manhattan	21	49
Queens	26	24
Staten Island	17	23

SOURCE 3

New York Boroughs: Crime Rate in 2000 (per 100 000 people)

	Person Crime	Property Crime	Total
Bronx	1112	2369	3481
Brooklyn	1024	2134	3158
Manhattan	895	3822	4717
Queens	583	2079	2662
Staten Island	332	1400	1732

SOURCE 4

New York Boroughs: Family Finances and Poverty Statistics in 2000

	Average Household Income ($)	Families in Poverty (%)
Bronx	28 000	27
Brooklyn	32 000	22
Manhattan	48 000	18
Queens	42 000	12
Staten Island	55 000	8

Using **only** the information about New York City and Sources 1, 2, 3, 4 above and opposite, what **conclusions** can be drawn about the ways in which the Boroughs are different from each other, and from the city as a whole?

You must **make** and **justify** a conclusion about **each** of the following headings.

- The Borough whose racial composition is **least** like that of the city as a whole
- The relationship between person crime rates and educational attainment
- The relationship between race and family finances
- The desirability of Manhattan as a Borough to live in

(Enquiry Skills, **8** marks)

[NOW GO TO QUESTION 4 ON PAGE 21]

[BLANK PAGE]

QUESTION 3 (CONTINUED)

(B) **RUSSIA**

(*a*) *In Russia, citizens have both political rights and the responsibilities that go with them.*

Describe, **in detail**, the ***political rights*** *of Russian citizens and the* ***responsibilities*** *that go with them.*

In your answer, you **must** use Russian examples.

(Knowledge and Understanding, **8** marks)

[Turn over

QUESTION 3 (B) (CONTINUED)

(*b*) Study Sources 1, 2, 3 and 4 and the information on Russia, then answer the question which follows.

Information about Russia

Russia is the biggest country in Asia with a total population of 144 million and a labour force of 72 million. It has large deposits of coal, natural gas, oil and many other valuable minerals. Russia is one of the major economic powers in the world. Its economy has grown fast since the end of Communist rule in 1991. It earns billions of dollars from oil and petrol exports and has a total GDP of $1282 billion. Russia relies on trade with several neighbouring countries and it sells over 16% of its exports to, and buys 19% of its imports from, just five of its neighbours.

Urban/Rural Divide

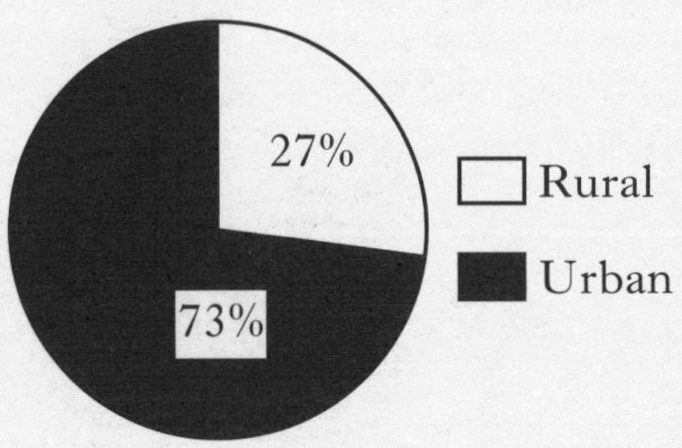

Russia and its neighbours

Economic Information		
Sector	**Employment (%)**	**Contribution to Wealth of Country (%)**
Agriculture	12	5
Industry	24	35
Services	64	60

SOURCE 1

Selected Countries: Trade with Russia (%)

	Imports from Russia	Exports to Russia
Japan	1·7	3·1
Mongolia	33·9	6·5
Kazakhstan	34·9	15·5
Norway	2·4	2·5
North Korea	2·1	8·1

QUESTION 3 (B) (*b*) (CONTINUED)

SOURCE 2

Urban/Rural Divide in some of Russia's neighbours (%)

	Urban	Rural
Japan	79	21
Mongolia	57	43
Kazakhstan	56	44
Norway	75	25
North Korea	61	39

SOURCE 3

Employment in different sectors of the economy for some of Russia's neighbours (%)

	Agriculture	Industry	Services
Japan	5	25	70
Mongolia	79	6	15
Kazakhstan	20	30	50
Norway	4	22	74
North Korea	36	48	16

SOURCE 4

Contribution of each sector to the GDP for some of Russia's neighbours (%)

	Agriculture	Industry	Services
Japan	1	26	73
Mongolia	20	21	59
Kazakhstan	8	37	55
Norway	2	36	62
North Korea	30	34	36

Using **only** the information on Russia and Sources 1, 2, 3, 4 above and opposite, what **conclusions** can be drawn about the relationship between **Russia and her neighbours**?

You must **make** and **justify** a conclusion about **each** of the following headings.

- The urban/rural divide in Russia compared with some of her neighbours
- The relationship between the urban/rural divide and employment in agriculture
- The relationship between employment in services and their contribution to GDP
- The importance of Russia to the economies of the neighbouring countries

(Enquiry Skills, **8** marks)

[NOW GO TO QUESTION 4 ON PAGE 21]

[BLANK PAGE]

QUESTION 3 (CONTINUED)

(C) **CHINA**

(*a*) *The Communist government in China gives citizens certain rights. In return, citizens are expected to accept their responsibilities.*

Describe, **in detail**, the ***rights*** *that Chinese citizens have and the* ***responsibilities*** *that go with them.*

In your answer, you **must** use Chinese examples.

(Knowledge and Understanding, **8** marks)

[Turn over

QUESTION 3 (C) (CONTINUED)

(*b*) Study Sources 1, 2, 3 and 4 and the information on China, then answer the question which follows.

Information about China

China is the second biggest country in Asia with a total population of 1·3 billion and a labour force of 744 million. It has large deposits of coal, natural gas, oil and many other valuable minerals. The government in China has turned the country into the major economic power in the region with the fastest growing economy in the world. China relies on trade with several countries in the region and has a total GDP of $6449 billion. It sells almost 21% of its exports to, and buys 25% of its imports from, just five of its neighbours.

China and its neighbours

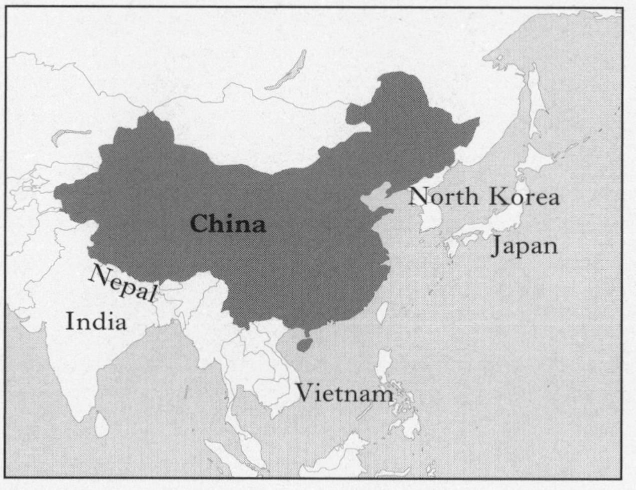

Urban/Rural Divide

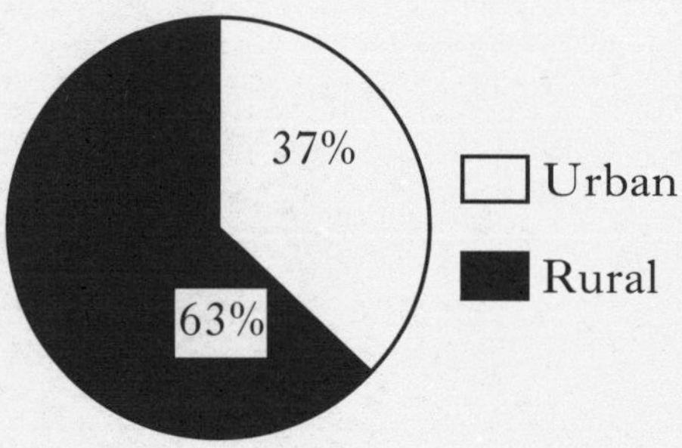

Economic Information

Sector	Employment (%)	Contribution to wealth of country (%)
Agriculture	50	15
Industry	22	53
Services	28	32

SOURCE 1

Selected Countries: Trade with China (%)

	Imports from China	Exports to China
Japan	19·7	12·1
India	4·5	6·3
Vietnam	13·6	6·2
Nepal	13·5	0·5
North Korea	39·7	28·4

QUESTION 3 (C) (*b*) (CONTINUED)

SOURCE 2

Urban/Rural Divide in some of China's neighbours (%)

	Urban	Rural
Japan	79	21
India	28	72
Vietnam	25	75
Nepal	12	88
North Korea	61	39

SOURCE 3

Employment in different sectors of the economy for some of China's neighbours (%)

	Agriculture	Industry	Services
Japan	5	25	70
India	60	17	23
Vietnam	63	23	14
Nepal	81	3	16
North Korea	36	48	16

SOURCE 4

Contribution of each sector to the GDP for some of China's neighbours (%)

	Agriculture	Industry	Services
Japan	1	26	73
India	24	28	48
Vietnam	22	40	38
Nepal	40	20	40
North Korea	30	34	36

Using **only** the information on China and Sources 1, 2, 3, 4 above and opposite, what **conclusions** can be drawn about the relationship between **China and her neighbours**?

You must **make** and **justify** a conclusion about **each** of the following headings.

- The urban/rural divide in China compared with some of her neighbours
- The relationship between the urban/rural divide and employment in agriculture
- The relationship between employment in services and their contribution to GDP
- The importance of China to the economies of the neighbouring countries

(Enquiry Skills, **8** marks)

[NOW GO TO QUESTION 4 ON PAGE 21]

[BLANK PAGE]

SYLLABUS AREA 4—INTERNATIONAL RELATIONS

QUESTION 4

(*a*) *In recent years some European countries and their allies have expanded their military actions beyond Europe.*

Explain, **in detail**, the reasons why *some European countries and their allies have expanded their military actions beyond Europe*.

In answering this question, you must refer to:

- A description of some of these actions.
- The reasons why such actions were taken.

Your answer **must** refer to recent examples you have studied.

(Knowledge & Understanding, **8** marks)

[Turn over

QUESTION 4 (CONTINUED)

(*b*) Study Sources 1, 2, 3 and 4 below and opposite, then answer the question which follows.

THE GREAT EUROPEAN DEBATE

SOURCE 1

Membership of the European Union (EU)

1958 Belgium, France, W Germany, Luxembourg, Italy and the Netherlands
1973 Denmark, Ireland and the UK
1981 Greece
1986 Portugal and Spain
1995 Austria, Finland and Sweden
2004 Cyprus, the Czech Republic, Estonia, Hungary, Latvia, Lithuania, Malta, Poland, Slovakia and Slovenia.

For the future, Bulgaria, Croatia, Romania and Turkey still wish to join the EU.

Opinion Poll carried out in selected countries
Question: If the EU were scrapped, how would you feel?

	Unhappy (%)	Delighted (%)	Don't care (%)	Don't know (%)
Belgium	29	7	53	11
Finland	22	28	41	9
Germany	30	14	40	16
Ireland	44	3	34	19
UK	16	27	45	12
EU average	28	14	45	13

The 2004 elections for the European Parliament highlighted many issues of importance to the people of Europe. Just over 44% of the 350 million eligible voters in 25 member states cast their ballots, making this one of the biggest democratic exercises in the world.

Many pro-Europeans had great hopes for the new member countries in these elections but only 20% of the electorate in Poland voted, despite the huge amount of EU funding the country is likely to receive over the next few years. The Poles, along with the majority of EU voters, rejected the party in government, using this as a protest vote about domestic issues.

SOURCE 2: Percentage of votes gained by selected parties in UK elections for the European Parliament (1999 and 2004)

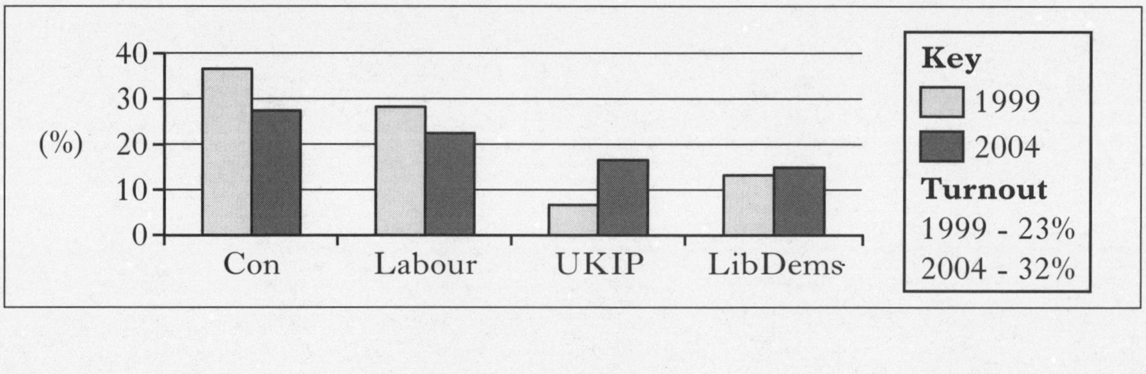

QUESTION 4 (*b*) (CONTINUED)

SOURCE 3: Attitude of selected political parties towards the European Union

SOURCE 4: Results of an Opinion Poll

Question: If there were a referendum on whether Britain should stay in or get out of the EU, how would you vote?

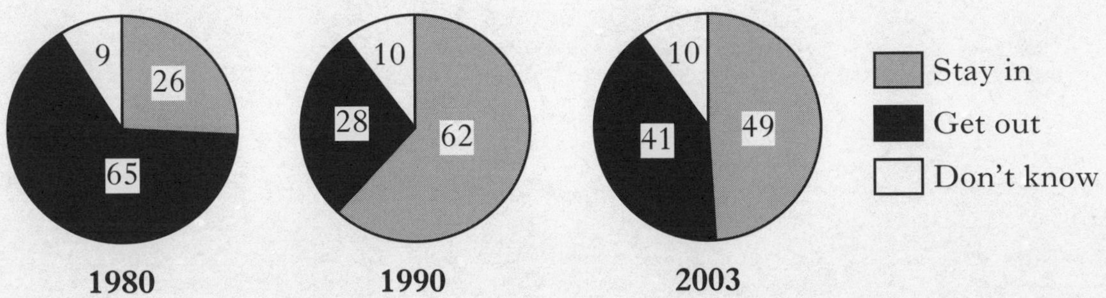

People in Britain and in other European countries no longer wish to be part of the European Union.

View of a UKIP voter

Using **only** sources 1, 2, 3 and 4 above and opposite, provide evidence **for** and **against** the view of the UKIP voter.

Overall, do you think the evidence **supports** the view? Give a reason for your answer.

(Enquiry Skills, **10** marks)

[*END OF QUESTION PAPER*]

[BLANK PAGE]

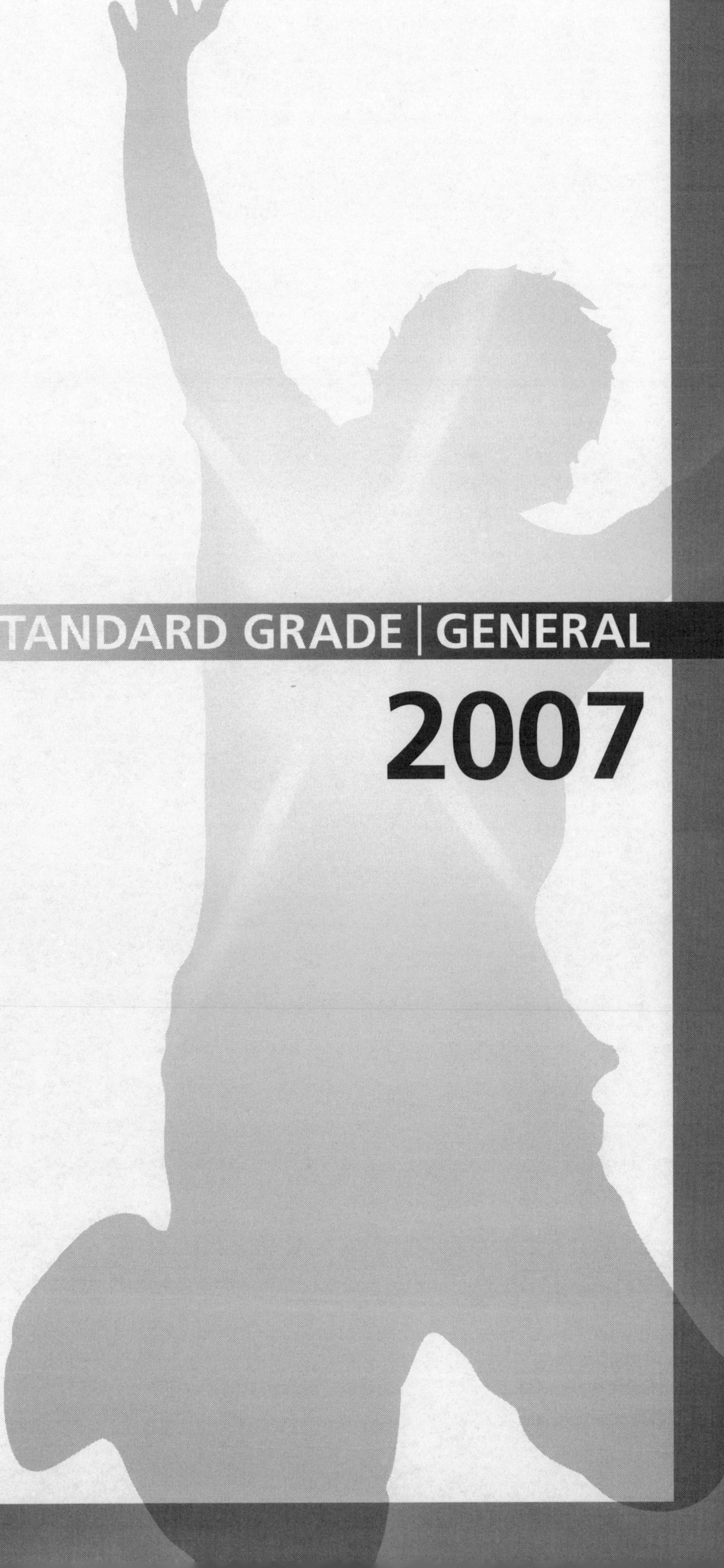

STANDARD GRADE | GENERAL

2007

[BLANK PAGE]

G

2640/402

NATIONAL QUALIFICATIONS 2007

TUESDAY, 22 MAY
10.20 AM – 11.50 AM

MODERN STUDIES
STANDARD GRADE
General Level

1 Read every question carefully.

2 Answer all questions as fully as you can.

3 If you cannot do a question, go on to the next one. Try again later.

4 In question 3, answer **one** section only; Section (A) The USA **or** Section (B) Russia **or** Section (C) China.

5 Write your answers in the answer book provided. Indicate clearly, in the left hand margin, the question and section of question being answered. Do not write in the right hand margin.

SCOTTISH QUALIFICATIONS AUTHORITY

LI 2640/402 6/22170

SYLLABUS AREA 1—LIVING IN A DEMOCRACY

QUESTION 1

(*a*)

Describe **two** ways in which supporters of a candidate can help during an election campaign.

To answer this question, you may wish to use the drawing above.

(Knowledge & Understanding, **4** marks)

QUESTION 1 (CONTINUED)

(*b*) Study the information below, then answer the question which follows.

Political Participation by British voters

Survey Result

Question: Which of the following political activities have you been involved in?

Activity	**2001**	**2005**
Signing a petition	43%	60%
Contacting your councillor	46%	43%
Attending a meeting or rally	38%	43%
Contacting a local council official	64%	41%
Taking part in a demonstration or protest	9%	22%
Contacting a government official	24%	20%
Contacting your Member of Parliament	33%	28%

Write down **two** conclusions about changes in political participation in Britain.

You must **only** use the information above.

You should write **one** conclusion about **each** of the following.

- The change in the most popular political activity from 2001 to 2005
- The activity which has shown the least change in participation from 2001 to 2005

(Enquiry Skills, **4** marks)

[Turn over

QUESTION 1 (CONTINUED)

(*c*)

Shop Stewards help union members in a number of different ways.

Give **two** problems that a *Shop Steward might help their members* with.

For **one** of these problems, describe how the Shop Steward might help.

To answer this question, you may wish to use the drawing above.

(Knowledge and Understanding, **4** marks)

QUESTION 1 (CONTINUED)

(*d*) Study Sources 1 and 2 below, then answer the question which follows.

SOURCE 1

UK Trade Union Membership 2001–2005

Year	Men	Women	Total
2001	3,636,000	3,210,000	6,846,000
2002	3,532,000	3,308,000	6,840,000
2003	3,500,000	3,320,000	6,820,000
2004	3,432,000	3,353,000	6,785,000
2005	3,311,000	3,356,000	6,667,000

SOURCE 2

The Daily Herald

Report About Pay

In 2005, the average hourly pay for all workers was £10·21 compared to only £8·75 in 2001. Workers who belong to a trade union enjoyed a pay rate of £11·38 in 2005, whereas workers who were not members got an average of £9·72. There are still big differences in the rates of pay received by different groups of workers.

Workers benefit from being members of a trade union. Membership of trade unions continued to increase for some groups of workers.

View of Salma Khan

Using **only** Sources 1 and 2, give **two** reasons to **support** the view of Salma Khan.

(Enquiry Skills, **4** marks)

[Turn over

SYLLABUS AREA 2—CHANGING SOCIETY

QUESTION 2

(*a*) Study the information below, then answer the question which follows.

Information on Millie Smith

Millie Smith is 72 years old and lives in a 4 bedroomed house which is too big for her. Her husband died recently and she feels lonely. She has always enjoyed having a garden. She has recently had a hip operation and finds it more difficult to move about or do the housework. Millie is starting to feel the cold more and more.

Millie wants to buy another house. She has seen the two houses below but is not sure whether **House A or House B** would **better meet her needs.**

House A — Ground Floor Flat

A ground floor, 2 bedroomed flat in a two-storey building with a shared central entrance.

There is double-glazing. Some more insulation and draught proofing is needed but this would be easy to do.

Elderly people live in the other 3 flats. All residents share a conservatory which looks onto a colourful garden.

House B — Bungalow

A one-storey, 2 bedroomed house. It would be straightforward to build a ramp and rails at the front to give easy access.

It has an overgrown garden, with many shrubs, that needs some work. There is a very pleasant garden summer-house for sitting in.

The bungalow is fully double glazed throughout and has full gas central heating. It is cheap to heat in the winter.

Using the information above, decide which house, **House A or House B**, would be the **better** choice for Millie Smith to **meet her needs**.

Give **two** reasons to **support** your decision.

You **must** link the information about Millie Smith to the house you have chosen.

(Enquiry Skills, **4** marks)

QUESTION 2 (CONTINUED)

(*b*) *Some elderly people are healthier than other elderly people.*

Give **two** reasons to explain why *some elderly people are healthier than other elderly people.*

(Knowledge & Understanding, **4** marks)

(*c*)

The government tries to help meet the needs of elderly people.

Describe **two** ways in which *the government tries to help meet the needs of elderly people.*

To answer this question, you may wish to use the drawings above.

(Knowledge and Understanding, **4** marks)

[Turn over

QUESTION 2 (CONTINUED)

(*d*) Study Sources 1 and 2 below, then answer the question which follows.

SOURCE 1

Scots spend too much time at work and work too hard!

Trade unions estimate that 16% of Scottish workers work more than 48 hours per week. Investigations have shown that regularly working more than 48 hours a week increases the risk of illness.

A survey on holidays found some interesting results. About 73% of Scottish workers said they often failed to take all their annual holidays. 37% of workers said they had been too busy to take their annual holidays, while 20% simply said that they had forgotten to take them. 50% also said that their annual holiday allowance of 20 to 25 days was not enough and should be increased.

SOURCE 2

Average weekly working hours for men	
Belgium	39·1
France	40·3
Greece	41·7
Italy	39·7
Portugal	42·1
Scotland	45·4
Sweden	40·2
EU Average	**41·3**

- Scottish men are the only men who work more than the EU weekly average.
- Working long hours can damage a worker's health.
- Very few Scottish workers fail to take all their annual holidays.
- Belgian men work the lowest number of hours.

Statements made by Sandy Brown

Using **only** Sources 1 and 2 above, write down **two** statements made by Sandy Brown which are **exaggerated.**

Using the information in the Sources, give **one** reason why **each** of the statements you have chosen is **exaggerated.**

(Enquiry Skills, **4** marks)

[Turn over for Question 3 on *Page ten*

SYLLABUS AREA 3—IDEOLOGIES

QUESTION 3

Answer **ONE** section only: Section (A)—The USA on pages *ten* and *eleven*

OR Section (B)—Russia on pages *twelve* and *thirteen*

OR Section (C)—China on pages *fourteen* and *fifteen*

(A) **THE USA**

(*a*) *People in the USA have many rights. They also have responsibilities that go with them.*

Describe **one** *right* that American people have.

Describe **one** *responsibility* that American people have.

In your answer you **must** use American examples.

(Knowledge & Understanding, **4** marks)

(*b*) Study the information below, then answer the question which follows.

The New York Herald

Bush wins again — 4 More Years

George Bush was returned to power for a second Presidential term in 2004.

Bush said to his opponents "To make this nation stronger and better, I will need your support and I will work to earn it." Bush told Kerry that he was "an admirable, worthy opponent."

Presidential Election Results (2004)

% vote for the candidates

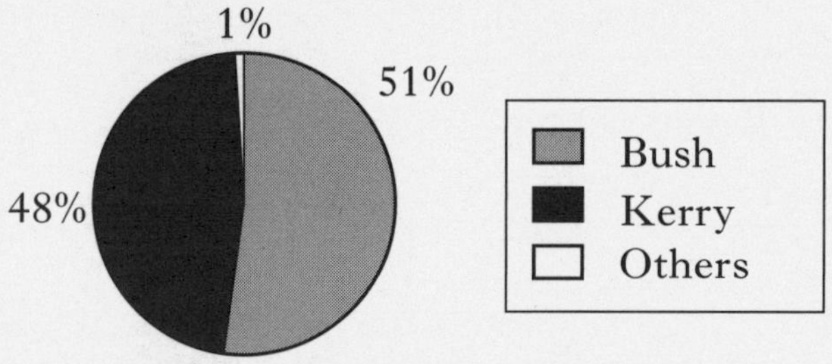

Percentage of voters turning out to vote

1996	**–**	**49·0%**
2000	**–**	**49·3%**
2004	**–**	**59·8%**

In the 2004 Presidential election, the winner had a large majority. It also showed greater participation in politics by voters in the USA.

View of Eva Kaye

Using **only** the information above, give **one** reason to **support** and **one** reason to **oppose** the view of Eva Kaye.

(Enquiry Skills, **4** marks)

QUESTION 3 (A) (CONTINUED)

(*c*)

Give **two** reasons to explain why many American people have become rich and successful.

In your answer you **must** use American examples.

(Knowledge & Understanding, **4** marks)

(*d*) Study the information below, then answer the question which follows.

Opinion Poll — A Comparison

The percentage of American people who are supportive of President Bush's performance in selected policy areas

Policy Areas	**2003**	**2004**	**2005**
The economy	42%	46%	35%
Handling of the war in Iraq	52%	48%	32%
US campaign against terrorism	70%	57%	58%
Overall performance as President	**52%**	**47%**	**40%**

Statements made by Martin Baxter, an American journalist

- The lowest level of support for President Bush has always been in his campaign against terrorism.
- In 2005 less people approved of Bush's handling of the war in Iraq.
- Support for his handling of the economy has steadily fallen each year.
- The electorate's support for the President's overall performance has declined each year.

Using **only** the information above, write down **two** statements made by Martin Baxter which are **exaggerated.**

Using the information in the Opinion Poll, give **one** reason why **each** of the statements you have chosen is **exaggerated.**

(Enquiry Skills, **4** marks)

NOW GO TO QUESTION 4 ON PAGE SIXTEEN

QUESTION 3 (CONTINUED)

(B) **RUSSIA**

(*a*) *People in Russia have many rights. They also have responsibilities that go with them.*

Describe **one** *right* that Russian people have.

Describe **one** *responsibility* that Russian people have.

In your answer you **must** use Russian examples.

(Knowledge & Understanding, **4** marks)

(*b*) Study the information below, then answer the question which follows.

MOSCOW JOURNAL

Putin Wins Again

President Putin has been returned to power by the Russian electorate. This represents a terrific result for him. Russia now has a strong President for the next four years.

The result means that he now has the backing of the Russian people to get all his policies into law.

Presidential Election Results (2004)

% vote for the candidates

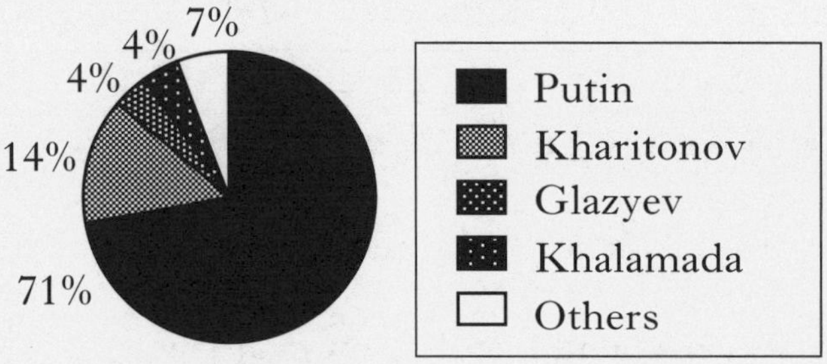

Percentage of voters turning out to vote

1996	**–**	**70%**
2000	**–**	**68%**
2004	**–**	**64%**

In the 2004 Presidential election, the winner had a large majority. It also showed greater participation in politics by voters in Russia.

View of Maria Chakvetadze

Using **only** the information above, give **one** reason to **support** and **one** reason to **oppose** the view of Maria Chakvetadze.

(Enquiry Skills, **4** marks)

QUESTION 3 (B) (CONTINUED)

(*c*)

Give **two** reasons to explain why many Russian people have become rich and successful.

In your answer you **must** use Russian examples.

(Knowledge & Understanding, **4** marks)

(*d*) Study the information below, then answer the question which follows.

Opinion Poll — A Comparison

Question: How good a job is President Putin doing?

Comment	**2000**	**2003**	**2005**
Doing a good job	36%	42%	39%
Doing a fair job	20%	27%	32%
Doing a poor job	35%	27%	24%
Don't know	9%	4%	5%

Statements made by Alexia Gudrun, a Russian journalist

- More Russians thought Putin was "doing a good job" in 2005 than in previous years.
- In all three years, the majority of Russian people asked did not think he was "doing a fair job".
- In 2003, most Russians thought Putin was "doing a poor job".
- More Russians answered "Don't know" in 2000 than in other years.

Using **only** the information above, write down **two** statements made by Alexia Gudrun which are **exaggerated.**

Using the information in the Opinion Poll, give **one** reason why **each** of the statements you have chosen is **exaggerated.**

(Enquiry Skills, **4** marks)

NOW GO TO QUESTION 4 ON PAGE SIXTEEN

QUESTION 3 (CONTINUED)

(C) **CHINA**

(*a*) *People in China have many rights. They also have responsibilities that go with them.*

Describe **one** *right* that Chinese people have.

Describe **one** *responsibility* that Chinese people have.

In your answer you **must** use Chinese examples.

(Knowledge & Understanding, **4** marks)

(*b*) Study the information below, then answer the question which follows.

Duyun Times

Amy Li's Surprise Win!

Communist Party candidate, Amy Li, won a place on the Duyun People's Congress yesterday.

She was not expected to win. Long serving representative, Zhao Lung, was a surprise loser. Amy has promised to work hard to improve the lives of all local people.

Duyun Peoples' Congress Elections (2005)

% vote for the candidates

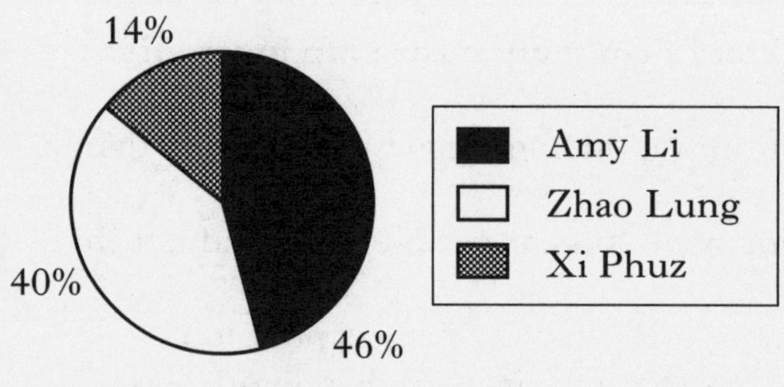

Percentage of voters turning out to vote

1995	**–**	**85%**
2000	**–**	**88%**
2005	**–**	**91%**

In the 2005 election, the winner had a large majority. It also showed greater participation in politics by voters in Duyun.

View of Zi Yan

Using **only** the information above, give **one** reason to **support** and **one** reason to **oppose** the view of Zi Yan.

(Enquiry Skills, **4** marks)

QUESTION 3 (C) (CONTINUED)

(*c*)

Give **two** reasons to explain why many Chinese people have become rich and successful.

In your answer you **must** use Chinese examples.

(Knowledge & Understanding, **4** marks)

(*d*) Study the information below, then answer the question which follows.

China's Urban/Rural split

Year	Total population	Urban population	Rural population
1995	1·21 billion	30%	70%
2000	1·29 billion	36%	64%
2005	1·30 billion	41%	59%
2010 (estimate)	1·31 billion	44%	56%

Statements made by Lye Zhang, a Chinese journalist

- The Chinese population has grown since 1995.
- The urban population of China will double between 1995 and 2010.
- The biggest rise in the total population came between 2000 and 2005.
- The urban population has always been smaller than the rural population.

Using **only** the information above, write down **two** statements made by Lye Zhang which are **exaggerated.**

Using **only** the information in the table, give **one** reason why **each** of the statements you have chosen is **exaggerated.**

(Enquiry Skills, **4** marks)

NOW GO TO QUESTION 4 ON PAGE SIXTEEN

SYLLABUS AREA 4—INTERNATIONAL RELATIONS

QUESTION 4

(*a*)

Many different types of aid can help to meet the ***needs*** *of some African countries.*

Describe **two** different types of aid which *help to meet the needs of some African countries.*

To answer this question, you may wish to use the drawing above.

(Knowledge & Understanding, **4** marks)

QUESTION 4 (CONTINUED)

(*b*) Study Sources 1 and 2 below, then answer the question which follows.

SOURCE 1	SOURCE 2
NATO protects Afghans	**Campaign proving difficult**
Afghanistan is a poor country in Asia with Pakistan and Iran as neighbours. The mission by NATO forces in Afghanistan is the first they have undertaken outwith Europe. They are there to help train, build up and support the Afghan army in the war against the Taliban. They are being successful in making the lives of the people better and more secure by fighting the Taliban. Some Afghans have had to flee from the fighting but they have been moved to clean, safe refugee camps.	NATO troops are involved in Afghanistan, a poor Asian country. Many local people have been forced to flee to refugee camps where the conditions are dangerous and filthy. This is the first NATO campaign outside Europe and involves troops from many countries, including the United Kingdom. The campaign is very difficult with casualties mounting. The Taliban are proving hard to defeat as they are based in the mountains. Afghanistan is now suffering from lawlessness, misery and starvation.

Sources 1 and 2 give different views about **the involvement of NATO troops in Afghanistan**.

Write down **two** differences between these views.

You **must** only use information from the Sources above.

(Enquiry Skills, **4** marks)

[Turn over

QUESTION 4 (CONTINUED)

You are investigating the topic in the box below.

Scotland and the European Union (EU)

Answer questions (*c*), (*d*) and (*e*) which follow.

(*c*) As part of the **Planning Stage**, give **two** relevant **aims** for your investigation.

(Enquiry Skills, **2** marks)

You decide to send an e-mail to your MEP to discover more about the topic.

(*d*) Give **two** advantages of sending an e-mail as a way of finding out information for your investigation.

(Enquiry Skills, **2** marks)

QUESTION 4 (CONTINUED)

Whilst researching your investigation you discover the following website.

Use the information below to answer question (*e*).

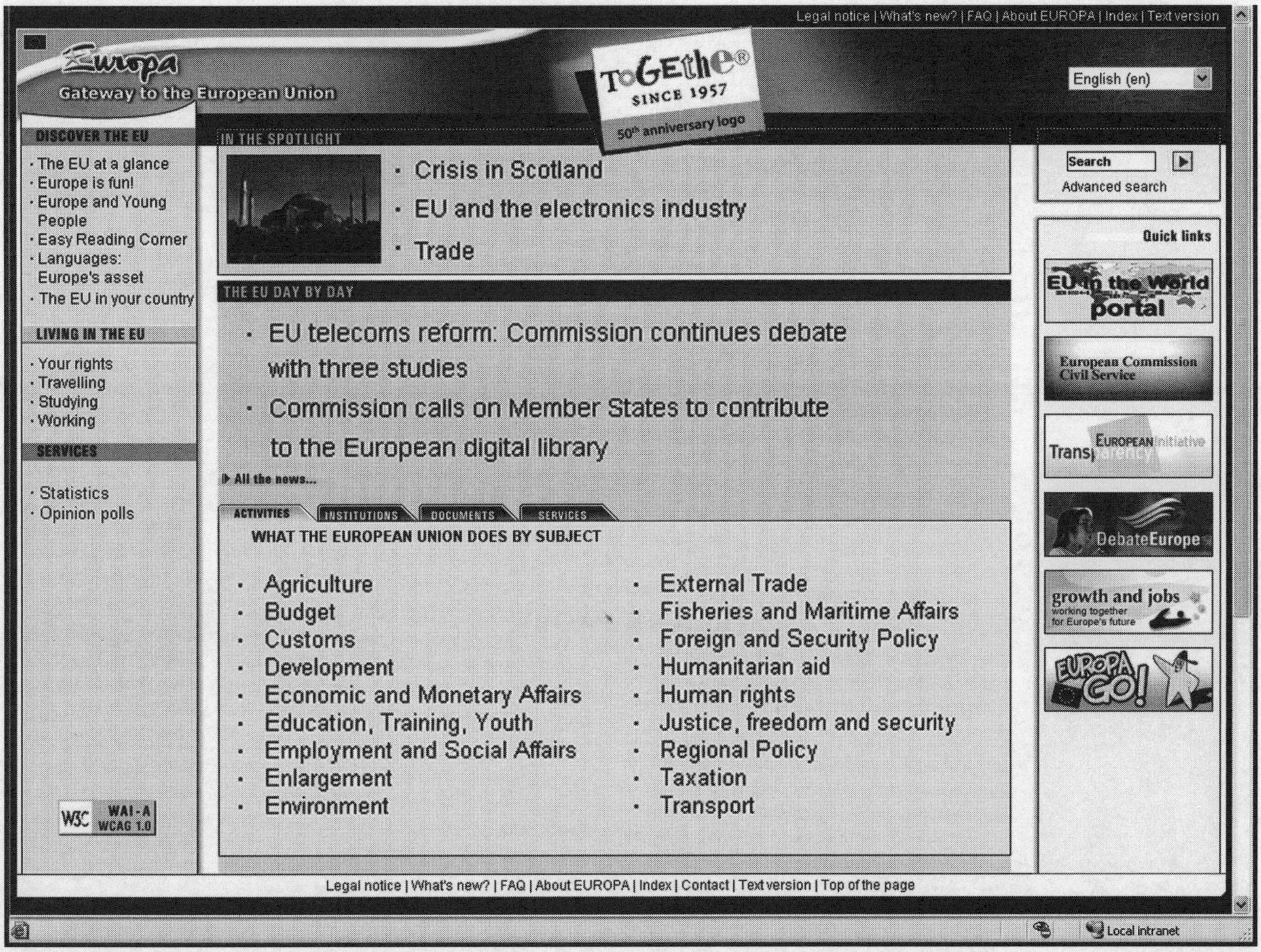

(*e*) Give **two** ways you could use this website to find out more information for your investigation.

For **each** way, explain why it would be a **good** way to find out this information.

(Enquiry Skills, **4** marks)

[*END OF QUESTION PAPER*]

[BLANK PAGE]

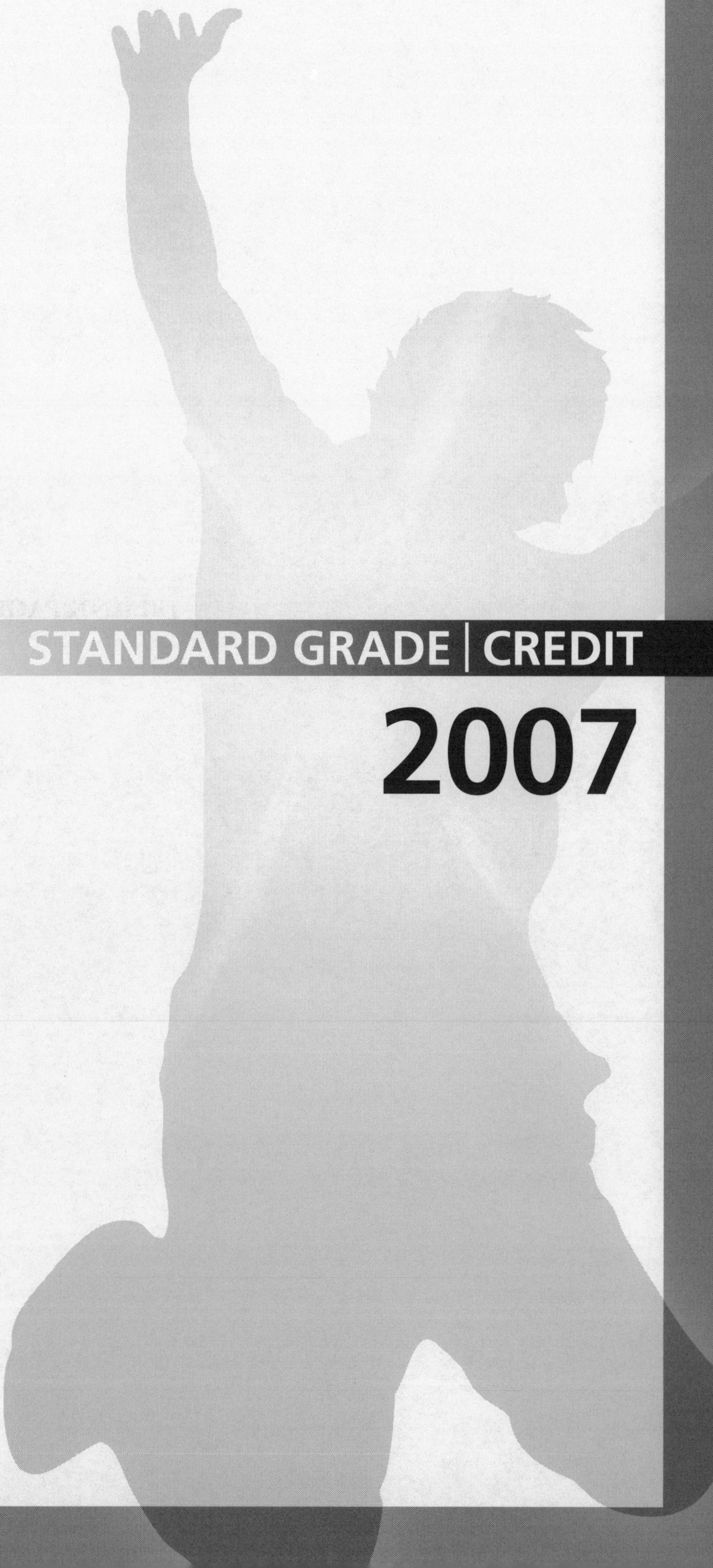

STANDARD GRADE | CREDIT

2007

[BLANK PAGE]

C

2640/403

NATIONAL QUALIFICATIONS 2007

TUESDAY, 22 MAY
1.00 PM – 3.00 PM

MODERN STUDIES
STANDARD GRADE
Credit Level

1 Read every question carefully.

2 Answer all questions as fully as you can.

3 If you cannot do a question, go on to the next one. Try again later.

4 In question 3, answer **one** section only: Section (A) The USA **or** Section (B) Russia **or** Section (C) China.

5 Write your answers in the answer book provided. Indicate clearly, in the left hand margin, the question and section of question being answered. Do not write in the right hand margin.

LI 2640/403 6/14570

[BLANK PAGE]

SYLLABUS AREA 1—LIVING IN A DEMOCRACY

QUESTION 1

(*a*)

The Daily Herald

OPPOSITION GROWS TO NEW GOVERNMENT LAWS

The Prime Minister has announced a package of new laws which he believes will improve the lives of the British people. They cover issues such as pensions, security and health. However, it is clear that many members of the public do not agree with these new laws and are ready to oppose the Government.

Describe, **in detail**, the rights that people have when opposing the introduction of new laws.

(Knowledge & Understanding, **4** marks)

(*b*) Choose **one** of the following electoral systems.

Explain, **in detail,** the **advantages** of the electoral system you have chosen.

(Knowledge & Understanding, **6** marks)

[Turn over

QUESTION 1 (CONTINUED)

(*c*) Study Sources 1, 2 and 3 below and opposite, then answer the question which follows.

SOURCE 1

UK General Election 2005: Selected Results

The UK RESULT

Party	Vote (%)	MPs	Seats (%)
Cons	32	198	31
Labour	35	356	55
Lib Dem	22	62	10
SNP	2	6	1
Others	9	24	3

Scotland

Party	Vote (%)	MPs	Seats (%)
Cons	16	1	2
Labour	39	41	69
Lib Dem	23	11	19
SNP	18	6	10
Others	4	0	0

Wales

Party	Vote (%)	MPs	Seats (%)
Cons	21	3	8
Labour	43	29	72
Lib Dem	18	4	10
Plaid Cymru	13	3	8
Others	5	1	2

England

Party	Vote (%)	MPs	Seats (%)
Cons	35·7	194	37
Labour	35·5	286	54
Lib Dem	22·9	47	8
Others	5·9	2	1

SOURCE 2

UK General Elections 1997 and 2005
Support for Selected Parties by Social class

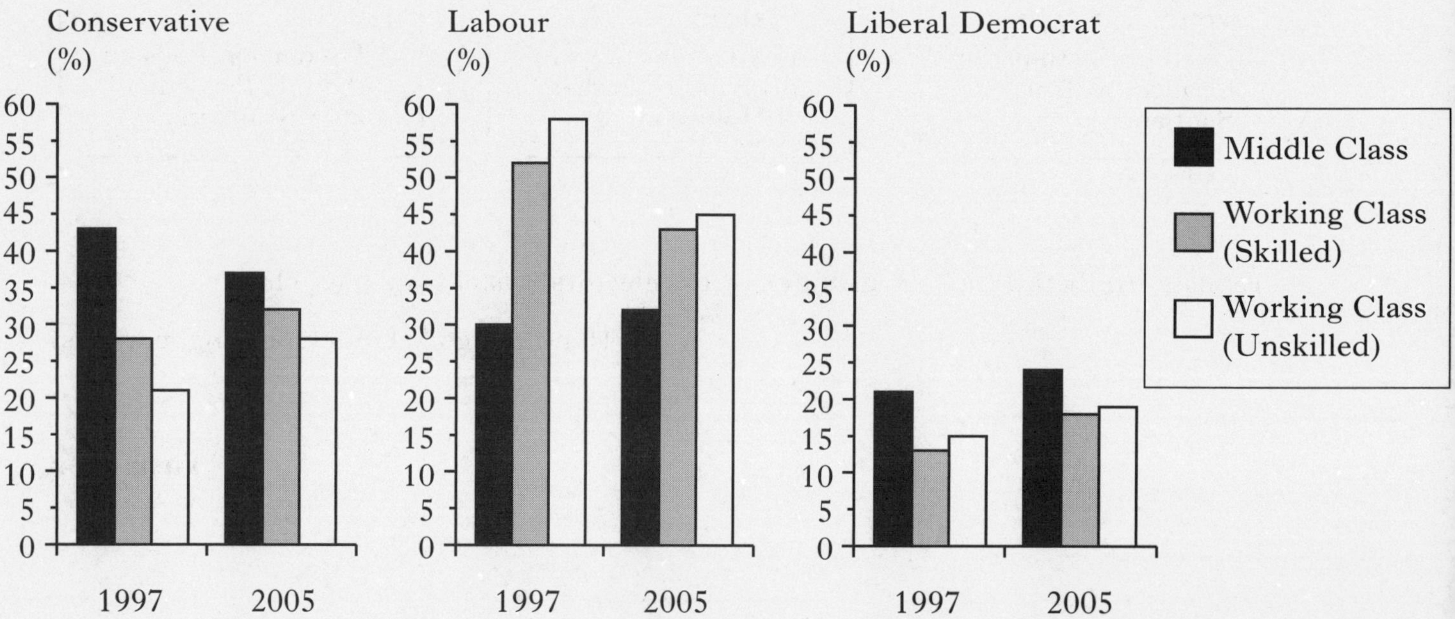

QUESTION 1 (*c*) (CONTINUED)

SOURCE 3

UK General Elections 1997 and 2005
Support for Selected Parties by Age Range

Age Range	Conservative 1997 %	Conservative 2005 %	Labour 1997 %	Labour 2005 %	Lib Dem 1997 %	Lib Dem 2005 %
18–24	25	24	50	42	17	26
25–34	27	24	50	42	17	26
35–64	31	33	43	38	18	22
65+	38	42	42	35	15	18

> The Conservative Party did badly in all areas of the country. The Liberal Democrats, on the other hand, are the only party whose support increased amongst different age ranges and within different social classes compared with other parties, between 1997 and 2005.

View of Karen Mitchell

Using **only** Sources 1, 2 and 3, explain **the extent to which** Karen Mitchell could be accused of being **selective in the use of facts.**

(Enquiry Skills, **8** marks)

[Turn over

[BLANK PAGE]

SYLLABUS AREA 2—CHANGING SOCIETY

QUESTION 2

(*a*) *Some families are unable to meet the needs of their children.*

Explain, **in detail**, the reasons why *some families are unable to meet the needs of their children*.

(Knowledge and Understanding, **6** marks)

(*b*) Study the information below, then answer the question which follows.

Regional Unemployment in the UK (%)

Regions — North	**1995**	**2005**
Scotland	8·3	5·7
Northern Ireland	10·9	4·6
North East England	11·3	6·4
North West England	8·9	4·2
Yorkshire and Humber	8·6	5·0
West Midlands	8·9	4·3
Wales	8·8	4·4
Regions — South		
East Midlands	7·4	4·0
Eastern England	7·5	3·6
London	11·6	6·7
South East England	6·4	3·6
South West England	7·8	3·2
UK Average	**8·6**	**4·6**

In 1995, unemployment was a bigger problem in the North than it was in the South. Ten years on, the situation was the complete opposite.

View of Tom Hicks

Give **one** reason to **support** and **one** reason to **oppose** the view of Tom Hicks.

(Enquiry Skills, **4** marks)

QUESTION 2 (CONTINUED)

(*c*) Study the information in the **"Focus on Families"** pamphlet below and opposite, then answer the question which follows.

Focus on Families

Introduction

Focus on Families looks at different types of families. Families in Britain have changed over the years.

Marriage and Divorce

More than 4 in 10 people over the age of 16 in the UK are married.

In 2005, the average age for first marriage was 31 for men and 29 for women. This had been 26 and 23 for men and women respectively 40 years earlier.

In 2005, the average age for divorce was 43 for men and 40 for women. This had been 39 and 37 for men and women respectively in 1995.

Marriages and Divorces in Britain

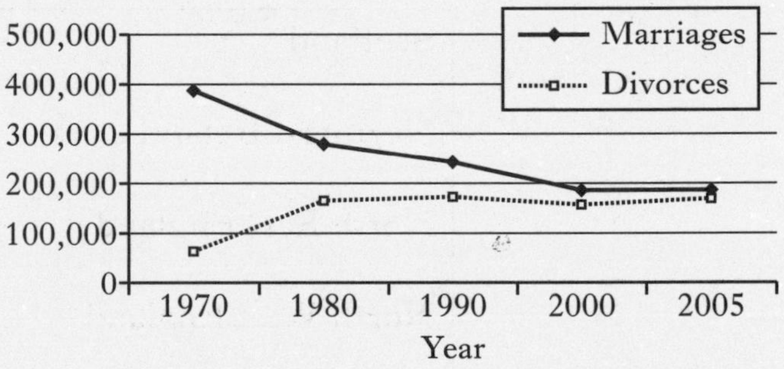

Family Structure

The total number of families reached 17 million in 2004. The "traditional" type of family has always been seen as a couple with dependent children. As the table shows, the percentage of families of each type in Britain has been changing. This may well have an impact on the welfare of dependent children.

People in each type of household (%)

	1971	1981	1991	2004
One person	6	8	11	14
Families:				
Couple no children	19	20	23	25
Couple with dependent children	52	47	41	37
Couple with non-dependent children only	10	10	11	8
Lone parent family	4	6	10	12
Other households	9	9	4	4

QUESTION 2 (*c*) (CONTINUED)

Focus on Families (continued)

% of families that are lone parent families (Scotland)

Lone Parent Families

The main cities have a younger age structure than the overall population. As the map shows, there are wide variations in the distribution of lone parent families across Scotland.

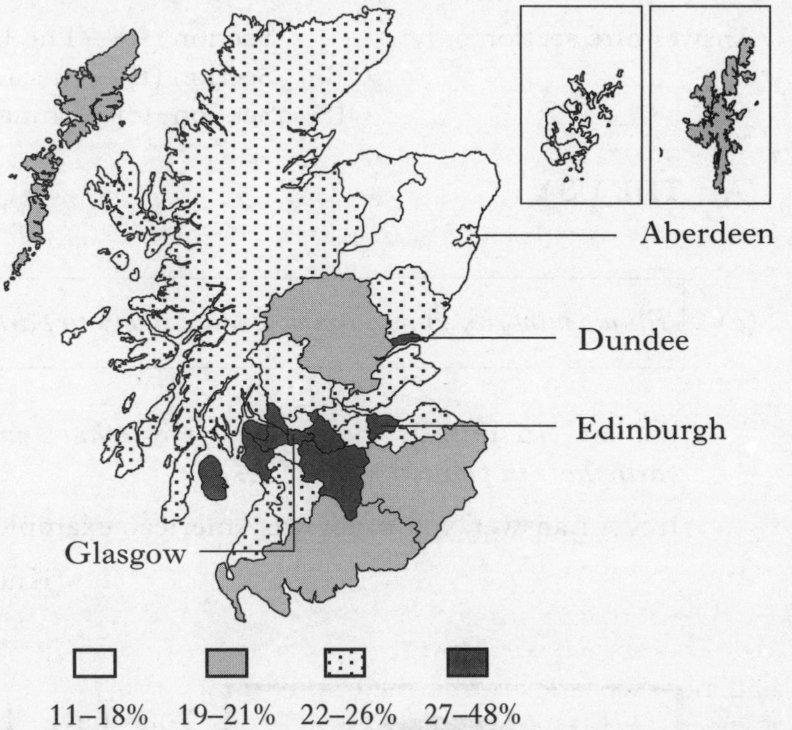

Families and Ethnicity

Some 9% of people in Britain are non-white. Ethnic groups differ in terms of family size and type.

62% of white families are married couples, 13% are cohabiting couples and 25% are lone parent families.

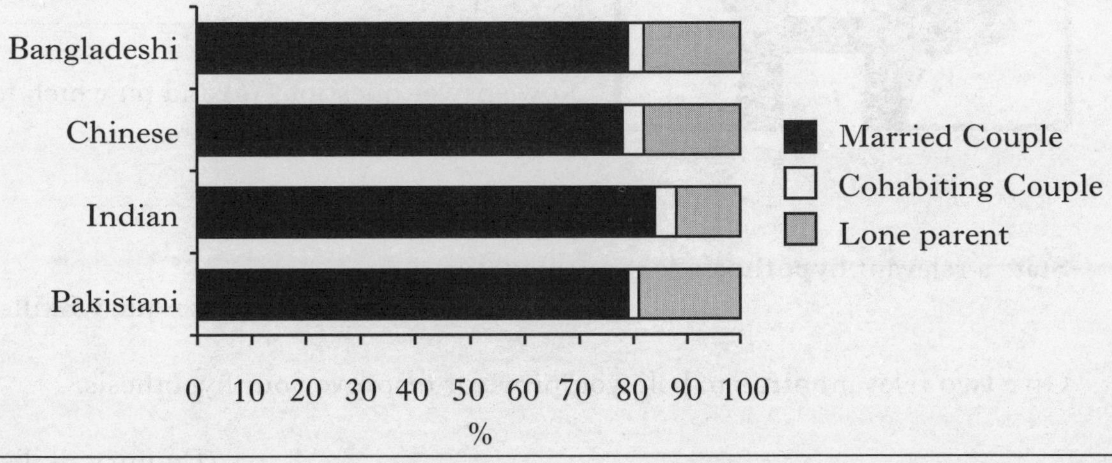

Using **only** the information from the "Focus on Families" pamphlet you must **make** and **justify** a conclusion about **all four** of the following headings.

- Changes in marriage and divorce in Britain.
- The link between changes in marriages and changes in the "traditional" family.
- The difference between the percentages of lone parent families in Britain and Scotland's four main cities.
- The main difference between ethnic minority families and white families.

(Enquiry Skills, **8** marks)

SYLLABUS AREA 3—IDEOLOGIES

QUESTION 3

Answer **one** section only: Section (A)—The USA on pages *ten* to *twelve*
OR Section (B)—Russia on pages *thirteen* to *fifteen*
OR Section (C)—China on pages *sixteen* to *eighteen*

(A) **THE USA**

(*a*) *Ethnic minority groups are now more likely to participate in politics in the USA.*

Explain, **in detail**, the reasons why *ethnic minority groups are now more likely to participate in politics in the USA.*

In your answer, you **must** use American examples.

(Knowledge and Understanding, **8** marks)

You have been asked to carry out **two** investigations.

The first investigation is on the topic in the box below.

Health care in the USA

Now answer questions (*b*) and (*c*) which follow.

(*b*) State a relevant **hypothesis** for your investigation.

(Enquiry Skills, **2** marks)

(*c*) Give **two** relevant **aims** to help you prove or disprove your hypothesis.

(Enquiry Skills, **2** marks)

QUESTION 3 (A) (CONTINUED)

The second investigation is on the topic in the box below.

Education in the USA

Now answer questions (*d*) and (*e*) which follow.

(*d*) While collecting information for your investigation you find out that your school has just started a twinning arrangement with a High School in the USA. You decide to **e-mail the Head Teacher** of the American school. You prepare the following e-mail. **Read it carefully**.

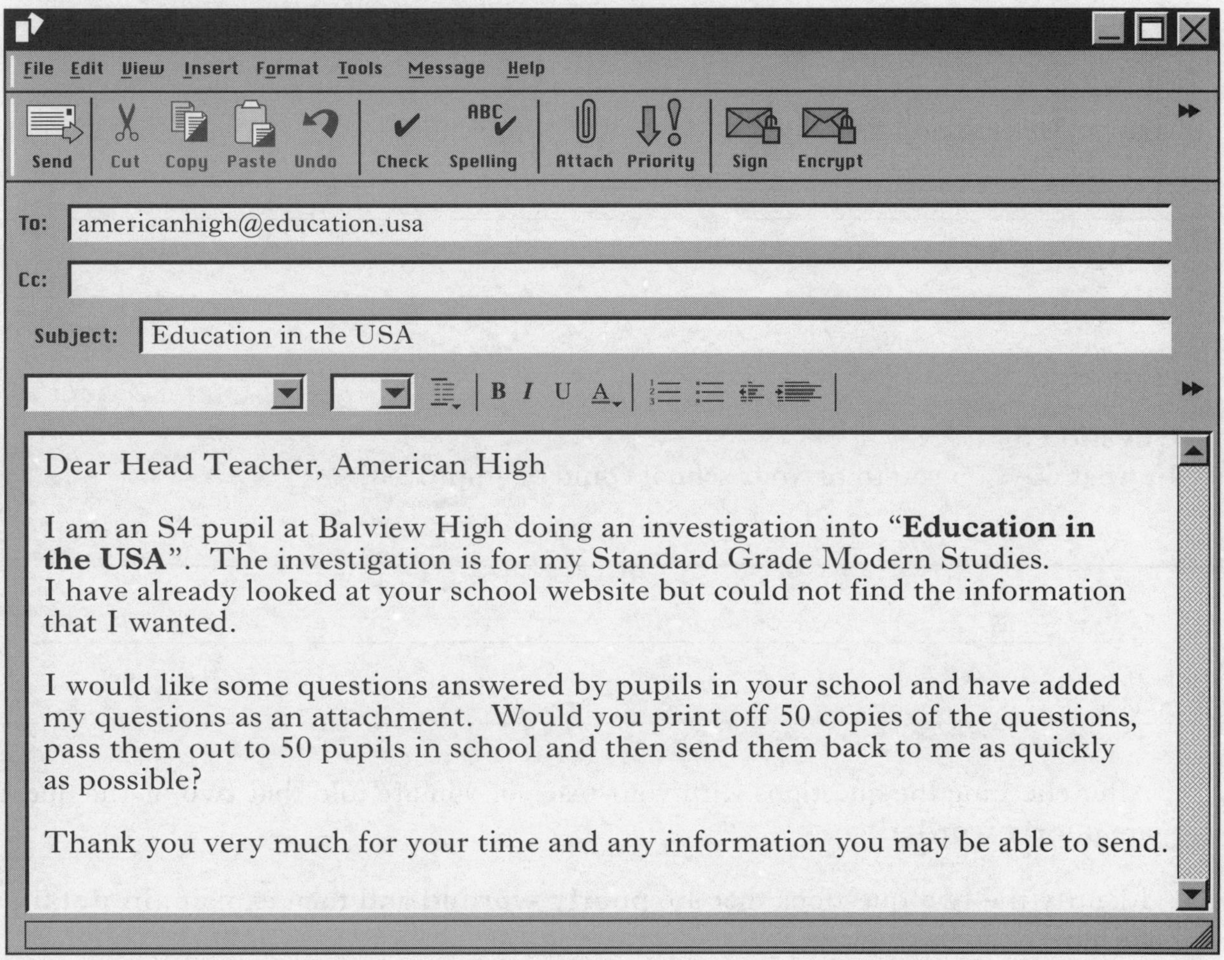

To: americanhigh@education.usa

Subject: Education in the USA

Dear Head Teacher, American High

I am an S4 pupil at Balview High doing an investigation into "**Education in the USA**". The investigation is for my Standard Grade Modern Studies. I have already looked at your school website but could not find the information that I wanted.

I would like some questions answered by pupils in your school and have added my questions as an attachment. Would you print off 50 copies of the questions, pass them out to 50 pupils in school and then send them back to me as quickly as possible?

Thank you very much for your time and any information you may be able to send.

Give **one good point** and **one bad point** about **the content of the e-mail** above.

(Enquiry Skills, **2** marks)

QUESTION 3 (A) (CONTINUED)

(*e*) Here is a copy of the questions you wish to send. **Read them carefully.**

EDUCATION IN THE USA
INVESTIGATION QUESTIONS FOR STUDENTS

Where there is a choice please circle your answer.

Question 1
Which racial group do you belong to?

White Black Hispanic Asian Native American Other

Question 2
How many students in your school wear school uniform?

All More than half Less than half None

Question 3
Are your school meals good and do students get them free?

Yes No Don't know

Question 4
Why do Blacks and Hispanics not do well at your school?

____

____

____

Question 5
In what ways do you think your school could be improved?

____

____

After checking the questions with your teacher, you are told that **two** of the questions are **poorly worded**.

Identify the **two** questions that are **poorly worded** and then explain, **in detail**, why each needs to be changed.

(Enquiry Skills, **4** marks)

[NOW GO TO QUESTION 4 ON PAGE 19]

QUESTION 3 (CONTINUED)

(B) **RUSSIA**

(*a*) *Many people in Russia like the fact that they can participate in politics.*

Explain, **in detail**, the reasons why Russian people *participate in politics*.

In your answer, you **must** use Russian examples.

(Knowledge and Understanding, **8** marks)

You have been asked to carry out **two** investigations.

The first investigation is on the topic in the box below.

Health care in Russia

Now answer questions (*b*) and (*c*) which follow.

(*b*) State a relevant **hypothesis** for your investigation.

(Enquiry Skills, **2** marks)

(*c*) Give **two** relevant **aims** to help you prove or disprove your hypothesis.

(Enquiry Skills, **2** marks)

[Turn over

QUESTION 3 (B) (CONTINUED)

The second investigation is on the topic in the box below.

Education in Russia

Now answer questions (*d*) and (*e*) which follow.

(*d*) While collecting information for your investigation you find out that your school has just started a twinning arrangement with a High School in Russia. You decide to **e-mail the Head Teacher** of the Russian school. You prepare the following e-mail. **Read it carefully**.

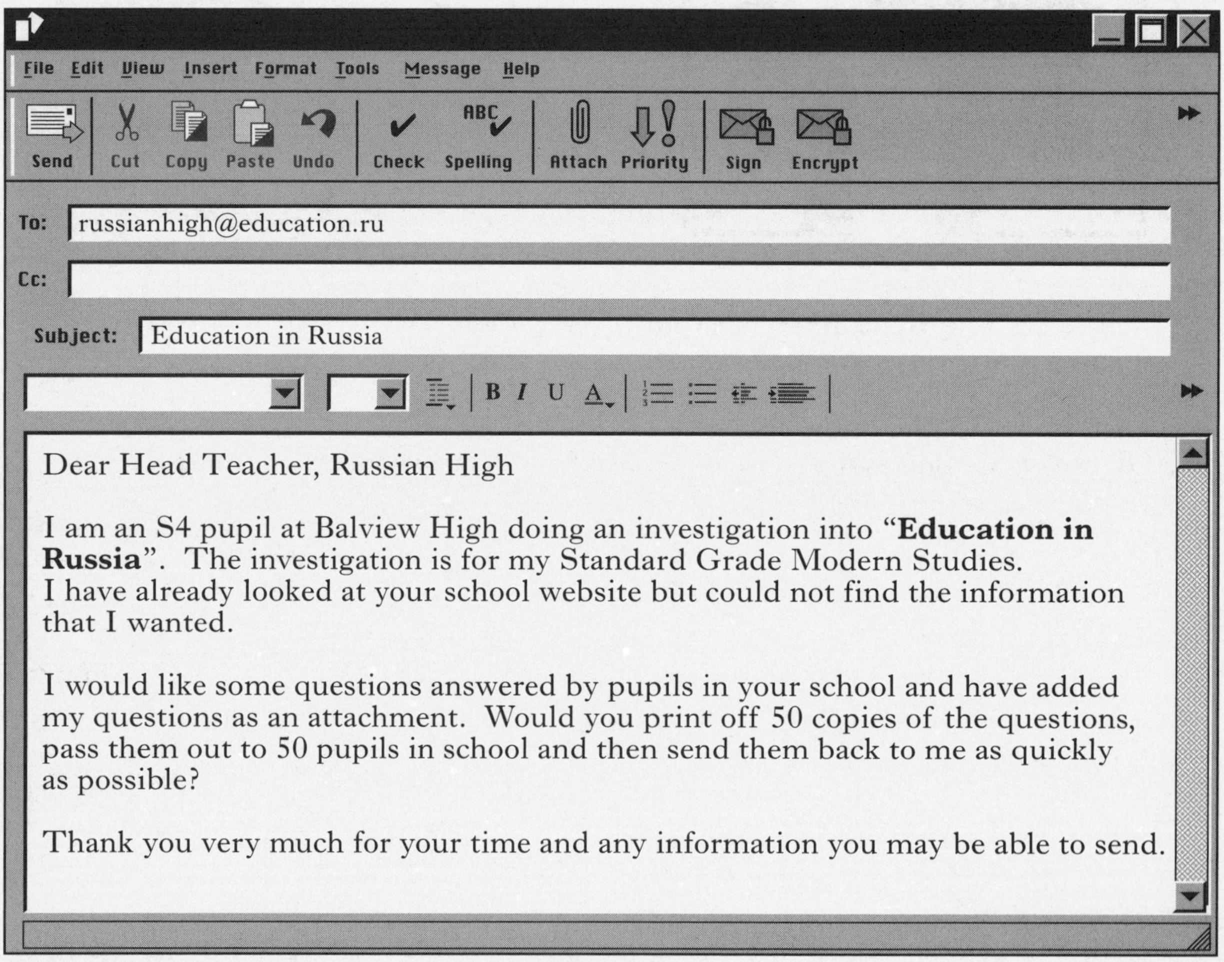

Dear Head Teacher, Russian High

I am an S4 pupil at Balview High doing an investigation into "**Education in Russia**". The investigation is for my Standard Grade Modern Studies. I have already looked at your school website but could not find the information that I wanted.

I would like some questions answered by pupils in your school and have added my questions as an attachment. Would you print off 50 copies of the questions, pass them out to 50 pupils in school and then send them back to me as quickly as possible?

Thank you very much for your time and any information you may be able to send.

Give **one good point** and **one bad point** about the **content of the e-mail** above.

(Enquiry Skills, **2** marks)

QUESTION 3 (B) (CONTINUED)

(*e*) Here is a copy of the questions you wish to send. **Read them carefully.**

EDUCATION IN RUSSIA
INVESTIGATION QUESTIONS FOR STUDENTS

Where there is a choice please circle your answer.

Question 1
Which age group do you belong to?

11–12 13–14 15–16 17–18 Over 18

Question 2
How many students in your school wear school uniform?

All More than half Less than half None

Question 3
Are your school meals good and do students get them free?

Yes No Don't know

Question 4
Why is it that girls always do better than boys at your school?

____

____

____

Question 5
In what ways do you think your school could be improved?

____

____

After checking the questions with your teacher, you are told that **two** of the questions are **poorly worded**.

Identify the **two** questions that are **poorly worded** and then explain, **in detail**, why each needs to be changed.

(Enquiry Skills, **4** marks)

[NOW GO TO QUESTION 4 ON PAGE 19]

[Turn over

QUESTION 3 (CONTINUED)

(C) **CHINA**

(*a*) *Many Chinese people have difficulties participating fully in politics.*

Explain, **in detail**, the reasons why *many Chinese people have difficulties participating fully in politics*.

In your answer, you **must** use Chinese examples.

(Knowledge and Understanding, **8** marks)

You have been asked to carry out **two** investigations.

The first investigation is on the topic in the box below.

Health care in China

Now answer questions (*b*) and (*c*) which follow.

(*b*) State a relevant **hypothesis** for your investigation.

(Enquiry Skills, **2** marks)

(*c*) Give **two** relevant **aims** to help you prove or disprove your hypothesis.

(Enquiry Skills, **2** marks)

QUESTION 3 (C) (CONTINUED)

The second investigation is on the topic in the box below.

Education in China

Now answer questions (*d*) and (*e*) which follow.

(*d*) While collecting information for your investigation you find out that your school has just started a twinning arrangement with a High School in China. You decide to **e-mail the Head Teacher** of the Chinese school. You prepare the following e-mail. **Read it carefully**.

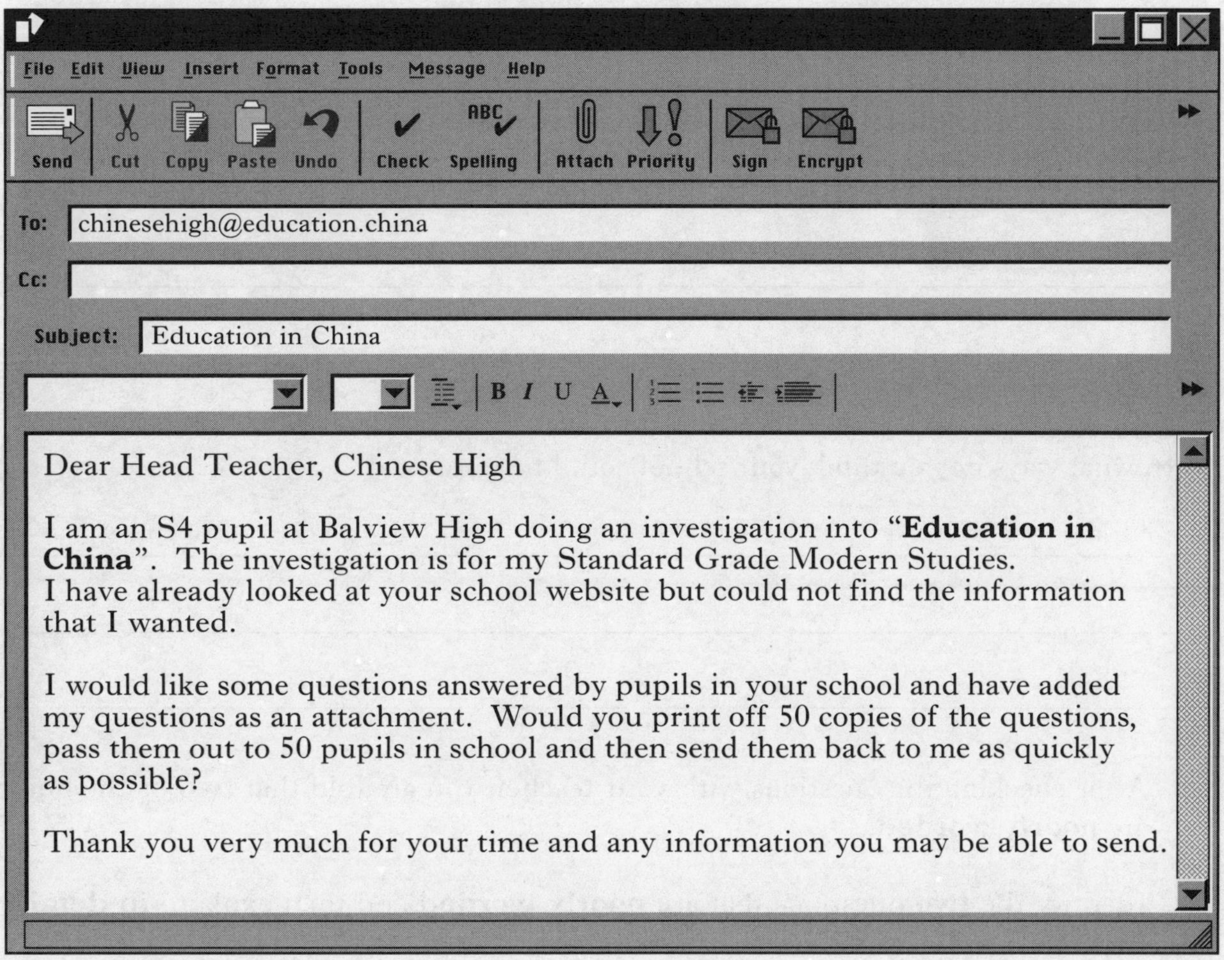

To: chinesehigh@education.china

Cc:

Subject: Education in China

Dear Head Teacher, Chinese High

I am an S4 pupil at Balview High doing an investigation into "**Education in China**". The investigation is for my Standard Grade Modern Studies. I have already looked at your school website but could not find the information that I wanted.

I would like some questions answered by pupils in your school and have added my questions as an attachment. Would you print off 50 copies of the questions, pass them out to 50 pupils in school and then send them back to me as quickly as possible?

Thank you very much for your time and any information you may be able to send.

Give **one good point** and **one bad point** about the **content of the e-mail** above.

(Enquiry Skills, **2** marks)

QUESTION 3 (C) (CONTINUED)

(*e*) Here is a copy of the questions you wish to send. **Read them carefully.**

EDUCATION IN CHINA
INVESTIGATION QUESTIONS FOR STUDENTS

Where there is a choice please circle your answer.

Question 1
Which ethnic group do you belong to?

Han Zhuang Uygur Hui Other

Question 2
How many students in your school wear school uniform?

All More than half Less than half None

Question 3
Are your school meals good and do students get them free?

Yes No Don't know

Question 4
Why is it that children from rural areas always do worse at your school?

____

____

____

Question 5
In what ways do you think your school could be improved?

____

____

After checking the questions with your teacher, you are told that **two** of the questions are **poorly worded**.

Identify the **two** questions that are **poorly worded** and then explain, **in detail**, why each needs to be changed.

(Enquiry Skills, **4** marks)

[NOW GO TO QUESTION 4 ON PAGE 19]

SYLLABUS AREA 4—INTERNATIONAL RELATIONS

QUESTION 4

(*a*) *The policies of the European Union (EU) try to meet the **needs** of member countries and their citizens.*

Choose **two** of the following policies.

- Single European Currency (Euro)
- Enlarged Membership
- Common Fisheries Policy
- Aid to the Regions
- European Defence Force
- Common Agricultural Policy

For **each** policy, describe, **in detail**, the ways in which it tries *to meet the **needs** of member countries and their citizens*.

In your answer, you **must** use recent examples you have studied.

(Knowledge & Understanding, **8** marks)

[Turn over

QUESTION 4 (CONTINUED)

(*b*) Study the article below and the information in the radio debate opposite, then answer the question which follows.

FOCUS ON CHAD

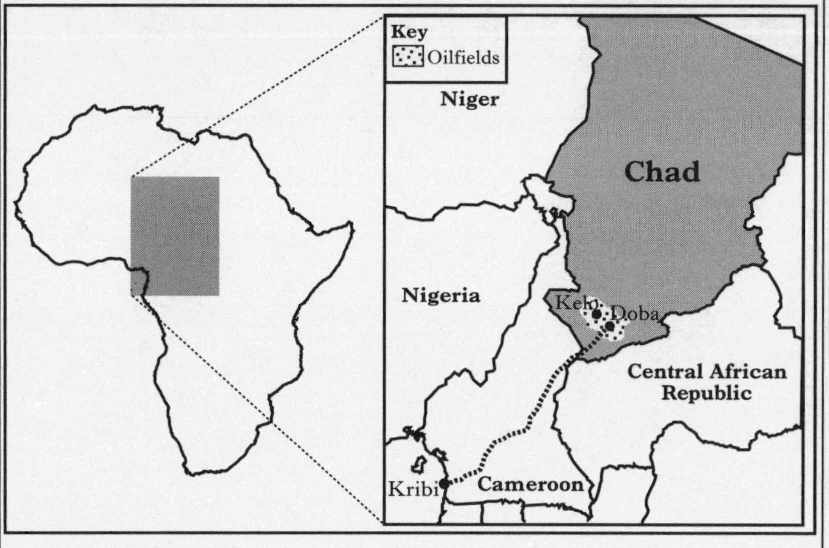

Introduction

Chad has many natural resources such as oil, uranium and gold which are under-developed. Only 200 sq km of farming land is currently irrigated and there are many natural hazards like drought. Lack of sanitation and clean water are major problems. The government is struggling to help its rapidly growing population.

Health Services

There is a lack of access to medical services. Many remote villages never see trained medical professionals and people cannot afford to travel to modern hospitals in the cities. They rely on local people who lack proper training. Doctors expect to be paid in advance by patients before treatment and there is a shortage of drugs.

Economy

Over 80% of the population rely on basic farming and livestock for survival. 75% of the population live on less than a dollar a day.

Few people are sufficiently qualified to leave the land to seek well-paid employment. 80% of the population live below the poverty line. Over $1 billion is owed in debt. The World Bank helped Western businesses to develop an oil pipeline from Chad to Cameroon.

People

Development Indicator	Chad	UK
Population	9·1 million	60·4 million
Population growth per year	3·0%	0·28%
Infant mortality per 1000 live births	94	5
Life expectancy	48 years	78 years
HIV/AIDS rate	5%	0·2%
Literacy rate	48%	99%

A conflict in Sudan has created a huge number of refugees which the government in Chad is trying to cope with.

Concerns of the people of Chad on selected issues

Question: What do you think is the most important issue facing Chad?

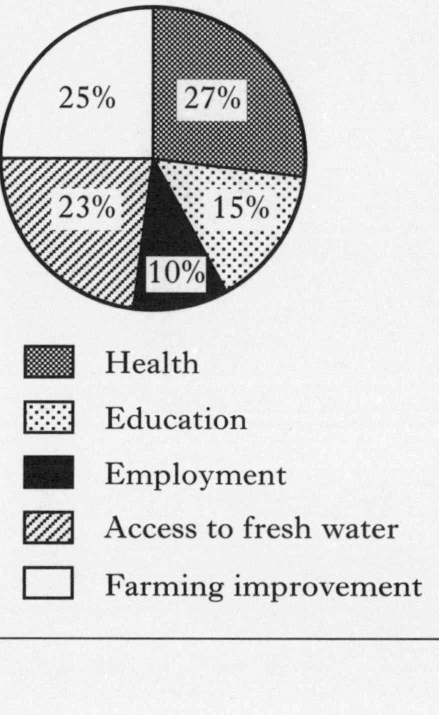

QUESTION 4 (*b*) (CONTINUED)

RADIO DEBATE

World Radio brings you a studio discussion about the best way to tackle poverty in Africa. Today's debate focuses on Chad.

What makes your project best for Chad?

Hello. I'm **Simon Rose** and I represent Rose Energy. We believe in supporting governments such as Chad's as they understand local conditions. Large-scale projects such as oil production are the best way to develop a country.

Good morning. My name is **Chrissie Smith** and I work for a non-governmental organisation called Helping Hands. We help local communities develop at their own pace. Small-scale projects provide a long-term solution.

What would be the main focus of your project?

We are prepared to invest $1 billion to create a second oil field in Chad. We will build a new road network in the south of the country, benefiting other industries. We hope to build a city hospital close to our proposed oilfield. Villages along the pipeline will have water pumps installed. 2% of our profits will go to the government as tax which could be spent repaying debts.

Helping Hands believes that health care and contraception are the key issues facing Chad. We will train local women to provide free community health care, reducing the spread of HIV/AIDS. Ten clinics across Chad will be set up, each costing $20 000.

What other issues do you believe are important for the development of Chad?

Without oil I see no future for the country. The economy currently relies on cotton and cattle. Jobs and improved services will only come with the development of the oil field and new infrastructure. Big schemes are best as the money spreads down through society.

The other key areas are farming and education. We must improve the income of farmers. This is a major obstacle to development. Also, very few children go to school as they are needed on the farm. It is crucial to begin teaching these children so they can be offered a better future. Small locally managed community projects are best suited to countries such as Chad.

Project One
Rose Energy

Project Two
Helping Hands

Which one of these projects is more suitable for Chad?

Using only **Focus on Chad** and the **radio debate**, explain which project, Rose Energy or Helping Hands, would be **more suitable** to help Chad develop.

Give **detailed reasons** to explain your choice and also why you **rejected** the other option.

In your answer you must **relate** the information about Chad to the information about the **two** projects.

(Enquiry Skills, **10** marks)

[*END OF QUESTION PAPER*]

[BLANK PAGE]

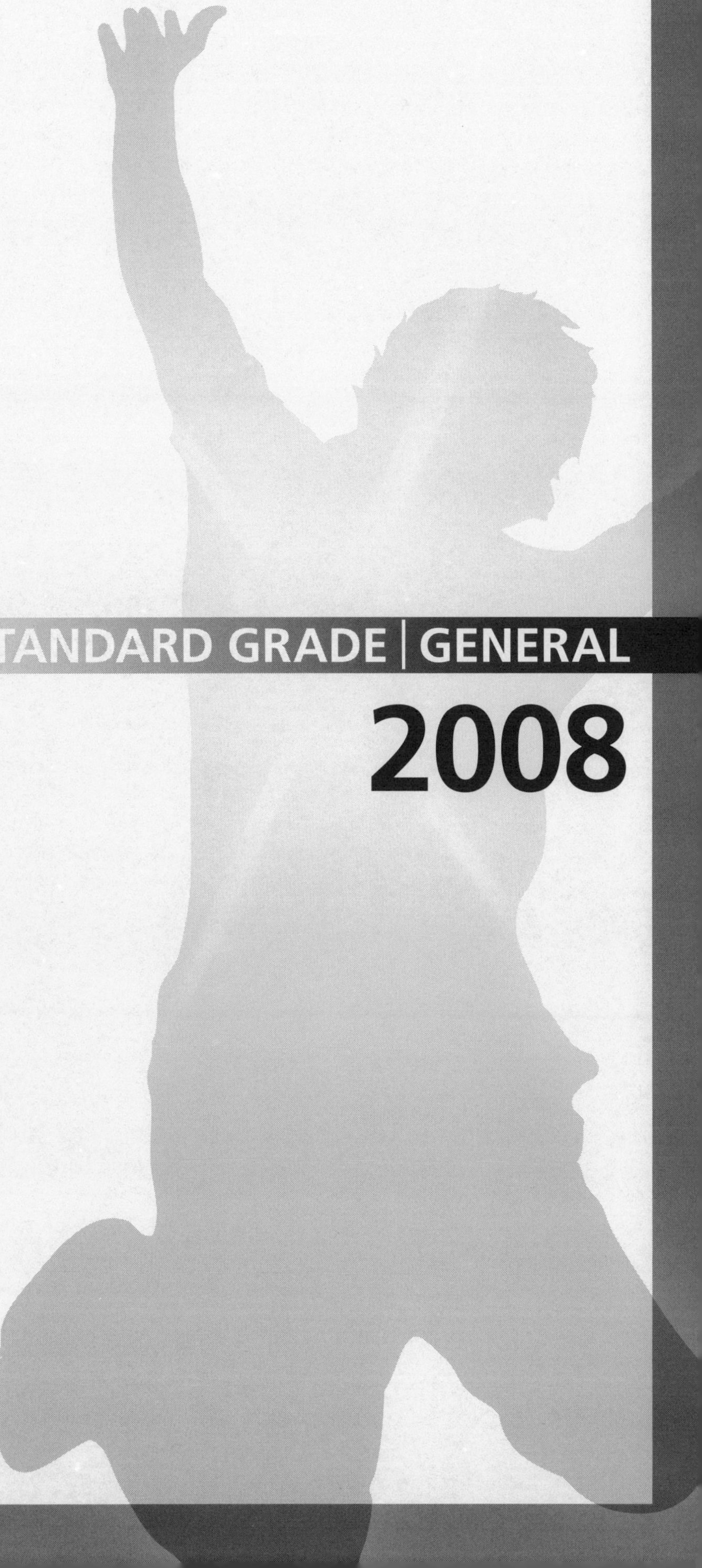

STANDARD GRADE | GENERAL

2008

[BLANK PAGE]

G

2640/402

NATIONAL QUALIFICATIONS 2008

THURSDAY, 22 MAY
10.20 AM – 11.50 AM

MODERN STUDIES STANDARD GRADE
General Level

1 Read every question carefully.

2 Answer all questions as fully as you can.

3 If you cannot do a question, go on to the next one. Try again later.

4 In question 3, answer **one** section only; Section (A) The USA **or** Section (B) Russia **or** Section (C) China.

5 Write your answers in the answer book provided. Indicate clearly, in the left hand margin, the question and section of question being answered. Do not write in the right hand margin.

SYLLABUS AREA 1—LIVING IN A DEMOCRACY

QUESTION 1

(*a*)

Members of pressure groups have rights and responsibilities.

Describe one **right** and one **responsibility** that members of a pressure group have.

To answer this question, you may wish to use the drawing above.

(Knowledge & Understanding, **4** marks)

(*b*) Study Sources 1 and 2 below, then answer the question which follows.

SOURCE 1

VIEW OF MALCOLM BROWN

There are about 5 million members of ethnic minority groups in Britain. The number of MPs from such ethnic groups rose slightly in 2005.

We do not need special arrangements to attract more women into Parliament. After the 2005 General Election, the number of women in the House of Commons rose to a historic high. 128 female MPs were elected. This shows that women are now well represented in the UK.

This was election win number three for Prime Minister Blair and his party.

SOURCE 2

VIEW OF JANE RENNIE

The 2005 election was the third win in a row for Tony Blair and the Labour Party.

With 128 MPs, there are more women in the House of Commons than ever before. However, with less than 20% of the total, women in the UK are still poorly represented when compared to other European countries. We must find new ways to encourage more women to become MPs.

The number of representatives from Britain's 5 million or so ethnic minority population has increased a little from 13 to 15 MPs.

Sources 1 and 2 give different views about **representation in the House of Commons**.

Write down **two** differences between these views.

You **must** only use information from the Sources above.

(Enquiry Skills, **4** marks)

QUESTION 1 (CONTINUED)

You are investigating the topic in the box below.

CAMPAIGNING IN ELECTIONS

Answer questions (*c*), (*d*) and (*e*) which follow.

(*c*) As part of the **Planning Stage**, give **two** relevant **aims** for your investigation.

(Enquiry Skills, **2** marks)

You decide to contact some political parties to help in your investigation.

SNP Conservatives

Labour LIBERAL DEMOCRATS

(*d*) Give **two** ways in which you could contact the political parties.

For **each** way you have chosen, explain why it is a **good** way to get information to help in your investigation.

(Enquiry Skills, **4** marks)

You decide to use your local library to help with your investigation.

(*e*) Describe **one** way in which you could use your local library.

(Enquiry Skills, **2** marks)

[Turn over

SYLLABUS AREA 2—CHANGING SOCIETY

QUESTION 2

(*a*)

The Government tries to help unemployed people find jobs.

Describe **two** ways in which *the Government tries to help unemployed people find jobs.*

To answer this question, you may wish to use the drawing above.

(Knowledge and Understanding, **4** marks)

QUESTION 2 (CONTINUED)

(*b*)

Technology has allowed many people to work from home.

Give **two** ways in which *technology has allowed many people to work from home.*

For **each** way, explain why it has allowed many people to work from home.

To answer this question, you may wish to use the drawing above.

(Knowledge and Understanding, **4** marks)

[Turn over

QUESTION 2 (CONTINUED)

(*c*) Study the information below, then answer the question which follows.

Inverdee Council

Inverdee Council to spend £150,000 on new scheme.

Inverdee wants to meet the needs of young unemployed people in one of its most deprived areas. These young people need help with completing job application forms. They also need to improve their interview skills and ICT skills.

Inverdee Council is not sure whether **Scheme A** or **Scheme B** would **best meet the needs of young unemployed people.**

Scheme A

A Digital Community Centre

This scheme digitally connects 12 local community centres in Inverdee. It aims to give local unemployed people basic to advanced ICT training. Locals will have access to multi-media technology, including computers, scanners, digital cameras and data projectors.

The community centres will provide training, promote employment and assist in setting up new businesses.

The scheme would target a range of groups including young people. Help will also be given in completing application forms for anyone who feels they need it.

Scheme B

Personal Advisors

Job hunters in Inverdee are to get help finding work. A local voluntary organisation wants to deliver a new service to help young people communicate better with possible employers. It will concentrate on improving interview skills but also offer work experience.

The programme will be available to young people, aged 18 to 24, who are unemployed for six months or more. It will also give advice on filling in application forms for new jobs.

The scheme is confident it will make a real difference in getting young people into quality employment in Inverdee.

Using the information above, decide whether **Scheme A** or **Scheme B**, would be the **better** choice for Inverdee Council to **meet the needs** of young unemployed people.

Give **two** reasons to **support** your decision.

You **must** link the information about the needs of the young unemployed people to the scheme you have chosen.

(Enquiry Skills, **4** marks)

QUESTION 2 (CONTINUED)

(*d*) Study the table below, then answer the question which follows.

Self-employment by ethnic group			
	2001	**2003**	**2005**
White	11·0%	11·9%	12·0%
Pakistani	21·8%	22·5%	21·0%
Indian	12·5%	13·1%	12·5%
Chinese	19·1%	18·3%	16·0%
Black Caribbean	7·1%	9·7%	8·0%
Black African	6·6%	6·2%	6·0%
Bangladeshi	12·3%	9·9%	14·0%

> Self-employment amongst Whites and Bangladeshis has grown every year.
> Pakistanis had the largest decrease in self-employment between 2003 and 2005

View of Abigail Smith

Using **only** the table above, give **two** reasons to **disagree** with the view of Abigail Smith.

(Enquiry Skills, **4** marks)

[Turn over

SYLLABUS AREA 3 — IDEOLOGIES

QUESTION 3

Answer **ONE** section only: Section (A)—The USA on pages *eight* to *eleven*

OR Section (B)—Russia on pages *twelve* to *fifteen*

OR Section (C)—China on pages *sixteen* to *nineteen*

(A) **THE USA**

(*a*)

MAX'S TYRES
Balance Sheet

Sales:	$550,000
Profit:	$240,000
Tax:	$ 25,000

Starting up a business can improve the lives of some Americans.

Describe **two** ways in which *starting up a business can improve the lives of some Americans.*

In your answer you **must** use American examples.

To answer this question, you may wish to use the drawings above.

(Knowledge & Understanding, **4** marks)

QUESTION 3 (A) (CONTINUED)

(*b*) Study Sources 1 and 2 below, then answer the question which follows.

SOURCE 1

Information about selected countries

Country	**Average Income ($)**	**Life Expectancy (Years)**
China	1,290	72
Japan	37,180	82
Russia	3,410	65
United Kingdom	33,940	79
United States	41,400	78

SOURCE 2

Percentage of children enrolled in primary school (2006)

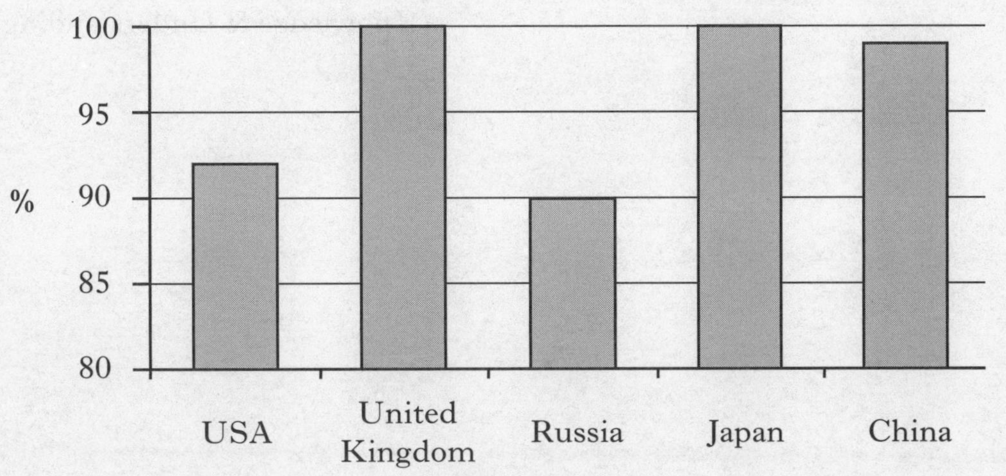

The USA enrolls less of its children in primary school than most other major countries. However, people in the USA have both the highest average income and live the longest.

View of Kelly Halcomb

Using **only** Source 1 and Source 2 above, give **one** reason to **support** and **one** reason to **oppose** the view of Kelly Halcomb.

(Enquiry Skills, **4** marks)

[Turn over

QUESTION 3 (A) (CONTINUED)

(*c*) **ISSUES IN THE USA**

Some Americans are worse off than others.

Choose **one** of the issues from the box above.

For the issue you have chosen, give **two** reasons why *some Americans are worse off than others.*

In your answer you **must** use American examples.

(Knowledge & Understanding, **4** marks)

QUESTION 3 (A) (CONTINUED)

(*d*) Study Sources 1 and 2 below, then answer the question which follows.

SOURCE 1

Hurricane Katrina hit the Gulf Coast of the United States on 29 August 2005, destroying towns in the states of Mississippi and Louisiana. It made one million people homeless, and killed almost 1,800 others. Americans were upset at the size of the disaster and how poorly prepared all levels of government were to deal with the problem. The President agreed that the government had been slow to respond. He promised "one of the largest re-building efforts the world has ever seen" to repair the damage.

SOURCE 2

Opinion Poll of American citizens

Question: How well has the government done in re-building the Gulf Coast after Hurricane Katrina?

Hurricane Katrina caused a great deal of damage to the Gulf Coast area. However, the government was well equipped to respond to the disaster. President Bush has promised to re-build these states. The majority of people agree that the government is doing a good re-building job.

View of Reed Johnson

Using **only** Source 1 and Source 2 above, write down **two** statements made by Reed Johnson which are **exaggerated**.

Using the information in the Sources, give **one** reason why **each** of the statements you have chosen is **exaggerated**.

(Enquiry Skills, **4** marks)

NOW GO TO QUESTION 4 ON PAGE TWENTY

QUESTION 3 (CONTINUED)

(B) **RUSSIA**

(*a*)

Starting up a new business can improve the lives of some Russians.

Describe **two** ways in which *starting up a business can improve the lives of some Russians.*

In your answer you **must** use Russian examples.

To answer this question, you may wish to use the drawings above.

(Knowledge & Understanding, **4** marks)

QUESTION 3 (B) (CONTINUED)

(*b*) Study Sources 1 and 2 below, then answer the question which follows.

SOURCE 1

Information about selected countries		
Country	**Average Income ($)**	**Life Expectancy (Years)**
China	1,290	72
Japan	37,180	82
Russia	3,410	65
United Kingdom	33,940	79
United States	41,400	78

SOURCE 2

Percentage of children enrolled in primary school (2006)

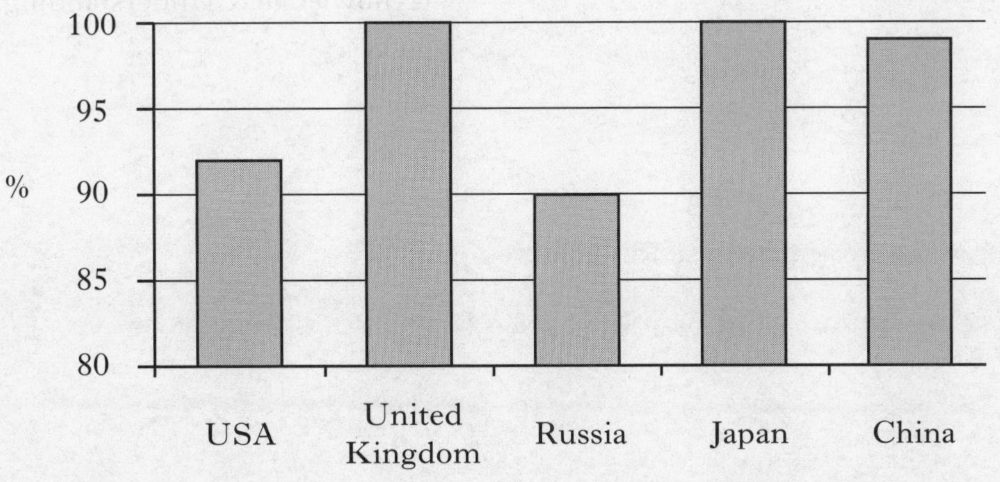

Russia enrolls less of its children in primary school than most other major countries. People in Russia also have both the lowest average income and shortest life expectancy.

View of Georgi Safin

Using **only** Source 1 and Source 2 above, give **one** reason to **support** and **one** reason to **oppose** the view of Georgi Safin.

(Enquiry Skills, **4** marks)

[Turn over

QUESTION 3 (B) (CONTINUED)

(*c*) **ISSUES IN RUSSIA**

Some Russians are worse off than others.

Choose **one** of the issues from the box above.

For the issue you have chosen, give **two** reasons why *some Russians are worse off than others.*

In your answer you **must** use Russian examples.

(Knowledge & Understanding, **4** marks)

QUESTION 3 (B) (CONTINUED)

(*d*) Study Sources 1 and 2 below, then answer the question which follows.

SOURCE 1

The cost of living in Moscow has risen in the past ten years. Some tourists can spend as much as $390 a day whilst on holiday. Foreigners who live and work in Moscow admit a few items such as perfume can cost a little more than in their own country. However, shopping costs can be reduced by using shops on the outskirts of Moscow instead of the centre of the city. The majority of foreigners enjoy life in the Russian capital.

SOURCE 2

Opinion poll of foreigners living in Moscow

Question: How expensive do you find living in Moscow?

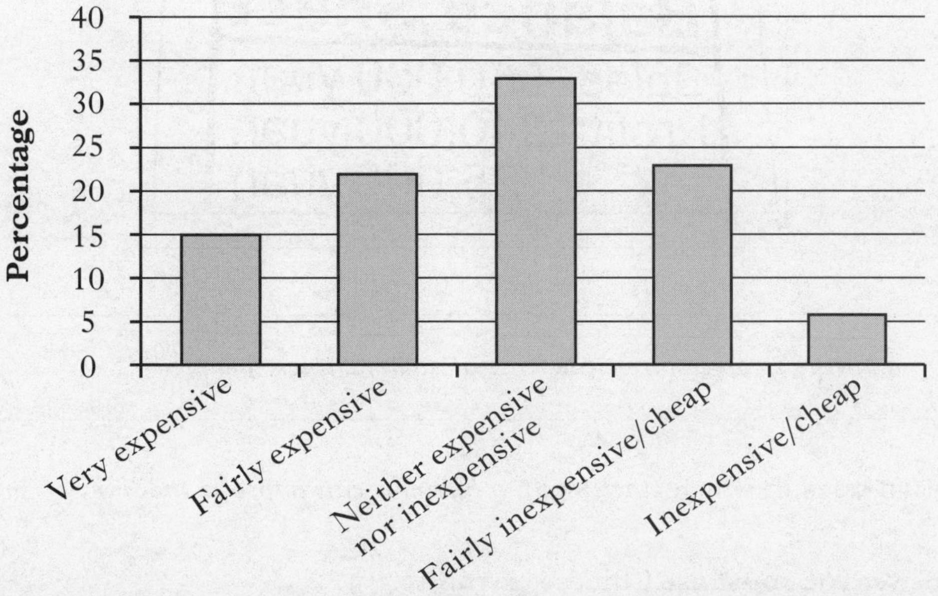

The cost of living continues to rise in Moscow. The majority of foreigners living in Moscow find the city expensive. Shopping costs are similar both in the centre and in the outskirts of Moscow. Foreign workers enjoy living and working in Moscow.

View of Maria Kirilenko

Using **only** Source 1 and Source 2 above, write down **two** statements made by Maria Kirilenko which are **exaggerated.**

Using the information in the Sources, give **one** reason why **each** of the statements you have chosen is **exaggerated**.

(Enquiry Skills, **4** marks)

NOW GO TO QUESTION 4 ON PAGE TWENTY

QUESTION 3 (CONTINUED)

(C) **CHINA**

(*a*)

Starting up a business can improve the lives of some Chinese people.

Describe **two** ways in which *starting up a business can improve the lives of some Chinese people.*

In your answer you **must** use Chinese examples.

To answer this question, you may wish to use the drawings above.

(Knowledge & Understanding, **4** marks)

QUESTION 3 (C) (CONTINUED)

(*b*) Study Sources 1 and 2 below, then answer the question which follows.

SOURCE 1

Information about selected countries		
Country	**Average Income ($)**	**Life Expectancy (Years)**
China	1,290	72
India	620	64
Russia	3,410	65
United Kingdom	33,940	79
United States	41,400	78

SOURCE 2

Percentage of children enrolled in primary school (2006)

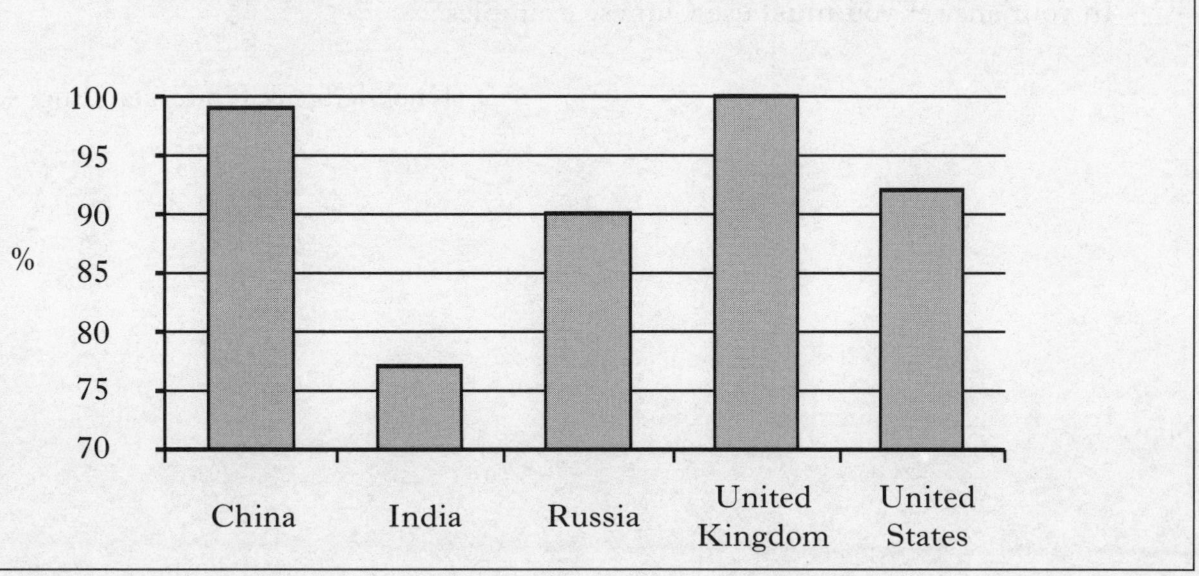

China enrolls more of its children in primary school than most other major countries. People in China also have both the second lowest average income and shortest life expectancy.

View of An Qi

Using **only** Source 1 and Source 2 above, give **one** reason to **support** and **one** reason to **oppose** the view of An Qi.

(Enquiry Skills, **4** marks)

[Turn over

QUESTION 3 (C) (CONTINUED)

(*c*) **ISSUES IN CHINA**

Education **Housing** **Health**

Some Chinese people are worse off than others.

Choose **one** of the issues from the box above.

For the issue you have chosen, give **two** reasons why *some Chinese people are worse off than others.*

In your answer you **must** use Chinese examples.

(Knowledge & Understanding, **4** marks)

QUESTION 3 (C) (CONTINUED)

(*d*) Study Sources 1 and 2 below, then answer the question which follows.

SOURCE 1

2008 Olympics – China spends big!

China has spent almost $39bn on preparations for the 2008 Olympic Games. Most of the cash was spent improving Beijing's transport links, with 132 kilometres of new rail and underground lines built. Beijing has also modernised roads, power stations and water supplies. Those in the countryside around Beijing have not been so fortunate as sixty-nine villages have been demolished to make way for the new Olympic facilities. China hopes to be the centre of attention in 2008 and attract more investment.

SOURCE 2

Opinion Poll of Chinese citizens

Question: **How happy are you that China has been awarded the 2008 Olympics?**

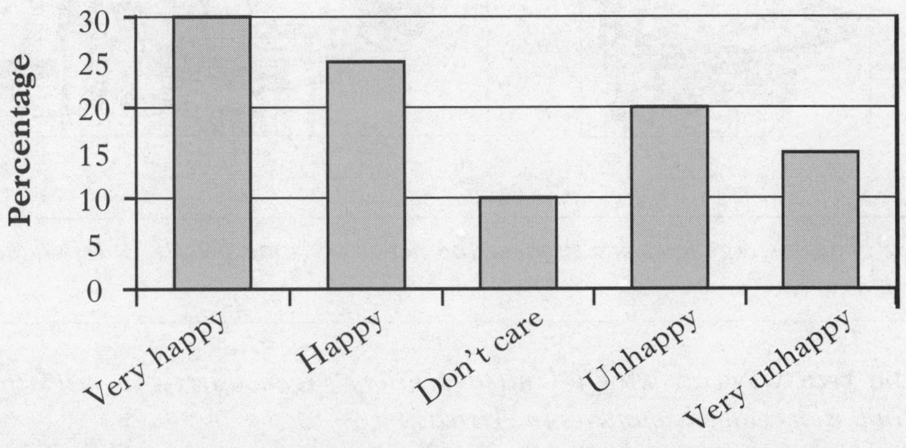

China has spent a lot of money preparing for the Olympics. The majority of Chinese people are not pleased about the Olympics coming to their country. However, everyone in the country should benefit from the Games. Beijing now has better transport links.

View of Zhan Zhenhua

Using **only** Source 1 and Source 2 above, write down **two** statements made by Zhan Zhenhua which are **exaggerated**.

Using the information in the Sources, give **one** reason why **each** of the statements you have chosen is **exaggerated**.

(Enquiry Skills, **4** marks)

NOW GO TO QUESTION 4 ON PAGE TWENTY

SYLLABUS AREA 4 - INTERNATIONAL RELATIONS

QUESTION 4

(*a*)

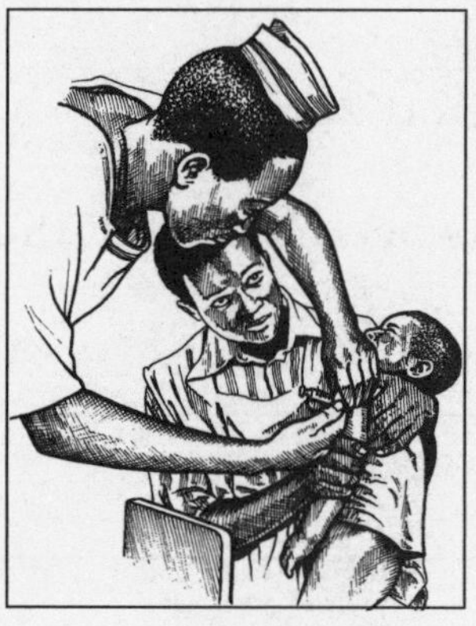

United Nations Agencies try to meet the needs of some people in less developed countries in Africa.

Describe **two** ways in which *United Nations Agencies try to meet the needs of some people in less developed countries in Africa.*

To answer this question, you may wish to use the drawings above.

(Knowledge & Understanding, **4** marks)

QUESTION 4 (CONTINUED)

(*b*) Study the information below, then answer the question which follows.

Data for selected NATO countries

Country	**1990**		**2005**	
	Numbers in Armed Forces ('000s)	**Defence spending per person ($)**	**Numbers in Armed Forces ('000s)**	**Defence spending per person ($)**
Greece	201	500	209	610
UK	308	770	216	530
USA	2,181	1,400	1,492	925
Turkey	769	110	816	115

Write down **two** conclusions about Armed Forces and Defence spending.

You should write **one** conclusion **with evidence** about **each** of the following.

- The country with the biggest change in the numbers in its armed forces.
- What happens to the numbers in the armed forces as defence spending rises.

You **must** only use the information above.

(Enquiry Skills, **4** marks)

[Turn over

QUESTION 4 (CONTINUED)

(*c*)

10 things you should know about the European Union (EU)

1. The European Union is a group of countries whose governments work together.
2. It's a bit like a club. To join you have to agree to follow the rules and in return you get certain benefits.
3. Each country has to pay money to be a member. They mostly do this through taxes.
4. The Single European Market has made trade between countries much easier.
5. There are 5 countries wishing to join at the moment.
6. 43% of all spending by the EU goes on Agriculture, Fisheries and helping the environment.
7. The EU has banned animal testing for cosmetics.
8. EU regional aid has raised living standards in poorer parts of Europe.
9. In 2006, 8 out of 10 EU citizens said they were fairly or very satisfied with living in the EU.
10. The EU has helped over 2 million young people study in another country.

Countries still wish to join the European Union.

Give **two** reasons why *countries still wish to join the European Union.*

To answer this question, you may wish to use the information above.

(Knowledge & Understanding, **4** marks)

QUESTION 4 (CONTINUED)

(*d*) Study the Timeline below, then answer the question which follows.

TIMELINE — NIGER FOOD CRISIS
KEY EVENTS 2004 – 2006

Date	Event
August 2004	Hardly any rain falls during what should be the rainy season. The crops which do grow are then eaten by several plagues of locusts.
November 2004	There are appeals for aid. Many people run out of food.
January 2005	Foodstocks are very low. There is very little food for people to buy. People march in the streets to draw attention to the problem.
July 2005	All Niger's debt is cancelled at the G8 summit. This should help greatly. Many children are dying of starvation.
August 2005	800,000 children under 5 are still going hungry. 40,000 tonnes of energy biscuits are sent to Niger by Italy.
September 2006	The rain fails to come again. A quarter of the population are reported to be hungry.

Niger has suffered greatly due to a lack of rain. People in Niger protested about the situation. No food aid was received by Niger. Debt is still a major problem for the government.

View of Lyz Graham

Using **only** the information above, write down **two** statements made by Lyz Graham which are **exaggerated**.

Using the Timeline, give **one** reason why **each** of the statements you have chosen is **exaggerated**.

(Enquiry Skills, **4** marks)

[*END OF QUESTION PAPER*]

[BLANK PAGE]

STANDARD GRADE | CREDIT

2008

[BLANK PAGE]

C

2640/403

NATIONAL QUALIFICATIONS 2008

THURSDAY, 22 MAY
1.00 PM – 3.00 PM

MODERN STUDIES
STANDARD GRADE
Credit Level

1 Read every question carefully.

2 Answer all questions as fully as you can.

3 If you cannot do a question, go on to the next one. Try again later.

4 In question 3, answer **one** section only: Section (A) The USA **or** Section (B) Russia **or** Section (C) China.

5 Write your answers in the answer book provided. Indicate clearly, in the left hand margin, the question and section of question being answered. Do not write in the right hand margin.

LI 2640/403 6/13970

SQA

[BLANK PAGE]

SYLLABUS AREA 1—LIVING IN A DEMOCRACY

QUESTION 1

(*a*) *Trade union members have **rights during a dispute** with their employers.*

Describe, **in detail**, the **rights** trade union members have **during a dispute** with their employers.

(Knowledge & Understanding, **4** marks)

(*b*) *Women are better **represented** in the Scottish Parliament than they are at Westminster.*

Explain, **in detail**, the reasons why women are better **represented** in the Scottish Parliament than at Westminster.

(Knowledge & Understanding, **4** marks)

[Turn over

QUESTION 1 (CONTINUED)

(*c*) Study the Background Information about Gleninch and Sources 1 and 2 on the next page, then answer the question which follows.

BACKGROUND INFORMATION ABOUT GLENINCH CONSTITUENCY

- Gleninch is a constituency in the north of Scotland with a population of 35 265 people. It is a largely rural area with only one town, Inverinch, and a large number of scattered villages. The traditional industries of farming and fishing have been in decline in recent years. The unemployment rate is well above the national average.
- Many young people leave the area, moving to the big cities throughout the UK to look for jobs or to attend college or university.
- Tourism is very important to the local economy, with a lot of people employed in hotels, bed and breakfast accommodation and restaurants. Tourists tend to visit the area for a few days on short breaks, attracted by rare wildlife and spectacular, unspoilt scenery. However, there are a number of transport problems in the constituency, including high petrol prices and poor public transport.
- There is a proposal to build a wind farm in the area. This would involve the construction of 6 large wind turbines along the coast, as well as a 15-mile long power line built on tall pylons to take electricity to the rest of the country. This would create a few temporary construction jobs but will disturb local wildlife and impact on the scenery of the area.
- An American mining company wants to build a huge "super-quarry" into a mountainside near Gleninch. This will produce crushed rock to build roads, railways and houses throughout the UK. The new quarry will create 150 new jobs in Gleninch.
- At the last General Election, the constituency was won by the Labour Party with a majority of just over 1000 votes. The Liberal Democrats came second. They are convinced that, with the right candidate, they can win the seat at the next election.

A Statistical Profile of Gleninch Constituency (2006)

	Gleninch	Comparison with Scottish Average
Average Income	£21 185	–14%
Income Support claimants	15·1%	+22%
Unemployment Rate	5·6%	+13%
School leavers with no qualifications	3·6%	–33%
School leavers with Highers	58·6%	+13%
Serious Assaults	8·8 (per 10 000 people)	–73%
Housebreaking	3·8 (per 10 000 people)	–93%
Road Accidents	57 casualties	–44%

Survey of Local Liberal Democrat Members

Question: *How important are these issues to people in the area?*

Issue	Unimportant	Not Very Important	Fairly Important	Very Important
Environment	5%	25%	40%	30%
Health	2%	10%	53%	35%
Jobs	0%	0%	48%	52%
Women in Parliament	15%	52%	22%	11%

QUESTION 1 (*c*) (CONTINUED)

There are two people hoping to be selected by the Liberal Democratic Party to be the Party's candidate at the next General Election. Here are extracts from speeches they have made.

SOURCE 1

EXTRACT FROM CAMPAIGN SPEECH BY KIRSTY REID

- I support the proposed wind farm as it will provide many local jobs and help the local environment.
- Our local schools provide an excellent education. If selected, I will work to ensure this continues.
- Women make up over half the country's population and yet there are still very few of us who are MPs. This is a major priority for local party members and is an important reason why I should be the candidate.
- The local economy has been in decline recently. We need more jobs to keep our young people in the area. The new quarry will help with this, and I will work hard to see that it is allowed to go ahead.
- To attract more people to the area we need to improve transport links. I will make this a priority.

SOURCE 2

EXTRACT FROM CAMPAIGN SPEECH BY ROBBIE McKAY

- Tourism is very important to the area and so I will oppose the new wind farm as it will be an ugly blot on the landscape and deter tourists.
- Crime in Gleninch is among the worst in Scotland. I will campaign to improve policing in the area.
- Although new jobs are important, local Liberal Democrats are much more concerned about the environment. The new quarry will put more heavy lorries on our roads which are already more dangerous than the rest of the country. I will oppose it going ahead.
- The issue of health will be one of my main concerns, just as it is for local party members.
- Compared to the rest of the country, the people of Gleninch are not well-off. I will do all I can to improve this.

Use **only** the information about Gleninch on *Page four* and Sources 1 and 2 above.

(i) State **which person** would be the **more suitable** to be selected by the Liberal Democratic Party as their candidate for this constituency at the next General Election.

(ii) Give **three detailed reasons to support your choice**.

(iii) Give **two detailed** reasons why you **rejected** the other candidate.

In your answer, you **must relate** information about the constituency to the information about the **two** candidates.

(Enquiry Skills, **10** marks)

SYLLABUS AREA 2—CHANGING SOCIETY

QUESTION 2

(*a*) **TYPES OF CARE FOR THE ELDERLY**

Community Care within their own home	Sheltered Housing	Residential Care Homes

Choose **one** type of care from the options above.

Explain, **in detail**, the ways in which this type of care **meets the needs** of some elderly people.

(Knowledge and Understanding, **8** marks)

QUESTION 2 (CONTINUED)

You have been asked to carry out an investigation on the topic in the box below.

Help for families in the UK

Now answer questions (*b*), (*c*), (*d*) and (*e*) which follow.

(*b*) State a relevant **hypothesis** for your investigation.

(Enquiry Skills, **2** marks)

(*c*) Give **two** relevant **aims** to help you prove or disprove your hypothesis.

(Enquiry Skills, **2** marks)

Your Modern Studies class decides to use **Video Conferencing** to do an interview to help the pupils with their investigations into "**Help for families in the UK**".

Your teacher contacted your MP at Westminster, who said she would be willing to be interviewed. The interview set up is shown below.

Your MP in her office at Westminster	**A secondary school classroom**

(*d*) Give **two relevant** questions which you could ask your MP to help with your investigation.

(Enquiry Skills, **4** marks)

[Turn over

QUESTION 2 (CONTINUED)

While collecting information for your investigation, you found the **Orinoco Web page** below which contained information about **Social Trends 2008**.

orinoco.co.uk

VIEW BASKET | WISH LIST | YOUR ACCOUNT | HELP

WELCOME | YOUR STORE | BOOKS | ELECTRONICS & PHOTO | MUSIC | DVD BUY & RENT | VIDEO | SOFTWARE | PC & VIDEO GAMES | HOME & GARDEN | TOYS & GAMES | SPORTS & LEISURE | NEW JEWELLERY & WATCHES

Search Books GO!

See larger image
Share your own customer images

Social Trends (Paperback)
by Office for National Statistics (Author)

Our Price: £45.00

Availability: Not in stock.
Pay now, delivered in 2 months.

Price: £45.00
out of stock
Dispatched from and sold by **Orinoco.co.uk**
Quantity: 1
Add to Shopping Basket
or
Sign in to turn on 1-Click ordering.

More Buying Choices

Social Trends 2008—book description

A reference source of 252 pages, "**Social Trends 2008**" draws together social and economic data from a range of government departments and other organisations. Social Trends has been published every year since 1970 by the Office for National Statistics. This annual publication provides a picture of life and lifestyle in the UK. Data is presented in a combination of tables, figures and text.

(*e*) Using **only** the Orinoco Web page, give one **disadvantage** of **buying** from this website and one **advantage** of **using** Social Trends 2008 in your investigation.

(Enquiry Skills, **2** marks)

[Turn over for Question 3 on *Page ten*

SYLLABUS AREA 3—IDEOLOGIES

QUESTION 3

Answer **one** section only: Section (A)—The USA on pages *ten* to *thirteen*
OR Section (B)—Russia on pages *fourteen* to *seventeen*
OR Section (C)—China on pages *eighteen* to *twenty-one*

(A) **THE USA**

(*a*) *American citizens can **participate** in politics in many ways.*

Describe, **in detail**, the ways in which *American citizens can **participate** in politics.*

In your answer, you **must** use American examples.

(Knowledge and Understanding, **8** marks)

QUESTION 3 (A) (CONTINUED)

(*b*) Study Sources 1 and 2 below, then answer the question which follows.

SOURCE 1

Average Personal Income Level Per Person in the 10 Wealthiest US States ($)

	2003	2004	2005
Colorado	34 500	36 000	37 500
Connecticut	42 000	45 400	47 500
Delaware	34 100	35 900	37 100
Maryland	37 500	39 200	42 000
Massachusetts	39 500	41 800	43 700
Minnesota	34 000	35 900	37 300
New Hampshire	35 100	37 000	37 800
New Jersey	39 600	41 300	43 800
New York	36 100	38 200	40 100
Virginia	33 700	35 500	37 600

SOURCE 2

Income Distribution in the USA

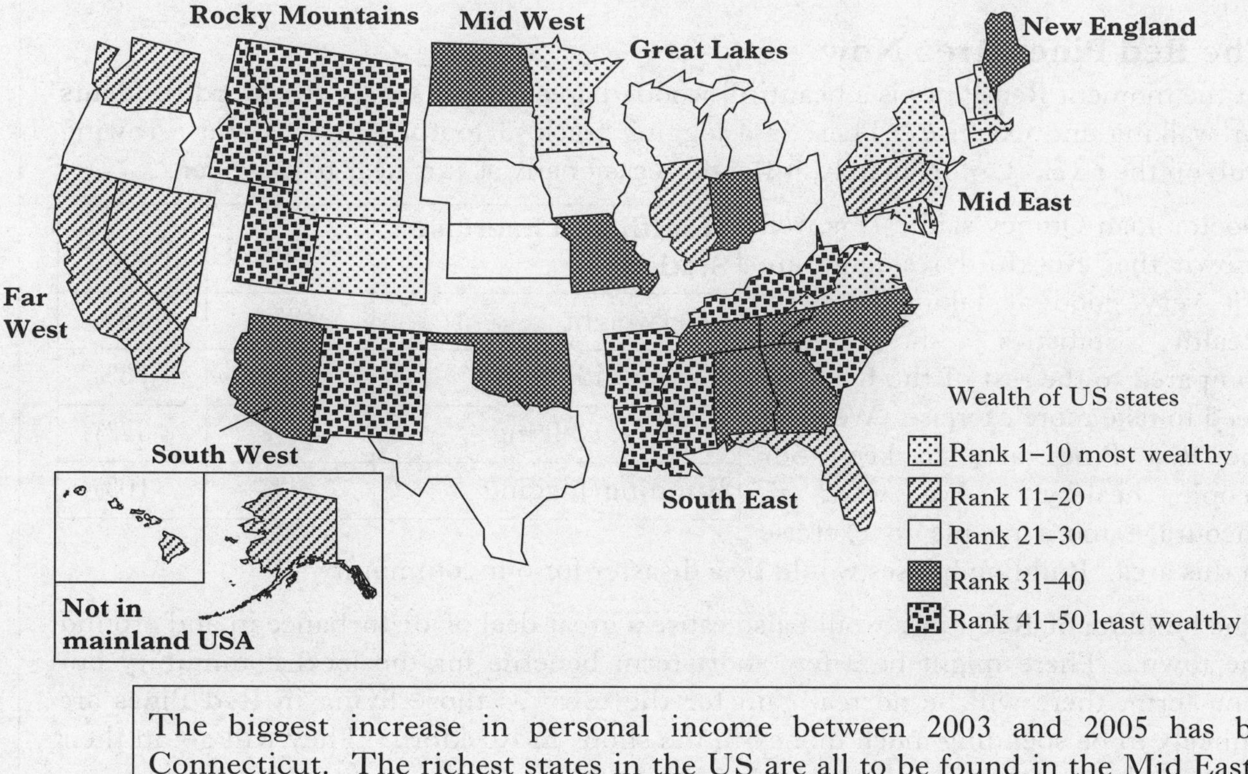

The biggest increase in personal income between 2003 and 2005 has been in Connecticut. The richest states in the US are all to be found in the Mid East of the country.

View of a Wall Street Economist

Using **only** the information above, give **one** reason to **support** and **one** reason to **oppose** the view of the Wall Street Economist.

(Enquiry Skills, **4** marks)

QUESTION 3 (A) (CONTINUED)

(*c*) Study the information in Sources 1, 2 and 3 below and on the next page, then answer the question which follows.

SOURCE 1

The Rockford Record

Your local voice, free to all 10 000 homes in Rockford City (23 May 2008)

New Housing Project Causes Local Anger

A recent public meeting in Rockford City Hall was attended by 500 local people. They were told about plans for a new gated community of 700 houses called "Red Pines". It is to be built by the Allan Building Company.

The gated community of Red Pines would be a walled housing development to which public access would be restricted. It would be guarded using CCTV and security personnel. The complex would have its own supermarkets, restaurants and bars.

The people at the meeting showed mixed feelings, for and against the possible development.

In 2004, gated communities housed 16 million Americans, about 6% of all households. Homeowners in gated communities live in upmarket and mostly white developments. Affluent black American homeowners are less likely than white people to live in gated communities.

The Red Pines Area Now

At the moment Red Pines is a beautiful wooded area. It is used by Rockford residents for walking and exercise. There is a jogging track, 3 football pitches and a rowing club on the river. Unfortunately, it floods occasionally as it is near to the river.

Doctor Joan Quincy said, "It is well known that Rockford residents are not very good at taking exercise. Health statistics show that compared to the rest of the USA we need to take more exercise. We need the Red Pines area to keep our people healthy. We want to encourage more people to exercise in this area. Building houses would be a disaster for our community."

Health and Exercise Statistics	Rockford	USA
Overweight	48%	35%
Bicycle riding	6%	16%
Exercise walking	16%	32%
Running/Jogging	4%	10%

The building of Red Pines would also cause a great deal of disturbance in and around the town. There might be a few short-term benefits for the local community but long-term, there will be no real gain for the town as those living in Red Pines are unlikely to be spending much money in the shops in Rockford. They will get in their cars and drive to the city which is only 15 miles away.

Doctor Quincy is also Chairperson of the Rockford Residents' Association.

QUESTION 3 (A) (*c*) (CONTINUED)

SOURCE 2

What the people want

The Rockford Record decided to find out the views of local people about the "Red Pines" development. We conducted an opinion poll and received 8900 replies from 10 000 homes and feel that this survey shows the real views of the people.

The Questions: How Important	Unimportant	Not very important	Important	Very important
is it that Rockford stays a racially mixed town?	20%	15%	25%	40%
a problem is jobs to the people of Rockford?	15%	25%	20%	40%
is the Red Pines area for exercise?	20%	10%	45%	25%

Ethnic origin of Rockford's Residents

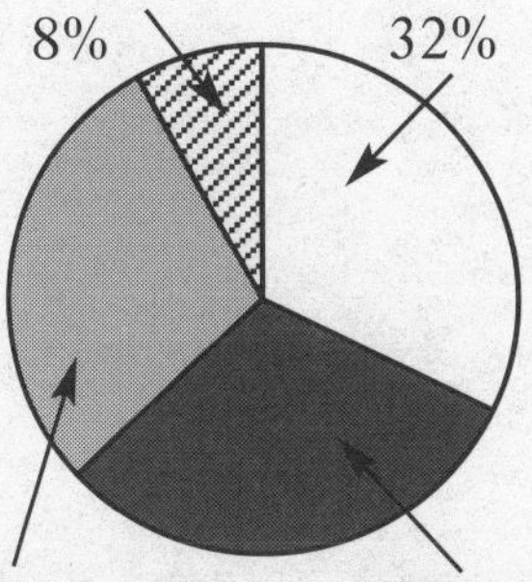

SOURCE 3

Leaflet from Allan Building Company

I am Chairman of the Allan Building Company and I was born in Rockford. I have stayed here all my life and want to do the best for Rockford. There is great demand for this type of housing from middle and upper income groups who would not live in Rockford because of their fear of rising crime there. We already have 500 new families from outwith Rockford, wanting to move into Red Pines whenever it is built. They are a mixture of young and old with an ethnic mix of 50% White, 25% Hispanic, 24% Black and 1% other groups.

Impact on Rockford

SHORT-TERM IMPACT

- Skilled workers employed in the building of Red Pines.
- Unskilled workers also needed.
- Workers on-site spend money in local shops.
- Building supply companies will increase trade.

LONG-TERM IMPACT

- Unskilled jobs will be available, eg cleaners.
- Jobs will be available in the new shops and restaurants.
- Shops in Rockford will gain extra business from the new residents close-by.
- Local shops have the opportunity to become suppliers to the new restaurants and bars which will open.
- Flood prevention measures will stop flooding.

The Red Pines gated development will cause many problems for our health and change the ethnic mix of Rockford. It will bring few benefits to the people of Rockford.

View of Findlay Smith, Editor, The Rockford Record

Using **only** the information in Sources 1, 2 and 3, explain, **in detail, the extent to which** Findlay Smith could be accused of being **selective in the use of facts**.

(Enquiry Skills, **8** marks)

[NOW GO TO QUESTION 4 ON PAGE 22]

QUESTION 3 (CONTINUED)

(B) **RUSSIA**

(*a*) *Russian citizens can* ***participate*** *in politics in many ways.*

Describe, **in detail**, the ways in which *Russian citizens can* ***participate*** *in politics.*

In your answer, you **must** use Russian examples.

(Knowledge and Understanding, **8** marks)

QUESTION 3 (B) (CONTINUED)

(*b*) Study Sources 1 and 2 below, then answer the question which follows.

SOURCE 1

Index of growth of Industry and Agriculture in Russia

Sector	**2001**	**2002**	**2003**	**2004**	**2005**
Industry	1108	1443	1601	1681	2995
Agriculture	204	287	309	302	625

SOURCE 2

The ways in which the Russian people spend their money
(% of total)

	2002	**2003**	**2004**	**2005**
Foodstuffs	50·2	45·8	53·4	53·7
Alcohol	2·5	2·8	2·6	2·5
Non-foods	31·3	36·5	30·1	30·8
Services	16·0	14·9	13·9	13·0

Both Industry and Agriculture have grown each year between 2002 and 2005. The amount spent on foodstuffs is the only one which has seen a rise between 2002 and 2005.

View of a Russian Economist

Using **only** the information above, give **one** reason to **support** and **one** reason to **oppose** the view of the Russian Economist.

(Enquiry Skills, **4** marks)

[Turn over

QUESTION 3 (B) (CONTINUED)

(*c*) Study the information from Sources 1, 2 and 3 below and on the next page, then answer the question which follows.

SOURCE 1

The Vorkuta Reporter

Your local voice, free to all 10 000 homes in Vorkuta (23 May 2008)

New Housing Project Causes Local Anger

A recent public meeting in Vorkuta Town Hall was attended by 500 local people. They were told about plans for a new gated community of 700 houses called "Sosny Woods". It is to be built by the Andropov Building Company.

The gated community of Sosny Woods would be a walled housing development to which public access would be restricted. It would be guarded using CCTV and security personnel. The complex would have its own supermarkets, restaurants and bars.

The people at the meeting showed mixed feelings, for and against the possible development.

Gated communities have been around for a long time in Russia. It used to be the case that they were only built for high-ranking political officials. This is changing and more and more are being built for Russians who are rich enough to be able to buy them.

The Sosny Woods Area Now

At the moment, the Sosny Woods area is a beautiful wooded area. It is used by Vorkuta residents for walking and exercise. There is a jogging track, 3 football pitches and a rowing club on the river. Unfortunately, it floods occasionally as it is near to the river.

Health and Exercise Statistics	Vorkuta	Russia
Overweight	48%	35%
Bicycle riding	6%	16%
Exercise walking	16%	32%
Running/Jogging	4%	10%

Doctor Yuri Press said, "It is well known that Vorkuta residents are not very good at taking exercise. Health statistics show that compared to the rest of Russia we need to take more exercise. We need the Sosny Woods area to keep our people healthy. We want to encourage more people to exercise in this area. Building houses would be a disaster for our community."

The building of Sosny Woods would also cause a great deal of disturbance in and around the town. There might be a few short-term benefits for the local community but long-term, there will be no real gain for the town as those living in Sosny Woods are unlikely to be spending much money in the shops in Vorkuta. They will get in their cars and drive to the city which is only 15 miles away.

Doctor Press is also chairperson of the Vorkuta Residents' Association.

QUESTION 3 (B) (*c*) (CONTINUED)

SOURCE 2

What the people want

The Vorkuta Record decided to find out the views of local people about the "Sosny Woods" development. We conducted an opinion poll and received 8900 replies from 10 000 homes and feel that this survey shows the real views of the people.

The Questions: How Important	Unimportant	Not very important	Important	Very important
is it that Vorkuta keeps in-comers to a minimum?	20%	15%	25%	40%
a problem is jobs to the people of Vorkuta?	20%	40%	25%	15%
is the Sosny Woods area for exercise?	20%	10%	45%	25%

SOURCE 3

Leaflet from Andropov Building Company

I am Chairman of the Andropov Building Company and I was born in Vorkuta. I have stayed here all my life and want to do the best for the town. There is a great demand for this type of housing from middle and upper income groups. They are keen to move to Vorkuta because of their fear of rising crime in nearby cities. We already have 500 new families wanting to move into Sosny Woods whenever it is built. They are a mixture of age ranges and backgrounds. 73% are people with no connection to the town, 17% are people who live in nearby towns and 10% are Vorkuta residents.

Benefits to Vorkuta

SHORT-TERM IMPACT

- Skilled workers employed in the building of Sosny Woods.
- Unskilled workers also needed.
- Workers on-site spend money in local shops.
- Building supply companies will increase trade.

LONG-TERM IMPACT

- Unskilled jobs will be available, eg cleaners.
- Jobs will be available in the new shops and restaurants.
- Shops in Vorkuta will gain extra business from the new residents close-by.
- Local shops have the opportunity to become suppliers to the new restaurants and bars which will open.
- Flood prevention measures will stop flooding.

The Sosny Woods Gated Development will cause many problems for our health and allow outsiders to dominate Vorkuta. It will bring few benefits to the people of Vorkuta.

View of Dmitri Arshavin, Editor, The Vorkuta Reporter

Using **only** the information in Sources 1, 2 and 3, explain, **in detail**, **the extent to which** Dmitri Arshavin could be accused of being **selective in the use of facts**.

(Enquiry Skills, **8** marks)

[NOW GO TO QUESTION 4 ON PAGE 22]

QUESTION 3 (CONTINUED)

(C) **CHINA**

(*a*) | *Chinese citizens can **participate** in politics in many ways.*

Describe, **in detail**, the ways in which *Chinese citizens can **participate** in politics.*

In your answer, you **must** use Chinese examples.

(Knowledge and Understanding, **8** marks)

QUESTION 3 (C) (CONTINUED)

(*b*) Study Sources 1 and 2 below, then answer the question which follows.

SOURCE 1
Average Personal Income
Top Ten Chinese Regions (Yuan)

Region	2003	2004	2005
Beijing	35 000	37 000	39 500
Tianjin	29 500	31 500	34 000
Hebei	13 000	13 500	13 500
Liaoning	15 000	16 500	17 000
Heilongjiang	13 000	14 000	15 500
Shanghai	51 000	55 500	61 000
Zhejiang	21 000	24 000	25 000
Fujian	15 500	17 000	18 000
Shangdong	16 000	17 000	17 500
Guangdong	18 500	20 000	21 000

SOURCE 2
China's Ten Richest Regions

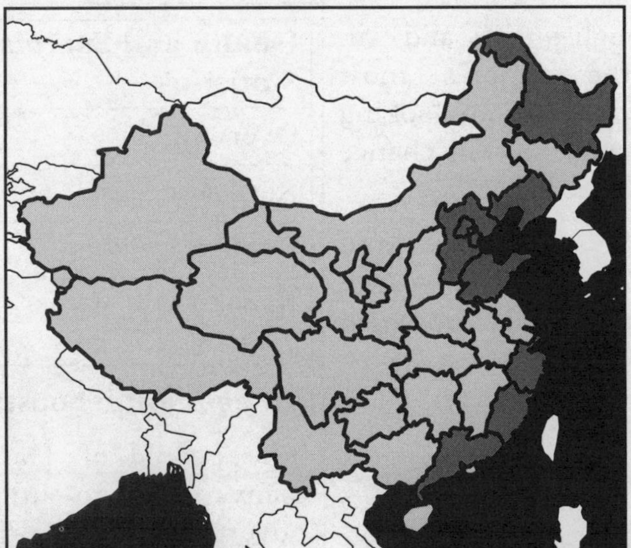

Ten richest regions of China
Rest of China

> The greatest increase in personal income has been experienced by those living in Shanghai. However, the wealthiest regions are evenly distributed throughout China.

View of Chinese Economist

Using **only** the information above, give **one** reason to **support** and **one** reason to **oppose** the view of the Chinese Economist.

(Enquiry Skills, **4** marks)

QUESTION 3 (C) (CONTINUED)

(*c*) Study the information from Sources 1, 2 and 3 below and on the next page, then answer the question which follows.

SOURCE 1

The Hankou Herald

Free to all 50 000 residents. Published by the Peoples' Congress of Hankou.

Joy as riverside housing is opened

The city authorities announced yesterday that the brand new "Riverside Garden" development of top quality houses is to open next month. The development (next to the Anze river) attracted 300 building jobs to the area, which have benefited Hankou's economy.

The new housing is known as a "Gated Community". This means that a wall will surround the 500 houses and local people will be employed as security guards and CCTV operators. Around 300 local people will have well-paid jobs in the community's facilities, eg medical centre, golf course, tennis courts, shops and gym.

The housing is very high quality and will attract many of the region's most successful business people who are looking for an escape from the city, and the chance to relax, play sport and socialise.

It will raise the profile of the area and possibly tempt more people to open new businesses in Hankou which is depressed economically and in need of a boost.

The Riverside area before

The area was only used by a few fishermen. Wages were poor and it was the only work available.

The town's people rarely went there. Sports facilities in all parts of the town, including the Riverside area, were very poor.

Local doctor speaks out

Dr Pu Zihao says, "It is well known that Hankou residents are not very good at taking exercise. Health statistics show that compared to the rest of China we need to be more active. We need new sporting facilities in the Riverside area to keep our people healthy. Building these houses is good for our community".

"Anyone will be able to use the sports facilities if they are willing to pay the yearly Sports Club membership fee of only 50 yuan."

(Dr Pu is a member of the "Healthy Hankou Campaign".)

Health and Exercise Statistics	Hankou	China
Overweight	27%	21%
Regular cyclists	64%	73%
Regular walkers	51%	78%
Regular golf/tennis players	1%	8%

An economic boost!

The people of Hankou have tried for many years to lift themselves out of poverty but they have not succeeded. Average wages are lower than the Chinese average and have shown little improvement in the last few years.

Average Wages (yuan)

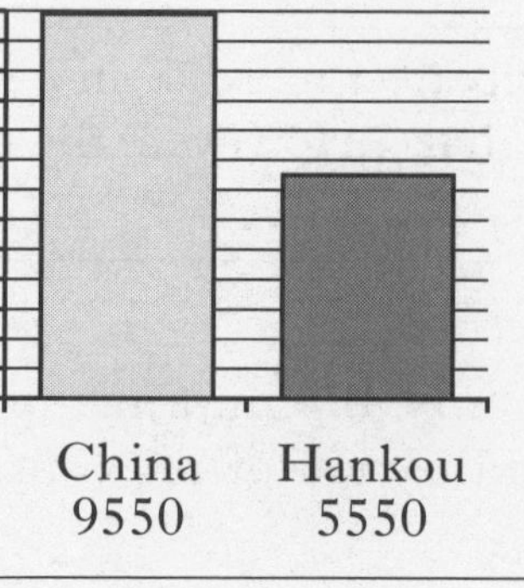

QUESTION 3 (C) (*c*) (CONTINUED)

SOURCE 2

What the people want

We decided to find out the views of the local people about the Riverside development. We sent questionnaires to 10 000 local homes and received 8900 replies. The views of local people really have been heard.

Question: How important are the following things for Hankou?

	Unimportant	Not very important	Important	Very important
Higher pay	13%	13%	20%	54%
Attracting new businesses	5%	14%	30%	51%
Protecting existing farmers and fishermen	40%	25%	26%	9%

View of Li Jie – a local fisherman

I have lost my job and so have six of my friends. Hankou fishermen are all against this new housing development. Riverside Garden might bring a few short-term benefits for the local community but, in the long term, there will be no real gain for the town. Those living in Riverside Garden are unlikely to be spending much money in the shops in Hankou. They will only use the shops in Riverside Garden as there will be little to interest them in Hankou or they will get in their cars and drive to the city which is only one hour's drive away.

SOURCE 3

Leaflet from Hankou Authorities

IMPACT ON HANKOU

- Unskilled jobs will be available, eg cleaners.
- Jobs will be available in the new shops and restaurants.
- Shops in Hankou will gain extra business from the new residents close-by.
- Local shops have the opportunity to become suppliers to the new restaurants and bars which will open.
- Affordable sports facilities

The Riverside Gated Development will improve the health of people living in Hankou. It will bring much needed benefits to the people of Hankou. Everyone living in Hankou is excited by the opening of Riverside Garden.

View of Pu Wei, Editor, The Hankou Herald

Using **only** the information in Sources 1, 2 and 3, explain, **in detail**, **the extent to which** Pu Wei could be accused of being **selective in the use of facts**.

(Enquiry Skills, **8** marks)

[NOW GO TO QUESTION 4 ON PAGE 22]

SYLLABUS AREA 4—INTERNATIONAL RELATIONS

QUESTION 4

(*a*) **SELECTED ISSUES IN AFRICA**

HIV/AIDS on the increase in large parts of Africa	Civil wars rage on in parts of Africa	Prices fall on a number of raw materials produced in some African countries

Choose **one** issue from the boxes above.

Explain, **in detail**, why your chosen issue may prevent some African governments **meeting the needs** of their people.

(Knowledge & Understanding, **4** marks)

QUESTION 4 (CONTINUED)

(*b*) *European governments have taken actions to protect their populations from possible threats to their security.*

Describe, **in detail**, some of the actions taken by *European governments to protect their populations from possible threats to their security*.

(Knowledge & Understanding, **4** marks)

[Turn over

QUESTION 4 (CONTINUED)

(*c*) Study the information in Sources 1, 2 and 3 below and on the next page, then answer the question which follows.

SOURCE 1
Millennium Development Goals

The Millennium Development Goals were agreed by 189 countries in New York in 2000.

Selected Millennium Development Goals

1: Reduce child mortality

2: Achieve primary education for all

3: Remove extreme poverty and hunger

4: Combat diseases

These goals represented a commitment by rich and poor nations to expand social and economic progress in all regions of the world, as well as creating a global partnership for reducing levels of poverty and suffering in less developed countries by 2015.

Many are now questioning the commitment of the More Developed Countries to making these goals a reality as few MDCs give the UN recommended 0·7% of Gross National Income (GNI).

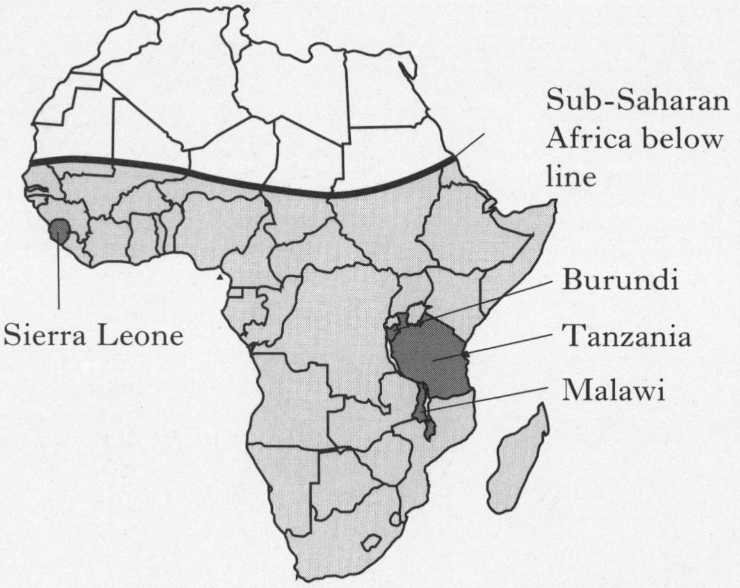

The World's Four Poorest Countries

Average Income Per Person ($)	
1. Sierra Leone	490
2. Tanzania	523
3. Burundi	591
4. Malawi	615

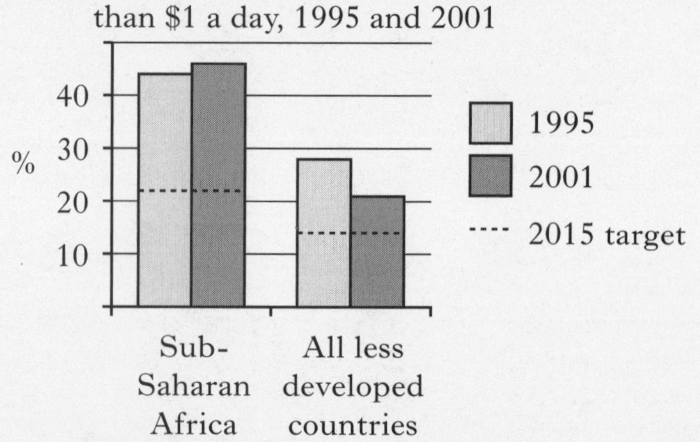

QUESTION 4 (*c*) (CONTINUED)

SOURCE 2: Aid given by selected Donor Countries

Selected Donor Countries	Aid Given 2004 $ billions (% of GNI)	2010 (prediction) $ billions (% of GNI)	% increase	Largest recipients ($ millions)
UK	7·88 (0·36)	14·60 (0·59)	85	1. India ($419) 2. Bangladesh ($267) 3. Tanzania ($265)
USA	19·7 (0·17)	24·00 (0·18)	22	1. Iraq ($2286) 2. Congo ($804) 3. Egypt ($767)
Portugal	1·03 (0·63)	0·93 (0·51)	–10	1. Angola ($367) 2. Cape Verde ($39) 3. Timor ($34)
Italy	2·46 (0·15)	9·26 (0·51)	276	1. Dem. Rep. Congo ($235) 2. China ($52) 3. Tunisia ($41)

SOURCE 3

Four Poorest African Countries – Progress on selected Millennium Development Goals

	Sierra Leone		Tanzania		Burundi		Malawi	
Selected Indicators / Year	1996	2006	1996	2006	1996	2006	1996	2006
% of population undernourished	44	50	50	44	63	67	50	34
Child Mortality (per 1000 births)	293	283	159	126	190	190	216	175
% 1 year olds vaccinated against measles	37	64	49	91	80	75	90	80
% Primary school enrolment	43	73	94	95	43	57	48	98

Using **only** the information above and opposite, you must **make** and **justify** conclusions about progress towards the Millennium Development Goals using the **four** headings below.

- Progress towards Millennium Development Goal 1
- Progress towards **all** of Millennium Development Goal 3
- The commitment of More Developed Countries to meeting the UN aid recommendation
- The commitment of Donor Countries to the world's **four poorest** nations

(Enquiry Skills, **8** marks)

[*END OF QUESTION PAPER*]

[BLANK PAGE]

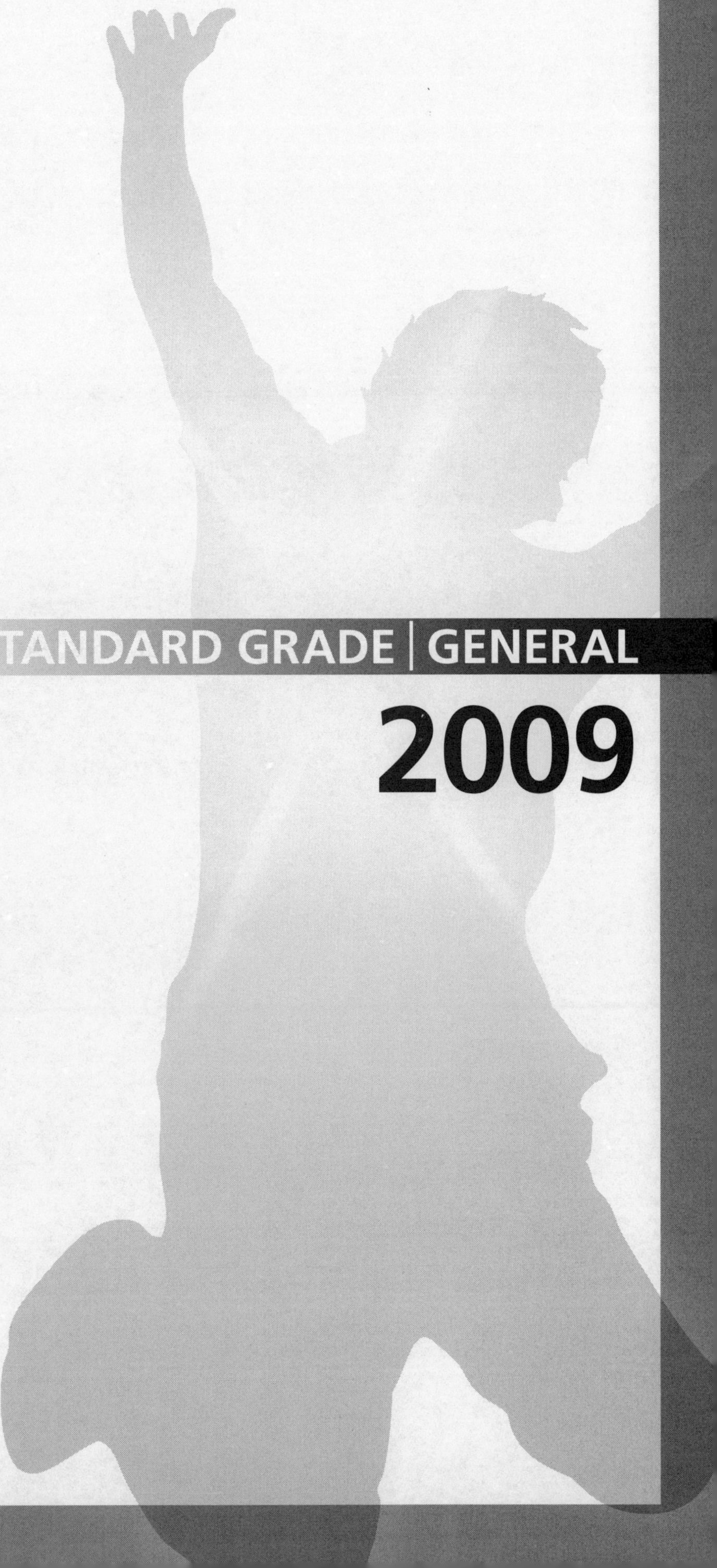

STANDARD GRADE | GENERAL

2009

[BLANK PAGE]

G

2640/402

NATIONAL QUALIFICATIONS 2009

MONDAY, 25 MAY
10.20 AM – 11.50 AM

MODERN STUDIES STANDARD GRADE
General Level

1 Read every question carefully.

2 Answer all questions as fully as you can.

3 If you cannot do a question, go on to the next one. Try again later.

4 In question 3, answer **one** section only: Section (A) The USA **or** Section (B) China.

5 Write your answers in the answer book provided. Indicate clearly, in the left hand margin, the question and section of question being answered. Do not write in the right hand margin.

SYLLABUS AREA 1—LIVING IN A DEMOCRACY

QUESTION 1

(*a*) *Members of the Scottish Parliament (MSPs) can represent their constituents in many ways.*

Extract from an MSP's diary

MAY 2009

Monday 18

2·00pm : Meet constituents at Holyrood

Tuesday 19

10·30 pm : Interview with journalist

Wednesday 20

11·00am : Health Committee Meeting in Room 2

Thursday 21

12 noon : First Minister's Questions

Friday 22

10·00am – 4·00pm : Constituency Office

Describe **two** ways in which MSPs **represent** their constituents.

To answer this question, you may wish to use the information above.

(Knowledge & Understanding, **4** marks)

QUESTION 1 (CONTINUED)

(*b*) Study Sources 1 and 2 below, then answer the question which follows.

Election Information, 2007 Scottish Parliament

SOURCE 1

Percentage of Spoilt Ballot Papers in the Scottish Parliament Election in 2007

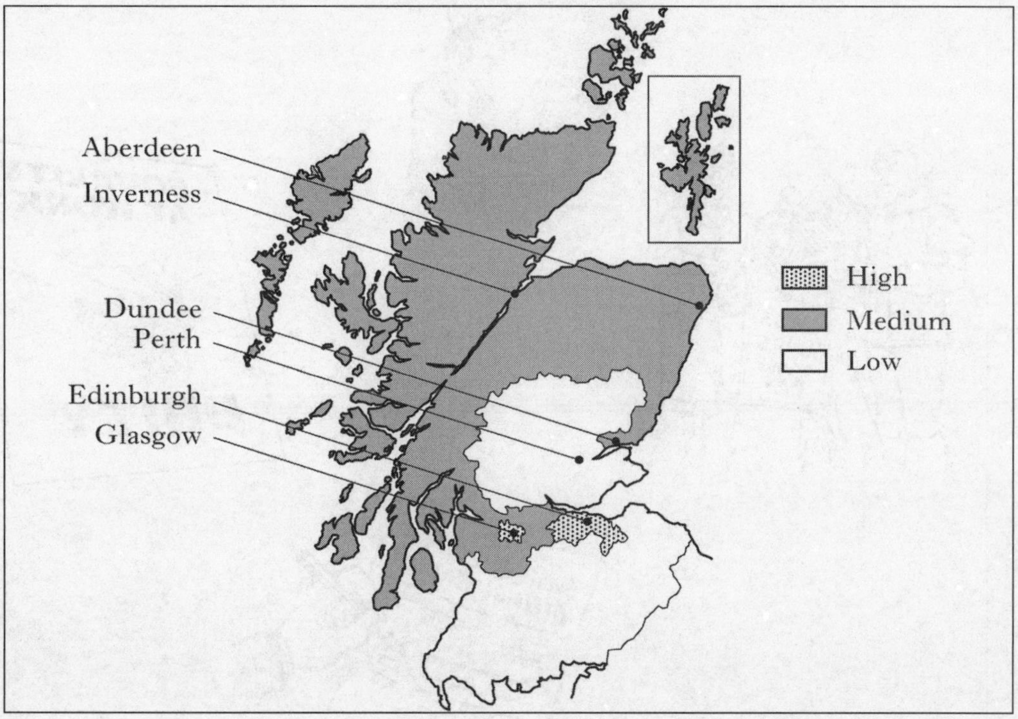

SOURCE 2

The Number of Spoilt Ballot Papers and Majorities in Selected Constituencies (2007)

Constituency	Spoilt Ballot Papers (Number of votes not counted in result)	Majority (Number of votes candidate won by)
Aberdeen North	1173	3749
Airdrie and Shotts	1536	1446
Cunninghame South	1055	2168
Dumfries	1006	2839
Midlothian	1649	1702

Edinburgh and Glasgow have the highest percentage of spoilt ballot papers. The number of spoilt ballot papers did not affect the result in any of the selected constituencies.

View of Holly Kerr

Using **only** Sources 1 and 2 above, give **one** reason to **support** and **one** reason to **oppose** the view of Holly Kerr.

(Enquiry Skills, **4** marks)

QUESTION 1 (CONTINUED)

(*c*)

Many workers choose to join a trade union. As members of a trade union, workers have rights that are important to them.

Give **two rights** that members of a trade union have.

Choose **one** of these **rights** and explain why it is important to workers.

To answer this question, you may wish to use the drawing above.

(Knowledge and Understanding, **4** marks)

QUESTION 1 (CONTINUED)

(*d*) Study Sources 1 and 2 below, then answer the question which follows.

Information about Industrial Disputes in the UK

SOURCE 1

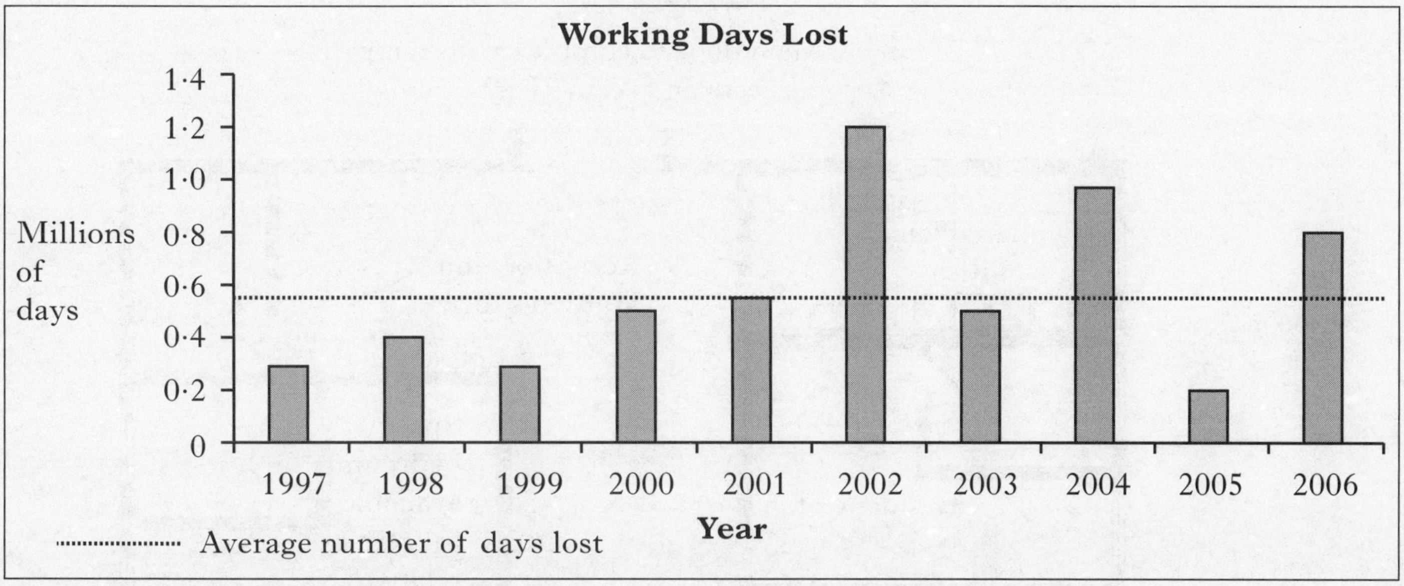

SOURCE 2

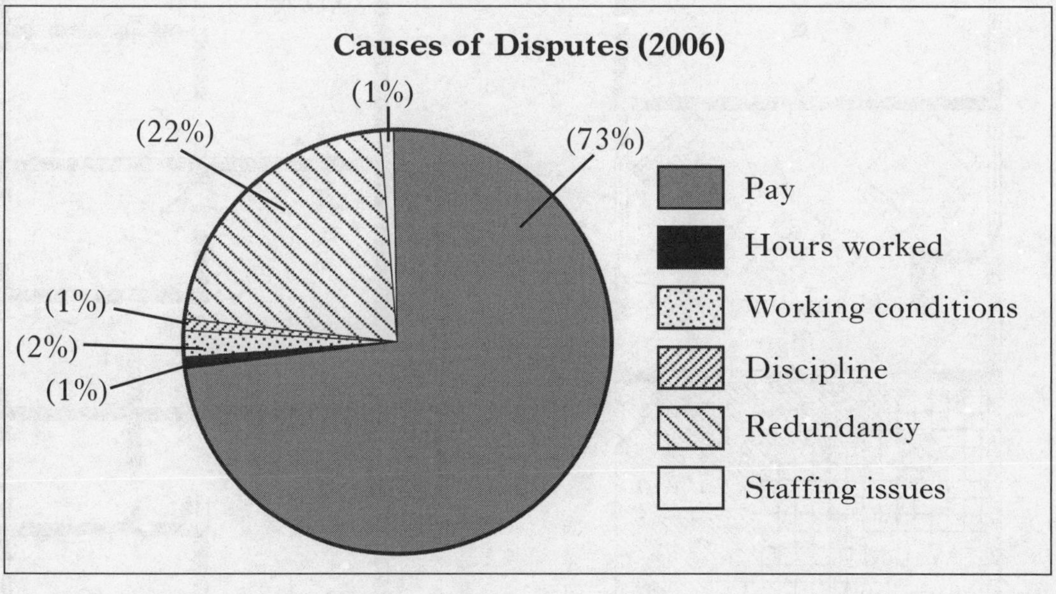

Write down **two** conclusions about industrial disputes in the UK.

You should write **one** conclusion **with evidence** about **each** of the following.

- The main cause of industrial disputes in 2006.
- The year which was the furthest from the average for working days lost.

Your answer **must** be based entirely on the Sources above.

(Enquiry Skills, **4** marks)

SYLLABUS AREA 2—CHANGING SOCIETY

QUESTION 2

(*a*) *Sheltered housing can help meet the **needs** of elderly people.*

Main door to complex with ramp access and security intercom

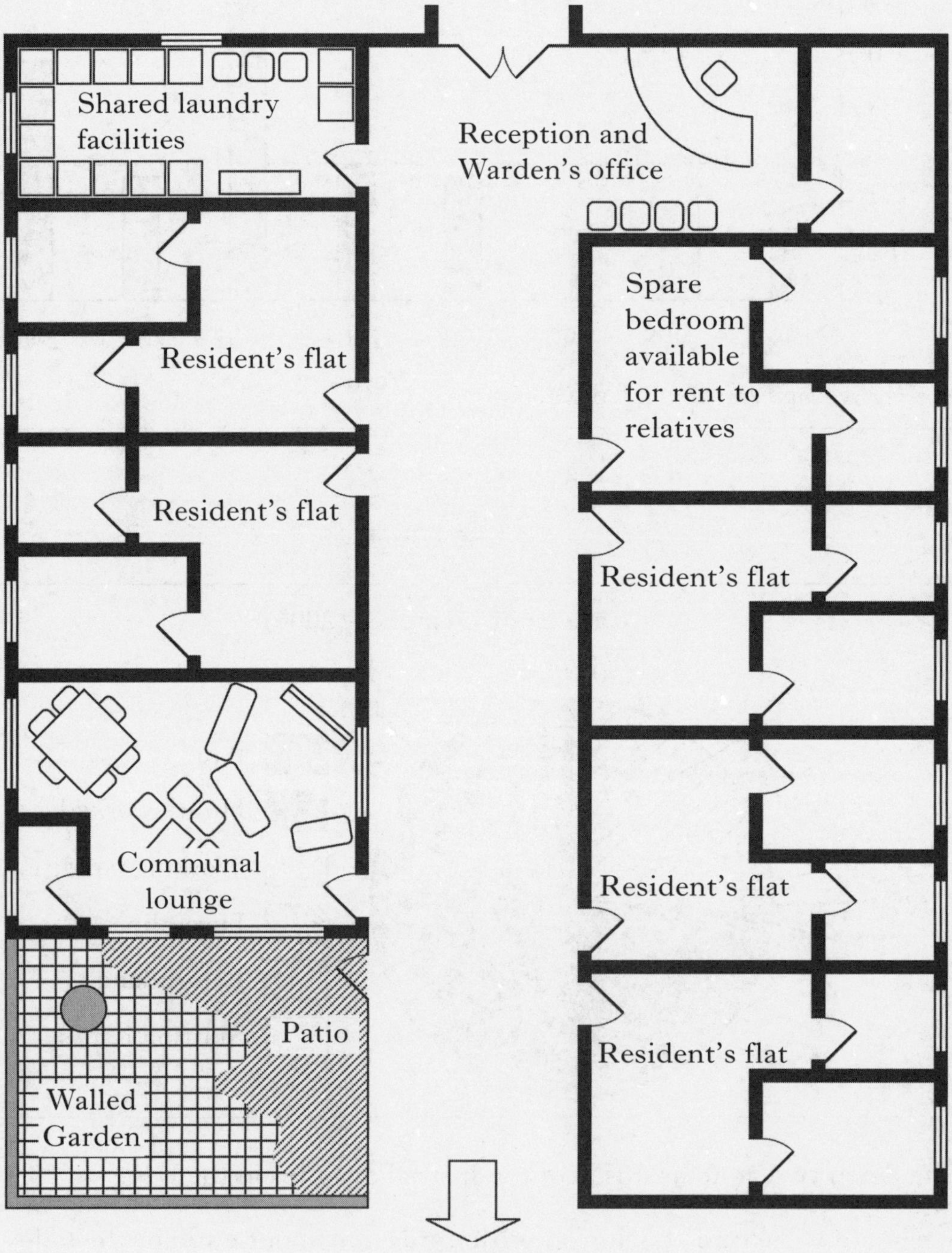

More flats this way

Describe **two** ways in which *sheltered housing can help meet the **needs** of elderly people.*

To answer this question you may wish to use the drawing above.

(Knowledge and Understanding, **4** marks)

QUESTION 2 (CONTINUED)

(*b*) Study Sources 1 and 2 below, then answer the question which follows.

SOURCE 1

The Scottish Workforce

In 2006, Scotland's population was 5,116,900. It was 5,094,800 the previous year, and 5,064,200 in 2001.

The number of people in employment is called the workforce. In 2006, there were 2,500,000 people in work in Scotland. The number of male workers had increased by 5·6% since 1996, and the number of females had gone up by 11·2%.

SOURCE 2

Unemployment in Scotland, 2000–2006 (%)			
Year	**Male**	**Female**	**Total**
2000	6·4	2·2	4·5
2001	5·9	1·9	4·0
2002	5·8	1·8	3·9
2003	5·5	1·8	3·7
2004	5·1	1·7	3·5
2005	4·7	1·6	3·2
2006	4·8	1·7	3·3

Statements made by Betty Hill

- The population has increased in recent years.
- The percentage of male workers has increased much more than the percentage of female workers.
- Female unemployment has always been lower than male unemployment.
- Total unemployment has fallen every year since 2000.

Using **only** Sources 1 and 2 above, write down **two** statements made by Betty Hill which are **exaggerated.**

Using the information in the Sources, give **one** reason why **each** of the statements you have chosen is **exaggerated**.

(Enquiry Skills, **4** marks)

[Turn over

QUESTION 2 (CONTINUED)

(*c*) *Some elderly people are wealthier than other elderly people.*

Give **two** reasons to explain why *some elderly people are wealthier than other elderly people*.

(Knowledge and Understanding, **4** marks)

(*d*) Study Sources 1 and 2 below, then answer the question which follows.

SOURCE 1

VIEW OF ALEX BROWN

The number of unemployed people in the United Kingdom has fallen in recent years.

Jobseeker's Allowance (JSA) was introduced by the Government to replace Unemployment Benefit. It is a weekly payment which is just enough to meet an unemployed person's basic needs.

To receive this benefit, an unemployed person must be aged 18 years or over, and actively seeking work.

JSA aims to get unemployed people into a job that best suits their qualifications.

SOURCE 2

VIEW OF NICOLA McLEAN

Jobseeker's Allowance (JSA) tries to push people off benefits and into any low paid job that's available.

Any unemployed person who is looking for a job, and is 18 or over, can apply.

The money is paid every week, but it is not enough for unemployed people to live on.

The Government brought in JSA as a replacement for Unemployment Benefit.

In the last few years there has been a decrease in the level of unemployment in the United Kingdom.

Sources 1 and 2 give different views about the **Jobseeker's Allowance**.

Write down **two** differences between these views.

You **must** only use information from the Sources above.

(Enquiry Skills, **4** marks)

SYLLABUS AREA 3 — IDEOLOGIES

QUESTION 3

Answer **ONE** section only: Section (A)—The USA on pages *nine* to *twelve*

OR Section (B)—China on pages *thirteen* to *sixteen*

(A) THE USA

(*a*) *American people can* ***participate*** *in politics in many ways.*

Describe **two** ways in which *American people can* ***participate*** *in politics* in the USA.

In your answer, you **must** use American examples.

To answer this question, you may wish to use the drawings above.

(Knowledge & Understanding, **4** marks)

[Turn over

QUESTION 3 (A) (CONTINUED)

(*b*) Study Sources 1 and 2 below, then answer the question which follows.

SOURCE 1
USA Ethnic Minority Unemployment Rate

Year	Ethnic Minority Groups		
	Black	**Hispanic**	**Asian**
1998	8·9%	7·2%	3·8%
2000	7·6%	5·7%	3·6%
2002	10·2%	7·5%	5·9%
2004	10·4%	7·0%	4·4%
2006	8·9%	5·2%	3·0%

SOURCE 2

The Rockford Record

Home Ownership Today

Home ownership is seen as an important part of the American Dream in the USA.

In 2006, home ownership was 75% for White families but only 47% for Black, 50% for Hispanic and 60% for Asian families. Compared to 1998, this is an increase of 3% for White families, 2% for Black families, 5% for Hispanic families and for Asian families the increase is 8%.

Today, there are still big differences in the rates of home ownership between whites and other ethnic minority groups.

In 2006, unemployment was at its lowest for all ethnic minority groups. The group with the lowest unemployment in 2006 has seen the greatest increase in home ownership.

View of Ann Struther

Using **only** Source 1 and Source 2 above, give **one** reason to **support** and **one** reason to **oppose** the view of Ann Struther.

(Enquiry Skills, **4** marks)

QUESTION 3 (A) (CONTINUED)

You are investigating the topic in the box below.

CRIME IN THE USA

Answer questions (*c*), (*d*) and (*e*) which follow.

(*c*) As part of the **Planning Stage**, give **two** relevant **aims** for your investigation.

(Enquiry Skills, **2** marks)

Relatives from the USA are visiting Scotland on holiday and you decide to talk to them about your investigation.

(*d*) Give **two** advantages of talking to your relatives from the USA as a way of finding out information for your investigation.

(Enquiry Skills, **2** marks)

[Turn over

QUESTION 3 (A) (CONTINUED)

You find out that your relatives have brought a copy of the "**Rockford Record**" with them. You find the page below in the newspaper.

Use the newspaper page below to answer question (*e*).

The Rockford Record **page 2**

	California	Texas	Mississippi	New York
High School Graduates	77%	76%	73%	79%
People living in poverty	13%	16%	19%	14%
Violent crimes per 100,000	526	529	278	445
Unemployment rate	5%	5%	7%	4%

Special Reports

America at War
Full coverage of the conflicts in Iraq and Afghanistan and of the "War on Terror" on pages 12 and 13.

Crime in the USA
See "Crime in the USA – Special Report" on pages 10 and 11.

The Top Schools
Find your school in our 2009 Index – is your school the best or the worst?

E-MAIL NEWSLETTERS
Sign up for your weekly newsletter. These specialised e-mails give extra information on each topic.

News – Breaking news
Politics – The 2008 Elections
Issues – Youth Crime
Life – Personal Health
Sports – Baseball

Crime in Rockford

There will be a public meeting about local crime in the town hall on Friday. Come along and make your views known to the Chief of Police who will be there.

(*e*) Give **two** ways in which you could use the newspaper page above to help with your investigation into "Crime in the USA".

For **each** way, explain why it would be a **good** way to help you with your investigation.

(Enquiry Skills, **4** marks)

NOW GO TO QUESTION 4 ON PAGE SEVENTEEN

QUESTION 3 (CONTINUED)

(B) **CHINA**

(*a*) *Chinese people can* ***participate*** *in politics in many ways.*

Describe **two** ways in which *Chinese people can* ***participate*** *in politics* in China.

In your answer, you **must** use Chinese examples.

To answer this question, you may wish to use the drawings above.

(Knowledge & Understanding, **4** marks)

[Turn over

QUESTION 3 (B) (CONTINUED)

(*b*) Study Sources 1 and 2 below, then answer the question which follows.

SOURCE 1
Unemployment Rate in Selected Chinese Regions

Year	Beijing	Guangdong	Henan
1998	0·8%	3·0%	3·0%
2000	0·9%	3·2%	3·1%
2002	1·4%	3·4%	3·5%
2004	2·3%	3·6%	4·7%
2006	2·5%	3·7%	4·8%

SOURCE 2

The Nanchong News

Report about the Wealth Gap

Unemployment in China is increasing the gap between rich and poor.

Unemployed people in Henan province struggle to live on $12 per month in benefits whereas the average monthly wage is $64. The average monthly wage in Beijing is $138 and in Guangdong it is $149.

Different education levels affect the differences in income.

The highest ownership of cars was in Beijing where 20% of households owned a car whereas in Guangdong it was 8% and in Henan 3%.

Since 1998, unemployment has increased in all the selected regions. The region with the lowest rate of unemployment in 2006 had the highest average monthly income.

View of Kathy Lou

Using **only** Source 1 and Source 2 above, give **one** reason to **support** and **one** reason to **oppose** the view of Kathy Lou.

(Enquiry Skills, **4** marks)

QUESTION 3 (B) (CONTINUED)

You are investigating the topic in the box below.

CRIME IN CHINA

Answer questions (*c*), (*d*) and (*e*) which follow.

(*c*) As part of the **Planning Stage**, give **two** relevant **aims** for your investigation.

(Enquiry Skills, **2** marks)

Relatives from China are visiting Scotland on holiday and you decide to talk to them about your investigation.

(*d*) Give **two** advantages of talking to your relatives from China as a way of finding out information for your investigation.

(Enquiry Skills, **2** marks)

[Turn over

QUESTION 3 (B) (CONTINUED)

You find out that your relatives have brought a copy of the "**Kowloon Herald**" with them. You find the page below in the newspaper.

Use the newspaper page below to answer question (*e*).

The Kowloon Herald **page 2**

Hong Kong's Biggest English Speaking Newspaper

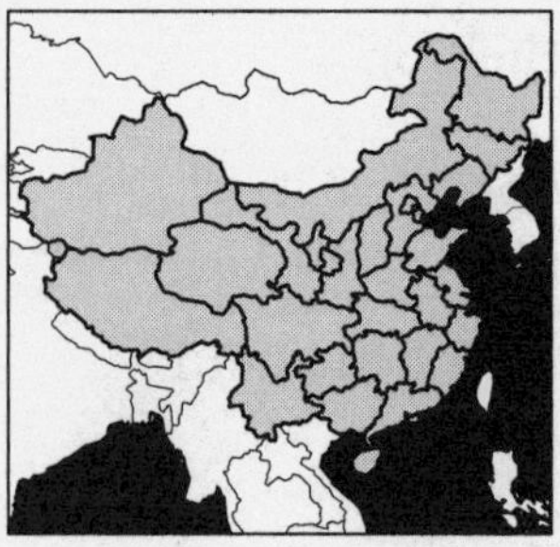

	Hong Kong	**Guangzhou**	**Sichuan**	**Henan**
High School Graduates	96%	91%	72%	75%
People living in poverty	18%	16%	27%	27%
Violent crimes per 100,000	138	147	68	62
Unemployment rate	4%	3%	4·5%	5%

Special Reports

The Chinese Economy
Analysis of the rapid growth in the Chinese economy. Could the economy "overheat"? Turn to pages 7 and 8 to find out.

Crime in China
See "Crime in China – Special Report" on pages 10 and 11.

Olympic Impact
Turn to pages 12 and 13 to find out how the Beijing Olympics boosted Chinese tourism.

E-MAIL NEWSLETTERS
Sign up for your weekly newsletter. These specialised e-mails give extra information on each topic.

News –	Breaking news
Politics –	Voting in the Party Congress
Issues –	Youth Crime
Life –	Has the One Child Policy worked?
Sports –	World Cup 2010

Crime in Hong Kong

The head of the Ministry for Public Security will be in Hong Kong on Friday to hear your views on the issue of crime. Come along and make your views known.

(*e*) Give **two** ways in which you could use the newspaper page above to help with your investigation into "Crime in China".

For **each** way, explain why it would be a **good** way to help you with your investigation.

(Enquiry Skills, **4** marks)

NOW GO TO QUESTION 4 ON PAGE SEVENTEEN

SYLLABUS AREA 4 - INTERNATIONAL RELATIONS

QUESTION 4

(*a*) **Problems faced by some African countries**

War/Conflict	Debt	HIV/AIDS	Unsafe water

Choose **two** of the problems shown above.

Describe how **each of the problems you have chosen** affects some African countries.

(Knowledge & Understanding, **4** marks)

[Turn over

QUESTION 4 (CONTINUED)

(*b*) Study Sources 1 and 2 below, then answer the question which follows.

SOURCE 1

EU Reform Treaty – The governments say "YES"

In 2007, all 27 European Union (EU) governments agreed a new treaty. It is called the EU Reform Treaty. European governments believe that it will give better security for all and help improve living standards for EU citizens. However, there are many people in Europe who do not support the Reform Treaty, particularly in France and Denmark.

The UK Government believes that British people support the treaty. They do not think a referendum on the EU Reform Treaty is necessary.

SOURCE 2

UK Public opinion poll on EU Reform Treaty (2007)

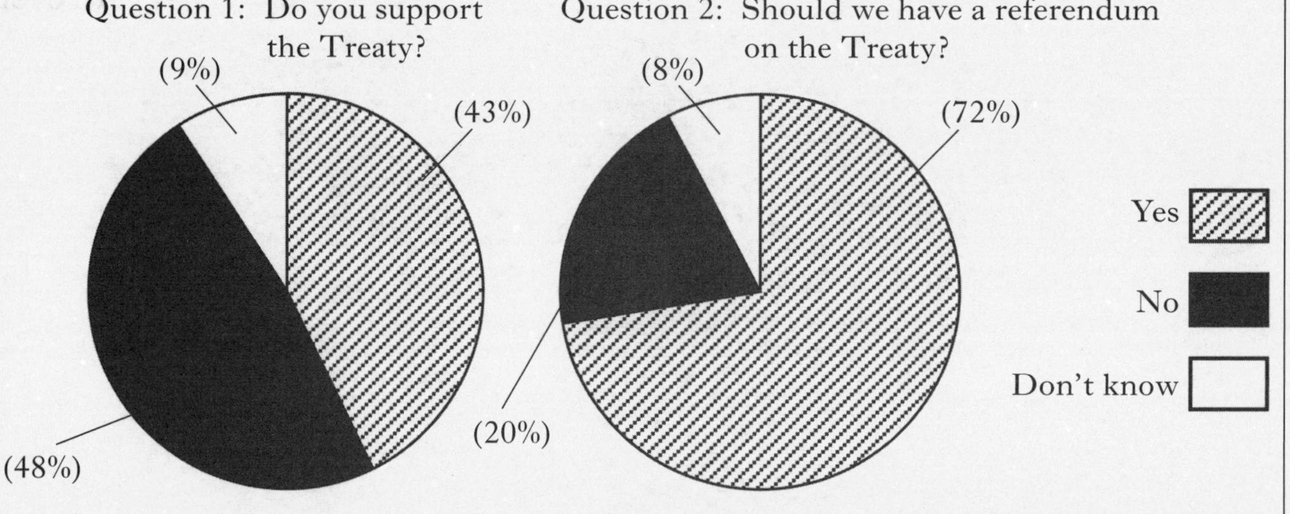

Statements made by John O'Donovan, Journalist

- All of the EU member governments have said "yes" to the Treaty.
- Almost half of the UK population are against the Reform Treaty.
- A large percentage of the UK's population are undecided about the Treaty.
- Most people agree with the UK government about a referendum on the Treaty.

Using **only** Source 1 and Source 2 above, write down **two** statements made by John O'Donovan which are **exaggerated**.

Using **only** the information in the Sources, give **one** reason why **each** of the statements you have chosen is **exaggerated**.

(Enquiry Skills, **4** marks)

QUESTION 4 (CONTINUED)

(*c*) *Countries like the UK can benefit from being members of the European Union.*

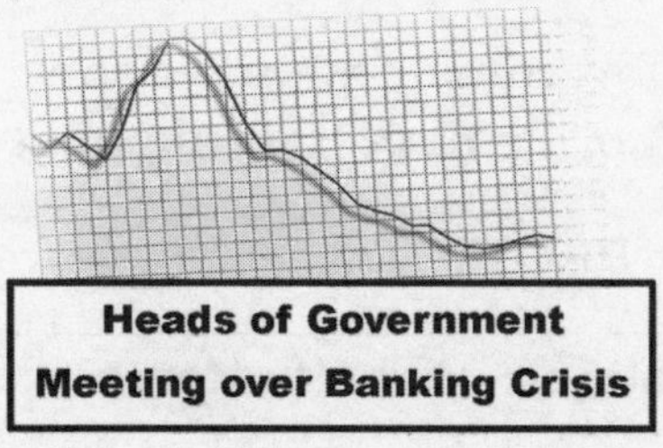

Give **two** ways in which a country *like the UK can benefit from being a member of the European Union.*

For **one** of these ways, describe how a country like the UK could benefit.

To answer this question, you may wish to use the drawings above.

(Knowledge & Understanding, **4** marks)

[Turn over for Question 4 (*d*) on *Page twenty*

QUESTION 4 (CONTINUED)

(*d*) Study the information below, then answer the question which follows.

Information about Tonu

Tonu is a town in the African country of Ghana. Tonu's population is around 23,000. Many of the people are very poor and half of them live on less than one dollar per day. The average income in the town is only $500 per year.

Ghana is a democratic country, with elections being held every four years. It is difficult to improve standards of living as only 58% of Tonu's population can read and write.

Ghana's government wants to solve some of Tonu's problems. They are not sure if **Project A** or **Project B** would **best solve these problems**.

PROJECT A

BS Industries – New factories

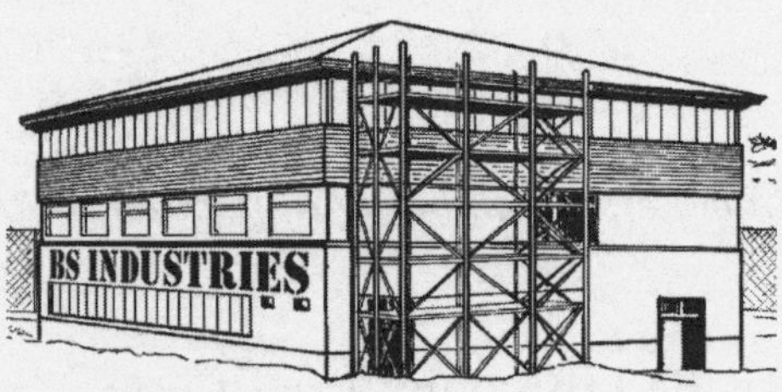

A new factory will be built in Tonu on land which will have to be cleared of rubbish. Electrical goods will be produced and sold throughout the world. Wages are likely to be around $1000 each per year for the 110 permanent workers.

The jobs will be low skilled and require little education. Some temporary jobs will be created to clear the land. The building work itself will take around four months to complete.

PROJECT B

Ghana Learning Foundation – Schools

This charity works in many different parts of Ghana. Five new primary schools will be built in Tonu, giving around two thousand children access to education for the first time.

Each school will serve a main housing area. Schools will be built on land that is not being currently used. The building work will take around 6 months to complete. 100 local people will be trained as teachers. They will then earn around $1200 per year.

Using **only** the information above, decide which project, **Project A** or **Project B**, would be the **better** choice for Ghana's government to **solve Tonu's problems**.

Give **two** reasons to **support** your decision.

You **must** link the information about Tonu to the project you have chosen.

(Enquiry Skills, **4** marks)

[*END OF QUESTION PAPER*]

STANDARD GRADE | CREDIT

2009

[BLANK PAGE]

C

2640/403

NATIONAL QUALIFICATIONS 2009

MONDAY, 25 MAY
1.00 PM – 3.00 PM

MODERN STUDIES STANDARD GRADE Credit Level

1 Read every question carefully.

2 Answer all questions as fully as you can.

3 If you cannot do a question, go on to the next one. Try again later.

4 In question 3, answer **one** section only: Section (A) The USA **or** Section (B) China.

5 Write your answers in the answer book provided. Indicate clearly, in the left hand margin, the question and section of question being answered. Do not write in the right hand margin.

LI 2640/403 6/13020

SQA

[BLANK PAGE]

SYLLABUS AREA 1—LIVING IN A DEMOCRACY

QUESTION 1

(*a*) *There are many ways for people in the UK to* ***participate*** *in* ***election campaigns****.*

Describe, **in detail**, the ways in which people in the UK can **participate** in **election campaigns**.

(Knowledge & Understanding, **6** marks)

(*b*) *Pressure Groups have many* ***responsibilities****.*

Choose **two** of the following **responsibilities.**

The pressure group should:

- inform the police before a demonstration
- keep protests within the law
- represent members' views
- only use accurate information during campaigns.

For **each responsibility** you have chosen, explain, **in detail**, why it is important.

(Knowledge & Understanding, **4** marks)

[Turn over

QUESTION 1 (CONTINUED)

(*c*) Study Sources 1, 2 and 3 below and on the next page, then answer the question which follows.

SOURCE 1

What should happen to Scotland after the 2007 Scottish Parliament Election
Views of Main Parties

LIBERAL DEMOCRATS	LABOUR	CONSERVATIVE	SNP	GREENS
Increased powers for the Scottish Parliament but "no" to independence	Scotland to remain in the United Kingdom	Scotland remains in the UK but willing to debate issues about devolved powers	Scotland to become independent after a referendum	Scotland to become an independent country

Seats in Scottish Parliament 2003 and 2007

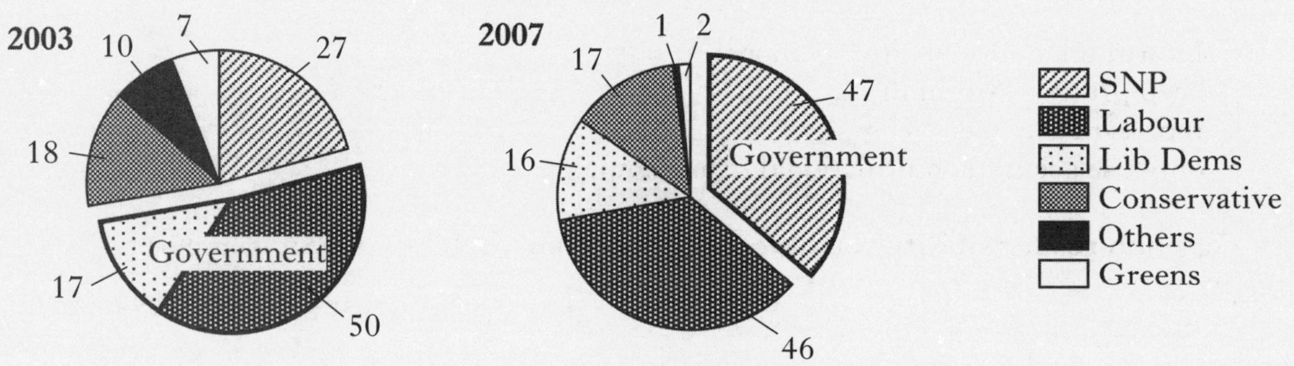

There are 129 MSPs

SOURCE 2

Scottish Parliament Elections (2003 & 2007)
Regional Turnout

Region	Turnout 2003	Turnout 2007
1. Central Scotland	48·5%	50·5%
2. Glasgow	41·5%	41·6%
3. Highlands and Islands	52·3%	54·7%
4. Lothians	50·5%	54·0%
5. Mid-Scotland and Fife	49·7%	52·8%
6. North East Scotland	48·3%	50·7%
7. South of Scotland	52·3%	53·6%
8. West of Scotland	53·3%	56·5%
Scotland (Total)	**49·4%**	**51·7%**

QUESTION 1 (*c*) (CONTINUED)

SOURCE 3

National Identity and the Scottish Parliament

People have different views on what makes a Scot. Is it supporting our football and rugby teams; is it a willingness to wear a kilt; is it a liking for traditional Scottish music or shortbread or the consumption of our national drink?

What makes a Scot?

A person's accent appears to be a very important factor when people are deciding if somebody is Scottish or not. A recent survey showed that 70% of Scottish people felt that a non-white person with a Scottish accent was Scottish whilst 54% believed that a person with an English accent living in Scotland, was not Scottish.

In 1999, prior to the opening of the Scottish Parliament, research carried out for the Government showed 25% of people in Scotland felt "Scottish not British" and 11% said they would describe themselves as "British not Scottish". SNP voters and young people were much more likely to say they were Scottish whilst the elderly and Conservative voters were more likely to say they were "British". When the research was repeated in 2006, 32% of Scottish people said they would describe themselves as "Scottish not British" and only 9% of those asked said that they were "British not Scottish".

The West of Scotland Region had the largest increase in voter turnout. In 2007, there were more MSPs in favour of independence than ever before and, since the opening of the Scottish Parliament, people feel more Scottish.

View of Callum Wishart

Using **only** Sources 1, 2 and 3, explain **the extent to which** Callum Wishart could be accused of being **selective in the use of facts.**

(Enquiry Skills, **8** marks)

[Turn over

SYLLABUS AREA 2—CHANGING SOCIETY

QUESTION 2

(*a*) **Government Policies to help Families with Dependent Children (2007)**

ema
Education Maintenance Allowance

SureStart

Child Benefit

CHILD TAX CREDITS

ctf
Child Trust Fund

new deal

Government policies help families with dependent children in different ways.

Choose **two** policies from the six above.

For **each** policy, describe, **in detail**, the ways in which it helps families with dependent children.

(Knowledge and Understanding, **6** marks)

QUESTION 2 (CONTINUED)

(*b*) Study Sources 1 and 2 below, then answer the question which follows.

SOURCE 1

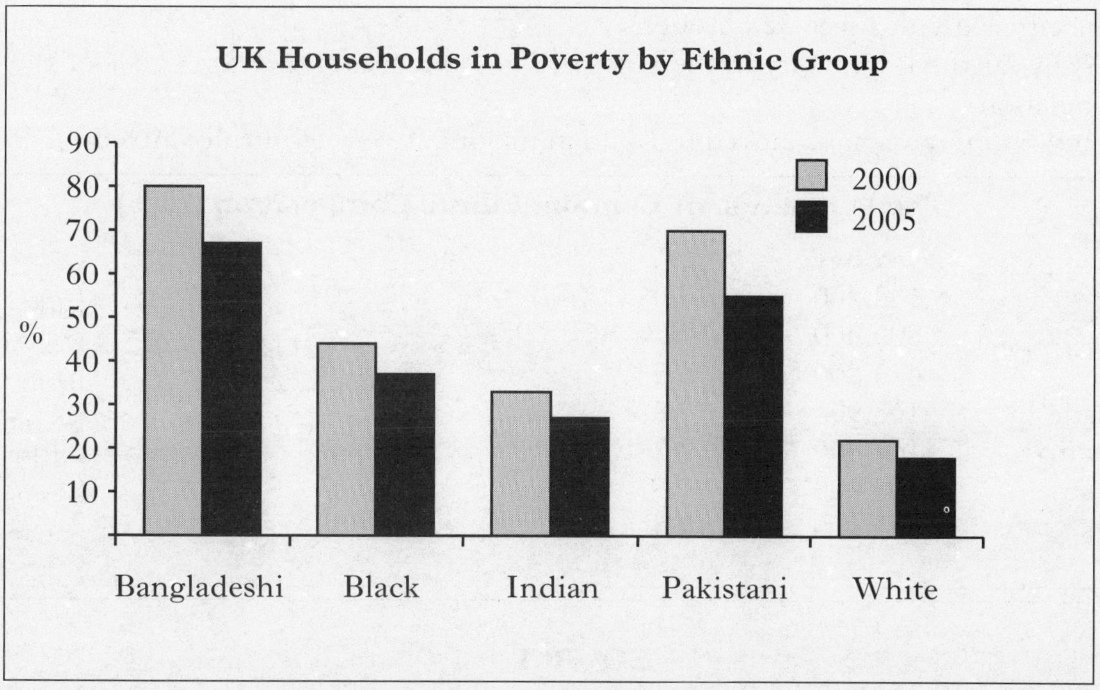

SOURCE 2

Average hourly Pay for Workers aged 18 and over (£ per hour)

	2000	**2005**
Bangladeshi	6·00	7·60
Black	7·04	7·33
Indian	6·57	8·41
Pakistani	4·94	6·25
White	6·76	8·00

Pakistani households have had a bigger fall in poverty than all other ethnic groups. The group with the smallest increase in hourly pay had the smallest drop in poverty.

View of Asif Iqbal

Give **one** reason to **support** and **one** reason to **oppose** the view of Asif Iqbal.

(Enquiry Skills, **4** marks)

QUESTION 2 (CONTINUED)

(*c*) Study the information about London and Sources 1, 2, 3 and 4 below and on the next page, then answer the question which follows.

Focus on London

- In 2005, there were 7,428,600 people in London.
- The city is divided into 32 boroughs.
- It is by far the largest city in the United Kingdom accounting for 12·5% of the country's population.
- Many immigrants have moved to London making it very ethnically mixed.

The Population of London: Ethnic Composition (2005)

	Number	%
White	5,182,200	70·0
Black	809,000	10·2
Indian	473,800	6·5
Bangladeshi	165,900	2·3
Pakistani	161,800	2·2
Chinese	103,000	1·5
Others	532,900	7·3

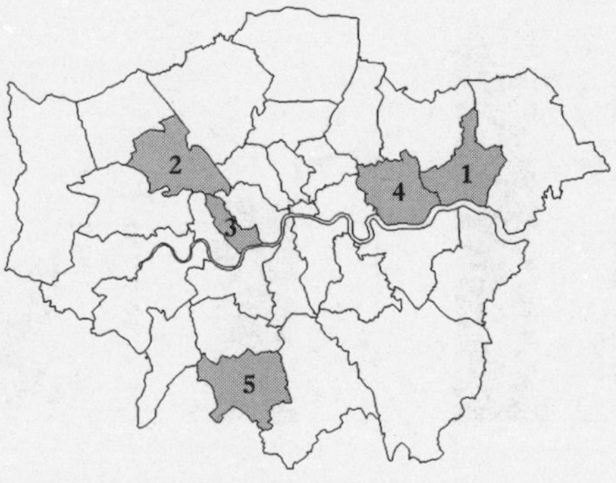

1 Barking and Dagenham
2 Brent
3 Kensington and Chelsea
4 Newham
5 Sutton

SOURCE 1

Resident Population by Ethnic Group in Selected London Boroughs (%)

Ethnic Group	Barking and Dagenham	Brent	Kensington and Chelsea	Newham	Sutton
White	85·2	45·3	78·6	39·4	89·2
Black	7·0	19·9	7·0	21·6	2·6
Indian	2·3	18·5	2·0	12·1	2·3
Bangladeshi	0·4	0·5	0·7	8·8	0·3
Pakistani	1·8	4·0	0·8	8·5	0·7
Chinese	0·5	1·0	1·6	1·0	0·7
Others	2·8	10·8	9·3	8·6	4·2

SOURCE 2

Crime in Selected London Boroughs (Rates per 10,000 people)

Type of Crime	Barking and Dagenham	Brent	Kensington and Chelsea	Newham	Sutton
Violence	321	308	181	340	178
Robbery	47	88	49	101	23
Burglary	68	96	85	108	38
Car Crime	200	180	169	282	132
Total Crime	**652**	**684**	**495**	**847**	**381**

QUESTION 2 (*c*) (CONTINUED)

SOURCE 3

Employment Statistics for Selected London Boroughs (%)

	Employment Rate	Self-employed	Unemployment Rate
Barking and Dagenham	62·0	12·8	9·6
Brent	68·3	17·1	7·7
Kensington and Chelsea	67·2	25·7	6·3
Newham	59·4	12·8	8·7
Sutton	88·3	11·6	4·9

SOURCE 4

Education and Earnings in Selected London Boroughs

	Percentage of pupils achieving 5 or more exam passes by age 16	Average Weekly Income
Barking and Dagenham	55·8	£478·30
Brent	61·4	£467·50
Kensington and Chelsea	63·0	£818·40
Newham	52·8	£460·40
Sutton	70·8	£506·00

Using **only** the information about London and Sources 1, 2, 3 and 4, what **conclusions** can be drawn about London and some of its boroughs?

You must **make** and **justify** a conclusion about **each** of the following headings.

- The relationship between education and unemployment
- The relationship between total crime and income
- The borough whose ethnic mix is **most** like that of London as a whole
- The borough that would be the most desirable to live in

(Enquiry Skills, **8** marks)

[Turn over

[BLANK PAGE]

SYLLABUS AREA 3—IDEOLOGIES

QUESTION 3

Answer **one** section only: Section (A)—The USA on pages *eleven* to *thirteen*
OR Section (B)—China on pages *fifteen* to *seventeen*

(A) **THE USA**

(*a*) *In the USA, social and economic inequalities continue to exist.*

Explain, **in detail**, why *in the USA, social and economic inequalities continue to exist.*

In answering this question, you must:

- describe the inequalities which exist
- explain the reasons why they exist.

In your answer, you **must** use American examples.

(Knowledge and Understanding, **8** marks)

[Turn over

QUESTION 3 (A) (CONTINUED)

(*b*) Study the information on **The Illegal Immigration Debate** and **Sources 1** and **2** on the next page, then answer the question which follows.

The Illegal Immigration Debate

For centuries, the USA has attracted immigrants in search of "The American Dream". Today, Americans are deeply divided about how to deal with the illegal immigrants who enter the USA through the border with Mexico. The best place to see, at first hand, the issue of immigration is in California. Here, for instance, you can find Mexican nannies collecting the children of rich Californians from suburban schools or Mexicans cleaning toilets. Many are part of the 7% of California's population that are illegal immigrants. California has one third of all illegal immigrants in the USA.

USA Illegal Immigrants (millions)

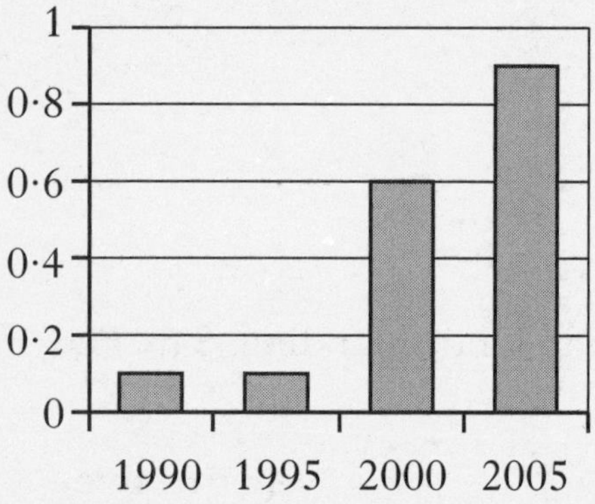

Illegal Immigrants – % of Californian workforce

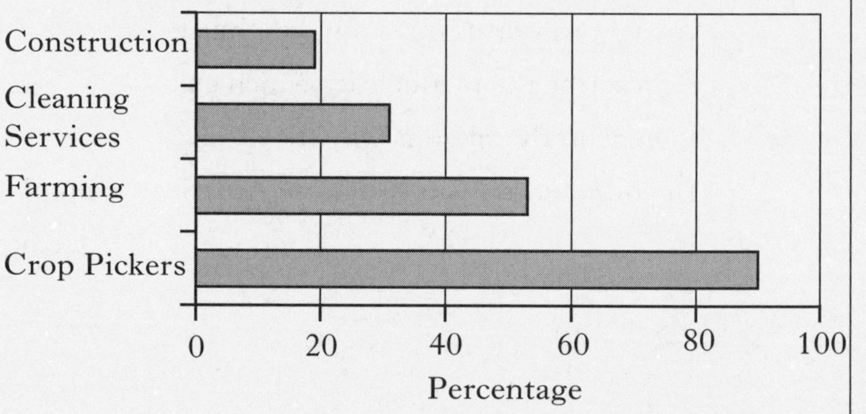

Unemployment is not a problem in California. It is less than 5%. 70% of Californians think that illegal immigrants are doing jobs that others do not want. Many Californians are concerned that illegal immigrants often live and work as "modern-day slaves" because they work for low wages and have no paid holidays or sick pay. However, some argue that illegal immigrants are a financial burden on California as they cost $650 million in health care, $2·2 billion in education with an overall cost of $5 billion a year.

One new suggestion to stop these illegal immigrants is to improve existing border security by building a high-tech fence at a cost of $5 billion to the Federal Government.

Proposed high-tech fence on the 140 mile Californian/Mexican Border

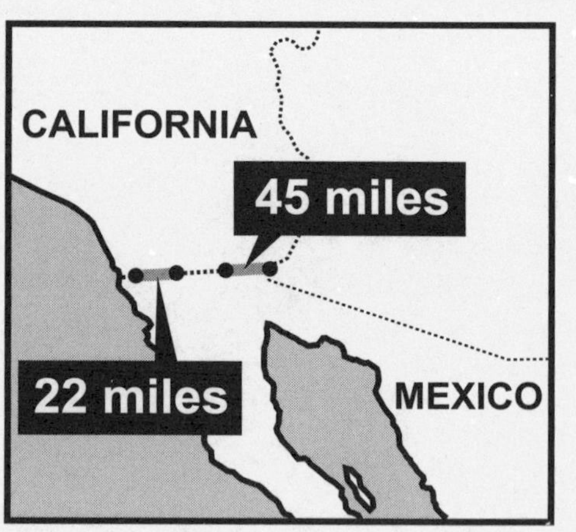

Californian voter opinion on how to deal with illegal immigrants	Yes	No	No opinion
Increase the number of border guards	71%	25%	4%
Introduce a Temporary Worker Programme	68%	28%	4%
Build a high-tech fence along sections of the border	36%	59%	5%

QUESTION 3 (A) (*b*) (CONTINUED)

The two people below are hoping to become Governor of California. Here are extracts from speeches they have made.

SOURCE 1

Corrine Padilla I am an American citizen but my Grandfather was an illegal immigrant from Mexico chasing the American Dream. I am not concerned about illegal immigration as the numbers entering the US are not rising steeply.

I, like many Californians, feel that illegal immigrants in California are exploited. My first priority will be to improve their pay and working conditions.

Although illegal immigration continues to occur, many Californians are not in favour of a high-tech fence. I agree with them as it will not prevent illegal immigration.

Border guards do a very difficult job but we do not need to increase their numbers and most Californians agree with me on this issue.

California needs workers to come and help our farmers pick their crops. If David Beckham can come and play football for LA Galaxy for a short time then a Mexican labourer should be able to come and work for a short time then go back to Mexico.

SOURCE 2

Peter Head My ancestors came from Scotland and I am proud of this. Although California only has a very small percentage of all US illegal immigrants, I am still concerned about this.

Illegal immigrants already in California cost a lot of money. Because of this they should become legal citizens so that they pay their taxes. This is my main aim.

I, like most Californians, believe that illegal immigrants take the jobs that Californians want, so we need to do something to stop it.

The high-tech fence should not be built as it will not protect all of the Californian/Mexican border. This means that illegal immigration would just continue.

The money saved by not having the high-tech fence would be better spent on more guards patrolling the border, which is what Californians want.

Use **only** the information about **The Illegal Immigration Debate** and **Sources 1** and **2** above.

(i) State **which person** would be the **more suitable** to become Governor of California.

(ii) Give **three detailed reasons to support your choice**.

(iii) Give **two detailed reasons** why you **rejected** the other person.

In your answer, you **must relate** information about the Illegal Immigration Debate to the information about the **two** people.

(Enquiry Skills, **10** marks)

NOW GO TO QUESTION 4 ON PAGE EIGHTEEN

[BLANK PAGE]

QUESTION 3 (CONTINUED)

(B) **CHINA**

(*a*)	*In China, social and economic inequalities continue to exist.*

Explain, **in detail**, why *in China, social and economic inequalities continue to exist.*

In answering this question, you must:

- describe the inequalities which exist
- explain the reasons why they exist.

In your answer, you **must** use Chinese examples.

(Knowledge and Understanding, **8** marks)

[Turn over

QUESTION 3 (B) (CONTINUED)

(*b*) Study the information on **The Migration Debate** and **Sources 1** and **2** on the next page, then answer the question which follows.

The Migration Debate

The difference in the standard of living between the cities and countryside in China is among the largest in the world. As a result, many poor farmers are moving to the eastern cities where a lot of new building is taking place. This migration is necessary to provide labour for the factories that are turning China into the "workshop of the world". Without these workers, China's economy would suffer. The most common destinations for migrants are the cities of Beijing, Shanghai and Guangzhou. It is estimated that 60% of China's population will live in towns and cities by 2020.

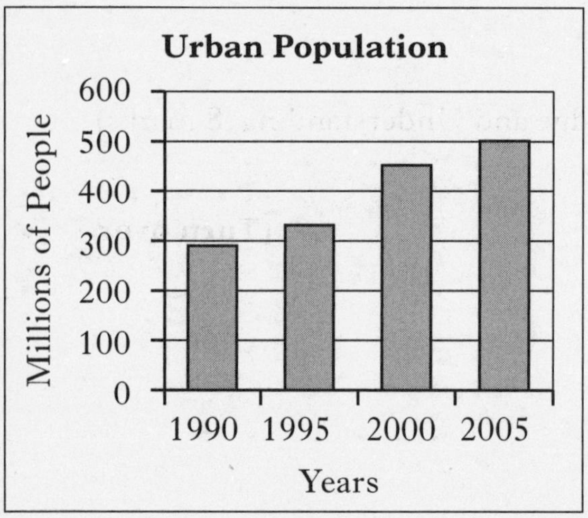

Educational Background of Rural Migrants

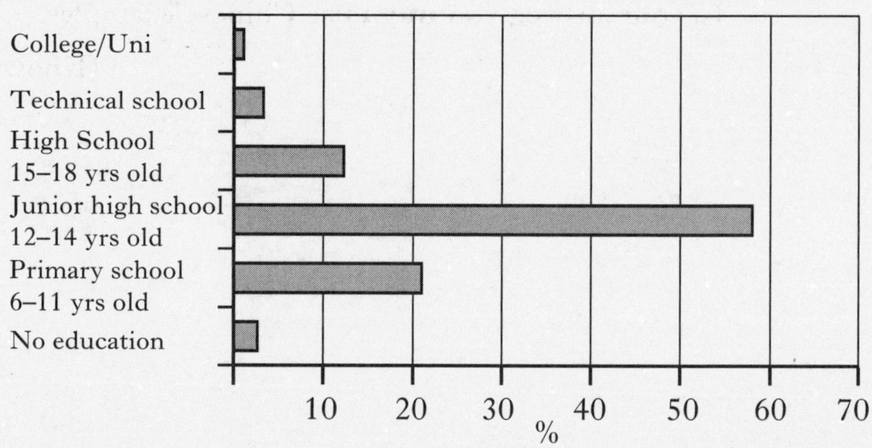

Unemployment is low in China. The rate in Beijing is 2·5% whilst it is 3·4% in Guangzhou. The migrants who move to these cities often work in clothing factories, shops, restaurants or in construction crews. Most plan to work for a year or two and then return home to have a family. Often they do not receive their whole wage on time as some is withheld to make sure that they stay for a full year. Since urban workers earn three times that of farmers, they send home part of their pay to help ageing parents or to educate younger brothers or sisters. Many Chinese are concerned about this wealth gap and President Hu Jintao has promised greater spending on health and education in rural areas in order to reduce the differences.

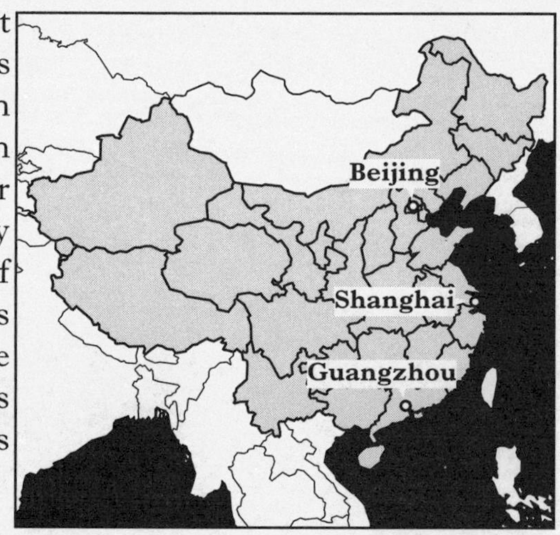

Many feel that the cities cannot cope with the growing numbers of migrants. Problems include a great shortage of housing, hospitals, power and transport. It is also claimed that in big cities more than 70% of crime is caused by temporary rural migrants.

Beijing residents' opinions on how to deal with migration	**Yes**	**No**	**No opinion**
Allow temporary migrant workers to become permanent	74%	14%	12%
Impose an additional tax on migrant workers in the city	24%	62%	14%
Make foreign firms invest in rural development when they locate in China	52%	27%	21%

QUESTION 3 (B) (CONTINUED)

The two people below are hoping to become the "Beijing Migration Officer". Here are extracts from speeches they have made.

SOURCE 1

Liu Wang I moved from the countryside to the city 15 years ago in order to improve my standard of living. Many migrants are college educated or better which is good for our cities and I will work to see this continue.

I, like many other Beijing residents, feel that temporary migrant workers are exploited. My first priority will be to make them permanent residents.

These migrant workers are required to fill jobs in construction, manufacturing and services. However, it is no good if only the cities are rich. I believe it is important that something is also done to raise the standard of living in the countryside.

In my opinion, it is no good punishing workers who continue to move to the city with additional taxes and most people agree with me on this issue.

As Chinese citizens, we believe that it is important to look after ourselves and most of Beijing realises that we should not rely on investment from foreign firms for development in rural areas.

SOURCE 2

Cho Yuen My ancestors moved from the countryside many years ago and I am proud of this. I am not concerned about rural migration as the numbers moving to the cities are small and not rising steeply.

I, like many others in Beijing, believe that temporary rural migrants fit in well and make Beijing a better place to live. My first priority will be to encourage further migration.

The income which these migrant workers send home is vital to the rural economy. I aim to allow this to continue so that city growth benefits those still living in the countryside.

Until President Hu Jintao has reduced the differences in education, I will work to allow migrants to come to Beijing in order to gain more than basic schooling so that better paid and better quality jobs are available to them.

Finally, China has become the "workshop of the world" and many international companies benefit from our labour. I am not alone in believing that we should make foreign firms invest in the development of rural China since they are using our labour to make profits.

Use **only** the information about **The Urban Migration Debate** and **Sources 1** and **2** above.

(i) State **which person** would be the **more suitable** to become Beijing Migration Officer.

(ii) Give **three detailed reasons to support your choice**.

(iii) Give **two detailed reasons** why you **rejected** the other person.

In your answer, you **must relate** information about The Migration Debate to the information about the **two** people.

(Enquiry Skills, **10** marks)

NOW GO TO QUESTION 4 ON PAGE EIGHTEEN

SYLLABUS AREA 4—INTERNATIONAL RELATIONS

QUESTION 4

(*a*) *A number of European countries have faced threats to their security. They have responded in different ways.*

Describe, **in detail**:

- the threats these countries have faced
- the ways in which they have responded to these threats.

(Knowledge & Understanding, **8** marks)

QUESTION 4 (CONTINUED)

You have been asked to carry out **two** investigations.

The first investigation is on the topic in the box below.

HIV/Aids in Africa

Now answer questions (*b*) and (*c*) which follow.

(*b*) State a relevant **hypothesis** for your investigation.

(Enquiry Skills, **2** marks)

(*c*) Give **two** relevant **aims** to help you prove or disprove your hypothesis.

(Enquiry Skills, **2** marks)

The second investigation is on the topic in the box below.

The benefits of EU expansion

Now answer questions (*d*) and (*e*) which follow.

(*d*) Describe, **in detail, two** factors that must be taken into account when designing and carrying out a survey.

(Enquiry Skills, **4** marks)

[Turn over for Question 4 (*e*) on *Page twenty*

QUESTION 4 (CONTINUED)

(*e*) You also decide to carry out a search on the Internet.

You enter the phrase, "Benefits of EU expansion" into an Internet search engine.

Six results are shown below.

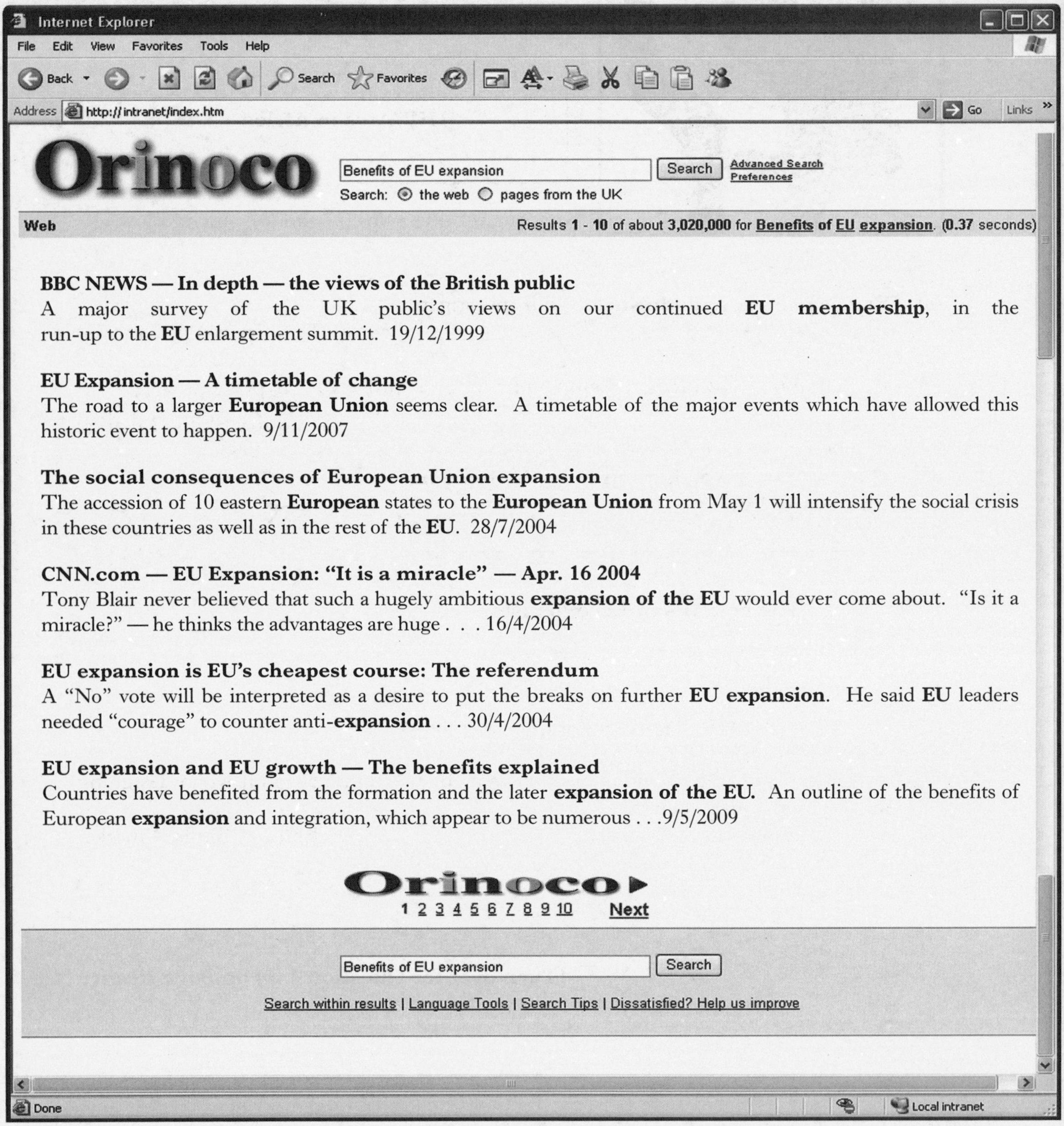

BBC NEWS — In depth — the views of the British public
A major survey of the UK public's views on our continued **EU membership**, in the run-up to the **EU** enlargement summit. 19/12/1999

EU Expansion — A timetable of change
The road to a larger **European Union** seems clear. A timetable of the major events which have allowed this historic event to happen. 9/11/2007

The social consequences of European Union expansion
The accession of 10 eastern **European** states to the **European Union** from May 1 will intensify the social crisis in these countries as well as in the rest of the **EU**. 28/7/2004

CNN.com — EU Expansion: "It is a miracle" — Apr. 16 2004
Tony Blair never believed that such a hugely ambitious **expansion of the EU** would ever come about. "Is it a miracle?" — he thinks the advantages are huge . . . 16/4/2004

EU expansion is EU's cheapest course: The referendum
A "No" vote will be interpreted as a desire to put the breaks on further **EU expansion**. He said **EU** leaders needed "courage" to counter anti-**expansion** . . . 30/4/2004

EU expansion and EU growth — The benefits explained
Countries have benefited from the formation and the later **expansion of the EU.** An outline of the benefits of European **expansion** and integration, which appear to be numerous . . .9/5/2009

Which result do you think would be **most useful**? **Explain** your answer.

(Enquiry Skills, **2** marks)

[*END OF QUESTION PAPER*]

BrightRED ANSWER SECTION FOR

SQA GENERAL AND CREDIT MODERN STUDIES 2006–2009

MODERN STUDIES GENERAL 2006

Syllabus Area 1 – Living In A Democracy

1. (*a*) The concept being assessed is Rights and Responsibilities. Candidates are required to provide detailed descriptions.
   Answers may include:
   - the right to take industrial action. The responsibility to keep within the law.
   - the right to vote for elected officials. The responsibility to do so in a responsible fashion.
   - the right to attend union meetings. The responsibility to take on board what is said.

   (*b*) Candidates are required to make comparisons within and between sources and draw conclusions.
   Answers may include:
   Changes in male or female trade union membership between 1999 and 2003
   - Trade union membership amongst males has gone down steadily from a high of 27.3% in 1999 down to 26.6% in 2001 and down even further to 25.5% in 2003.
   - Trade union membership amongst females has remained almost constant in each of the 3 years. The percentage went up slightly by 0.1% in 2003.

   Changes in male and female trade union membership in one of the jobs between 1998 and 2002
   - amongst Managers and Administrators, the percentage of males has gone down from 18% in 1998 to 16% in 2002 whilst the percentage of females has risen from 21% in 1998 to 22% in 2002.
   - within Secretarial, the percentage of males has risen from 30% in 1998 to 31% in 2002 whilst the percentage of females has also risen from 22% in 1998 to 23% in 2002.
   - within Sales and Customer Services, the percentage of males has gone down from 18% in 1998 to 13% in 2002 whilst the percentage of females has risen from 12% in 1998 to 13% in 2002.
   - any other valid conclusion.

   (*c*) Candidates are required to provide evidence to support a given point of view.
   Answers may include:
   - Anne Hall says that trade unions play an important part in the election of Labour MSPs. This point is supported by the fact that some trade unions give money to and campaign for Labour party candidates in elections.
   - Anne Hall also says that trade unions play a part in policy making for the Labour party. This point is supported by the fact that a committee of the Labour party in Scotland, which has trade union representatives on it, writes policies on which the Labour party fights elections.

   (*d*) The concept being assessed is Representation. Candidates are required to provide detailed descriptions.
   Answers may include:
   Local Councillors
   - attend Council meetings and vote on issues which have an effect on local people.
   - Councillors deal with local problems such as a housing query from a voter in his/her ward.
   - they hold regular surgeries to find out the views of local people.
   - they attend local functions in an official capacity.

   MSPs
   - they work on behalf of their constituents both at Holyrood and also within the constituency.
   - they attend debates in Parliament and try to put across views of the people they represent.
   - they hold regular surgeries to find out the views of local people.
   - they attend local functions in an official capacity.
   - they sit on Committees.
   - any other valid point for either of the representatives.

Syllabus Area 2 – Changing Society

2. (*a*) The concept being assessed is Need. Candidates are required to provide detailed descriptions.
   Answers may include:
   - easy use lever taps can be installed – this helps an elderly person who has arthritis and therefore might have difficulty turning on ordinary taps.
   - a stair lift, on which an elderly person can sit and be taken up stairs at the push of a button, can be installed – this helps an elderly person who may have a hip problem and who has difficulty getting up or down ordinary stairs.
   - a walk in bath can be installed which allows an elderly person to open a door, walk into the bath, close the door and then fill up the bath – this helps an elderly person with a bad back or has difficulty climbing in and out of an ordinary bath.
   - any other valid point.

   (*b*) Candidates are required to detect exaggeration and provide explanations.

The correct responses are:
Statement 1
'Most grandmothers use very little modern technology.'
Reason 1
The statement is exaggerated because in Source 2 it shows that 75% of grandmothers have a mobile phone and 55% have a home computer. Therefore, they use a lot of modern technology.

Statement 2
'When people retire, they just want to meet friends, travel and play golf.'
Reason 2
The statement is exaggerated because in Source 1 most people who retire want to garden, (60%), then meet friends (58%) and travel (57%). More wish to garden than play golf (11%).

(*c*) Candidates are required to give relevant aims for an investigative topic.
Two correct responses are:
- to find out which local groups help the elderly the most.
- to find out why some local people volunteer to help the elderly.

The following are not acceptable:
- who are the elderly?
- to find out about Sheltered Housing.

(*d*) Candidates are required to state two relevant ways to gather information.
Answers may include:
- interview some local elderly people.
- send a letter to some local group.
- go to one of the local group meetings.
- any other valid point.

(*e*) Candidates are required to justify the use of a method of enquiry.
Answers may include:
Interview some local elderly people
They would be able to tell me how local groups meet their needs. I could also ask extra questions if I felt it was necessary.
Send a letter to some local group
I could prepare specific questions to put in the letter. The letter would give the local group time to think of good answers to my questions before they replied. They could also send me some information or booklets about their work.
Go to one of the local group meetings
The questions would be asked directly and I could also ask supplementary questions if I felt it was necessary. Local groups would also know a lot about the local area and how they meet the needs of local elderly people.
Any other valid point.

(*f*) Candidates are required to give a disadvantage of a given method of enquiry.
Answers may include:
- the road show is during school time and you would need to get permission and then arrange time out of school.
- it is only on one day of the week which might not be suitable.
- you do not know where it is held and it may be too far away.
- you might not be allowed in as the advert is unclear.
- any other valid point.

Syllabus Area 3 – Ideologies

THE USA

3A. (*a*) The concept being assessed is Participation. Candidates are required to provide detailed descriptions.
Answers may include:
- write to letters pages/editor of local and national newspapers such as The New York Times or The Washington Post, to complain about an issue such as illegal immigration.
- taking part in 'phone-ins' to local radio stations to criticise a decision taken by the City Mayor or State Governor.
- contact the local TV station to tell them about a demonstration to encourage them to cover it.
- use the Internet to set-up a website to get their point across and send an e-mail to their representatives such as Senators, the Governor or the President at the White House.
- any other valid point.

(*b*) Candidates are required to support and oppose a given point of view.
Answers may include:
Reasons to **support** the view:
- Nancy Holstein says that the smallest drop in smoking has been amongst white females. Evidence to support this is that in 1990, 23.5% of white females smoked but by 2001, the figure had gone down to 22.1% which was a drop of 1.4%. This was the smallest drop in figures with the next smallest being 2.7% for white males.

Reasons to **oppose** the view:
- Nancy Holstein says that men are less likely to smoke than women. Evidence to oppose this is that in 2001, 24.7% of males smoked compared to only 20.8% of females.
- in both 1990 and 2001 the percentage smoking for all groups of men were higher than all groups of women.

(*c*) The concept being assessed is Equality. Candidates are required to provide detailed explanations.
Answers may include:
- by working hard at high school and college, and gaining good qualifications many more ethnic minority Americans have got a good job with high pay.
- by setting up their own business, working hard and making a big profit, more have achieved the 'American Dream'.

- affirmative action policies have encouraged more Black and Hispanic Americans into skilled jobs.
- any other valid point.

(*d*) Candidates are required to detect exaggeration and provide explanations.
The correct responses are:
Statement 1
Since September 11 2002, US troops have only invaded one country.
Reason 1
The timeline shows that US forces have invaded two countries - Afghanistan in October 2001 and Iraq in March 2003.

Statement 2
America is the only country to have suffered terrorist attacks.
Reason 2
In July 2005 terrorists also attacked London by exploding bombs on a bus and on the Underground.

RUSSIA

3B. (*a*) The concept being assessed is Participation. Candidates are required to provide detailed descriptions.
Answers may include:
- write to letters pages/editor of local and national newspapers such as Pravda, to complain about an issue such as the war in Chechnya.
- taking part in 'phone-ins' to local radio stations to criticise a decision taken by local officials.
- contact TV and Radio stations to let them know about a demonstration and to encourage them to cover it.
- use the Internet to set-up a website to get their point across and send an e-mail to their representative in Parliament.
- any other valid point.

(*b*) Candidates are required to support and oppose a given point of view.
Two correct responses are:
Reason to **support** the view:
It is true that jobs in IT and the Law have the highest salaries. In both 2002 and 2003, this was the case. Personnel Director came next with an average salary of $2 000 in 2003. This was $100 behind the figure for lawyers.

Reason to **oppose** this view:
It is untrue that jobs in IT and the Law have seen the biggest change in salaries between 2002 and 2003. Sales Managers have seen salaries rise by 125% between the two years whereas the figures for IT and the Law are only an increase of 50% and 20%.

(*c*) The concept being assessed is Equality. Candidates are required to provide detailed explanations.
Answers may include:
- by working hard at school and college, and gaining good qualifications many more Russians have got a good job with high pay. These jobs tend to be in the major cities.
- by setting up their own business, working hard and making a big profit. This has happened for many more Russians recently as opportunities are now available.
- the break-up of the Soviet Union allowed a number of Russians to get involved in taking over former state-run companies. Many have made a great success out of this opportunity.
- any other valid point.

(*d*) Candidates are required to detect exaggeration and provide explanations.
The correct responses are:
Statement 1
It is the Chechen rebels who have carried out all the killings.
Reason 1
In October 2002, Russian forces stormed a theatre in Moscow and killed most of the rebels in the theatre.

Statement 2
A settlement between the two sides is within reach.
Reason 2
In November 2001, peace talks between the two sides broke up without agreement.

CHINA

3C. (*a*) The concept being assessed is Participation. Candidates are required to provide detailed descriptions.
Answers may include:
- detention by the police without charge for up to three months.
- evidence of torture and beatings at the hands of the police.
- forced labour camps hold many political prisoners
- environmental campaigners who have gone too far in their criticism have found themselves evicted from their homes, sacked from their jobs and their children denied education and medical care.
- any other valid point.

(*b*) Candidates are required to support and oppose a given point of view.
Two correct responses are:
Reasons to **support** the view:
- China did have the fastest growth in Internet access. It has more than trebled from 8% to 25%. No other country shown has even doubled.

Reasons to **oppose** the view:

- China has not always had the lowest levels of Internet access. In 2005 China had 25% but Russia was lower at 24%.

(*c*) The concept being assessed is Equality. Candidates are required to give detailed explanations.
Answers may include:

- recent investment by foreign businesses has tended to be concentrated around larger towns and cities especially along the coast. Higher pay is more likely in these areas eg Special Economic Zones (SEZs).
- companies set up by Chinese entrepreneurs are much more common in these areas.
- less unemployment in towns than in rural farming areas.
- towns and cities have more modern hospitals with more qualified doctors, nurses, specialist equipment etc. There is a shortage of medical staff in rural areas.
- the cities have better schools and universities, with more qualified staff, than the countryside.
- the major cities have a better choice of housing with access to electricity, running water etc. Many rural Chinese cannot afford such luxuries.
- there is much easier access to foreign consumer goods in the towns.
- any other valid point.

(*d*) Candidates are required to detect exaggeration and provide explanations.
The correct responses are:

Statement 1
Every Chinese person will benefit when the project is finished.
Reason 1
In the source (2003) its shows that between 1.2 million and 2 million people will have lost their homes when the dam is finished, so 'every' person will not benefit.

Statement 2
Everyone in China supports the project.
Reason 2
In the source (July 1993) it shows that hundreds of people have been jailed for criticising the dam, so not 'everyone' supports the project.

Syllabus Area 4 – International Relations

4. (*a*) The concept being assessed is Need. Candidates are required to provide detailed descriptions.
Answers may include:

FAO

- advice on farming methods.
- support to improve technology.

UNICEF

- campaign on children's rights.
- supporting mothers eg breastfeeding programmes.
- against child labour/child soldiers.

WHO

- immunisation programmes.
- advice and support on health related matters.
- training in basic medical skills for community health workers.
- any other valid point for any of the agencies.

(*b*) Candidates are required to make comparisons between sources and draws conclusions.
The two correct responses are:

Difference 1
Source 1 says a large number of people have been forced to leave their homes but Source 2 says that a large number of people have chosen to leave.

Difference 2
Source 1 says children are dying of hunger but Source 2 says everybody has enough to eat.

(*c*) The concept being assessed is Power. Candidates are required to provide detailed descriptions.
Answers may include:

- 80% of the money donated comes back to the donor country.
- there is prestige involved. It makes the donor country look good.
- the donor country profits from the relationship eg creating employment in their own country.
- all the powers remain with the donor. Recipients cannot say how the money is spent.
- any other valid point.

(*d*) Candidates are required to make comparisons between sources and draw conclusions.
The correct responses are:

Statement 1
Benin has a smaller percentage of its population living in poverty than Kenya or Nigeria.
Reason 1
Benin has only 37% of the population below the poverty line compared to 50% in Kenya and 60% in Nigeria.

Statement 2
Life expectancy is lowest in Kenya.
Reason 2
Life expectancy in Kenya is only 45 years compared to 51 in Benin and 50 in Nigeria.

MODERN STUDIES CREDIT 2006

Syllabus Area 1 – Living In A Democracy

1. (*a*) The concept being assessed is Participation. Candidates are required to use understanding of the concept to provide detailed descriptions with relevant examples and appropriate generalisations.

Answers may include:

- driving people to the polling station.
- canvassing – going round door to door.
- leafleting and putting up posters.
- organising meetings.
- any other valid point.

(*b*) The concept being assessed is Rights and Responsibilities. Candidates are required to use understanding of the concept to provide detailed explanations with relevant examples and appropriate generalisations.

Answers may include:

- if you don't vote, you can't complain.
- the government spends taxes collected, so you should have your say on how it is spent.
- low turnout might allow an unrepresentative government into power.
- failure to vote might allow extremist parties to win seats in Parliament.
- a democracy only works properly if people vote.
- people in the past fought for this fundamental right. Voters today should respect this fact.
- any other valid point.

(*c*) Candidates are required to state a hypothesis relevant to the issue of 'Voting systems used in elections in Scotland'.

The following receive no marks:

- Who votes in Scottish Elections?
- young people do not vote in Scottish Elections.

The following receive one mark:

- there are many different voting systems in the Scottish elections.
- first past the post is a voting system used in Scotland.

The following receive two marks:

- STV will be a good voting system for Local Government elections in Scotland.
- people in Scotland are confused by the many different voting systems.

(*d*) Candidates are required to state aims relevant to the issue.

For example:

Hypothesis: STV will be a good voting system for Local Government elections in Scotland.

- to find out how the STV system will work.
- to find out if people in my town think it will be a good voting system.

Hypothesis: People in Scotland are confused by many different voting systems.

- to find out the differing voting systems used in Scotland.
- to find out what people in my town think about the different voting systems that they use.
- any other valid aim.

(*e*) Candidates are required to justify the use of a given method of enquiry relevant to the issue of 'Peoples' attitude towards voting'.

The following reasons receive one mark:

- the survey has a wide range of ages.
- the survey shows the answers from a lot of people.
- the survey has been carried out by the Home Office.
- it was done fairly recently.

The following reasons receive two marks:

- the survey has a wide range of ages so that it compares what people of different ages think.
- the survey shows the answer from 9 600 people which is a very large amount and much larger than I could ask.
- the survey has been done by the Home Office and will be trustworthy information from a government source.
- it was done in September 2004 which is not very long ago so the information is relatively up-to-date.
- any other valid reason.

(*f*) Candidates are required to state a relevant question for a given method of enquiry.

The following questions receive one mark:

- Do you vote?

The following questions receive two marks:

- Do you think you can influence decisions in the local area by voting?
- Do you think that young people aged over 16 should be allowed to vote?
- How important do you think it is to vote? (Please tick)
  Very Important... Important...
  Fairly Important... Not Important...
- If you do not vote can you please tick your reason for not voting.
  It is a waste of time...
  Not bothered...
  The policies are all the same...
  I do not like the people who stood to be elected...
  Other reason...
  If you ticked 'other reason' please explain...
- any other valid question.

Syllabus Area 2 – Changing Society

2. (*a*) The concept being assessed is Ideology. Candidates are required to use understanding of the concept to provide detailed descriptions with relevant examples and appropriate generalisations.

Answers may include:

Education Maintenance Allowance (EMA)

- financial help for eligible youngsters in S5 and S6.
- it is a weekly payment of up to £30, paid directly to young people.
- this is to enable them to stay in post-16 education in order to get as many qualifications as possible as this is a route into Higher education or into paid employment.

Skillseekers

- it is a training programme for young people.
- training is to nationally recognised standards.
- the cost of the training is covered.
- it is open to 16 – 18 year olds who have left school.
- most skillseekers are in work but if they are not, it can still be used through work experience. A work placement can be organised for the trainee.
- training normally lasts about two years.
- the object of the scheme is to make a young person more employable due to the gaining of qualifications.

Modern Apprentices (MA)

- MA's offer those over 16 paid employment.
- they offer the opportunity to train for jobs at craft, technician and management level.
- they allow a person to gain skills and qualifications to help start a career without having to study full-time. The apprentices, themselves, should be capable of achieving a Vocational Qualification at Level 3 or above.
- MA's are available across a wide range of industries.

New Deal (ND)

- this is a Government programme that aims to give unemployed people the help and support they need to get into work.
- everyone on ND gets a personal adviser who is their point of contact throughout the programme.
- the personal adviser, after discussions, prepares a plan to try and get the person into a suitable job.
- there are different programmes designed for different categories of people eg ND for Young People, ND for Lone Parents, ND for Disabled People or ND for 50 plus.

Jobcentre Plus (JCP)

- launched in April 2002 by the Labour Government.
- it brought together the Employment Service and parts of the Benefits Agency.
- the aim of JCP was to increase the effective labour supply by helping as many unemployed and economically inactive people of working age as possible to move into jobs by making available to them job vacancies, information, advice, training and support, and encouraging employers to open up more opportunities to them.
- help was also to be provided for people of working age in the most disadvantaged groups and areas so that they moved closer to the labour market, were able to compete effectively for, and remain in work.
- JCPs were also to pay people of working age the correct amount of benefit to which they were entitled throughout the period of their claim. They were also expected to protect the benefit system from fraud, error and abuse.
- any other valid point

(*b*) Candidates are required to provide evidence to oppose a given point of view.

Answers may include:

Sandy Mathieson says **'Households consisting of pensioners have grown the most in percentage terms'**

Source 1 shows that in 1981 there were 28.9% pensioner households and this rose to 30.8% in 2003, a rise of 1.9%. However the biggest rise was shown by Single Adult households which rose by 8.7% over the same period. This **opposes** the view.

Sandy Mathieson says **'.... they (Pensioner households) have experienced less of an improvement in the quality of their lives than other groups'**

Source 2 shows that from 1994 to 2002 pensioner households in poverty fell from 32% to 9%, a drop of 23%. This is the biggest drop in poverty of any household group. This **opposes** the view.

(*c*) Candidates are required to detect and explain examples of lack of objectivity in complex sources, giving developed argument when required.

Answers may include:

'Women are becoming more important to the Scottish economy in the 21st century'.

- *From Source 1:* new growth industries are mainly service industries such as call centres where the % of women has grown from 42% to 67%.
  women becoming more important
- *From Source 2:* more men than women were employed in 1998 but in 2002 it was more women than men employed in Scotland
  women becoming more important
- *From Source 2:* more women than men employed in Banking, Distribution, Public Administration and other services, ie all the new growth service sectors, in 2002.
  women becoming more important
- *From Source 3:* there are far more women than men in part-time employment and it is increasing.
  women becoming more important as numbers are increasing

'Furthermore, this is reflected in the changes in their pay and conditions'.

- *From Source 3:* there are far more women than

men in part-time employment and it is increasing. However, possibly poorer working conditions as not full-time.
women's growing importance not reflected

- *From Source 4:* women on average, for every year mentioned still have less pay than men.
women still lagging behind men as they are not as well paid
- *From Source 4:* women's pay as a % of men's pay is increasing.
women's growing importance is reflected in improving pay and conditions

The Sources tend to show that Tom Anderson is really only being selective in the use of facts to a fairly small degree. The evidence tends to support a lot of what he has to say. Women are becoming more important to the Scottish economy but this may not be fully reflected in their pay and conditions.

Syllabus Area 3 – Ideologies

THE USA

3A. (*a*) The concept being assessed is Rights and Responsibilities. Candidates are required to use understanding of the concept to provide detailed descriptions with relevant examples and appropriate generalisations.

Answers may include:

- the right to vote in city, local, state and federal elections for a large variety of elected posts BUT the responsibility is to register for elections, use their vote, and to do so in a considered way.
- the right to freedom of speech means that Americans can express their opinions at meetings and through the media BUT the responsibility is to respect the views of others and not tell lies – America has powerful laws against libel and slander.
- the right to protest and demonstrate to gain attention for your views. For example a march outside the White House or the Capitol building in Washington DC, BUT the responsibility is to do so peacefully, to stay within the law and to follow a prearranged route.
- the right to join a political party or an interest group with other people who have similar opinions. For example the Republican and Democratic Parties and/or an interest group such as the National Rifle Association, BUT the responsibility is to support these groups financially and to help with their campaigns, and to stay within the law.
- any other valid point.

(*b*) Candidates are required to make comparisons within and between complex sources and draw valid conclusions from them, with justification by developed argument when required.

Answers may include:

The borough whose racial composition is least like that of the city as a whole

Bronx

Racial composition in the Bronx is least like the city as a whole because:

- Hispanics are the largest ethnic group in the Bronx with 48.4%. In all the other boroughs Whites are the largest group, just as for the city of New York as a whole.
- in New York the largest group is White, followed by Hispanic then Black. 3 boroughs – Manhattan, Queens and Staten Island - show this same pattern. Brooklyn has 2 groups in a different order, but only the Bronx has all 3 in different positions, ie Hispanic, Black, then White.

Staten Island

Racial composition in Staten Island is least like the city as a whole because:

- although the population groups from largest to smallest follow the same sequence as New York, the figures are very different. For example, the White group at 71.3% is over twice that of the city which is only 35.0%. Both the Hispanic and Black groups are less than half the figures for the city as a whole. These differences are much larger than for any other borough.

The relationship between person crime rates and educational attainment

- the Sources show that as the rate of person crime increases educational attainment gets poorer. For example, Staten Island has the lowest crime rate at 332 per 100 000 people and has the lowest rate for not completing high school.
- the Bronx is the borough with the highest rate of person crime (1 112 per 100 000 people) and also has the highest % of those who did not complete high school (38%) and the lowest % who were college graduates (15%).

The relationship between race and family finances

- Staten Island has the lowest rate of family poverty (8%). It also has by far the highest proportion of Whites in the city at 71.3%.
- Bronx has the lowest level of income ($28 000). It also has the lowest proportion of Whites in the city at only 14.5 %. (Or the highest level of Hispanics at 48.4%)

The desirability of Manhattan as a Borough to live in

Manhattan would be a desirable place to live in because:

- educational attainment is very high as 49% of those aged 25+ are college graduates and it has the second lowest rate for those not finishing high school (21%).

- average income is $48 000 which is the second highest in New York. This is only $7 000 behind the highest, Staten Island, but $20 000 more than the Bronx which is the lowest at $28 000.

Manhattan would not be a desirable place to live because:

- it has the highest crime rate in New York at 4 717 per 100 000 people. The rate for person crime is 3rd highest behind Bronx and Brooklyn, but property crime is by far the highest in the city at 3 822 per 100 000.
- any other valid point for any of the headings.

RUSSIA

3B. (*a*) The concept being assessed is Rights and Responsibilities. Candidates are required to use understanding of the concept to provide detailed descriptions with relevant examples and appropriate generalisations.

Answers may include:

- the right to vote in local and national elections for a large variety of elected posts BUT the responsibility is to use their vote, and to do so in a considered way.
- the right to freedom of speech means that Russians can express their opinions at meetings and through the media BUT the responsibility is to respect the views of others.
- the right to protest and demonstrate to gain attention for your views. For example a march outside the Kremlin building in Moscow, BUT the responsibility is to do so peacefully, to stay within the law and to follow a prearranged route.
- the right to join a political party with other people who have similar opinions. For example the Liberal Democratic Party of Russia or Yabloko or United Russia BUT the responsibility is to support these parties financially and to help with their campaigns, and to stay within the law.
- any other valid point.

(*b*) Candidates are required to make comparisons within and between complex sources, and draw valid conclusions from them, with justification by developed argument when required.

Answers may include:

The urban/rural divide in Russia compared with some of her neighbours

- the urban/rural split in Russia is very similar to that in both Japan and Norway. In all 3 countries it is almost 75% urban compared to 25% rural.
- Kazakhstan, North Korea and Mongolia also all have fairly similar urban/rural divides with approximately 60% urban as opposed to 40% rural.

The relationship between the urban/rural divide and employment in agriculture

- although Japan and Norway have similar urban/rural divides, the percentage of the Russian population employed in Agriculture is much higher than in either of the other 2 countries. It is 12% in Russia compared to 5% in Japan and only 4% in Norway.
- North Korea has 3 times the percentage of Russian people in Agriculture whilst Mongolia is completely different from Russia with 79% compared to 12%.

The relationship between employment in services and their contribution to GDP

- both Japan and Norway have a bigger percentage of their workforce employed in Services. In Russia, 64% of the workforce contributes 60% of the wealth whereas in Japan, 70% of the workforce contributes an even higher percentage of the wealth at 73%. In Norway, it is different as 74% of the workforce only contributes 62% of the wealth. This is a figure much closer to that in Russia.
- Mongolia and North Korea have a much smaller percentage of their workforces involved in Services but in the case of Mongolia, it contributes almost the same percentage of the country's wealth as is the case in Russia.

The importance of Russia to the economies of the neighbouring countries

- The importance of Russia to the economies of the neighbouring countries varies greatly.
- Japan, Norway and North Korea import very little from Russia and in all 3 cases, they sell more to Russia than they buy from Russia.
- Both Mongolia and Kazakhstan get one third of all their imports from Russia which means that Russia is vitally important to them.
- Russia is a very important export market for Kazakhstan with over 15% of all exports going to Russia.

CHINA

3C. (*a*) The concept being assessed is Rights and Responsibilities. Candidates are required to use understanding of the concept to provide detailed descriptions with relevant examples and appropriate generalisations.

Answers may include:

- the right to start a business. Ever since the early 1980's Chinese people have been encouraged to open their own businesses. Estimates of 2 million privately owned enterprises. However, there is a responsibility to employ people on a living wage and to contribute to the growth and strength of the economy.
- the right to elect village/local representatives/ deputies to Peoples' Congresses at city,

provincial and national level. However, there is a responsibility for individuals themselves to take part in the running of villages, towns etc by voting or perhaps by becoming a candidate either for the Communist Party or for one of the approved opposition parties.

- the right to protest in pressure groups but the responsibility is to ensure that the authority of the Communist Party isn't challenged. Chinese people also have a responsibility to obey the law and to support the communist revolution by educating others and by reporting counter revolutionaries.
- any other valid point.

(*b*) Candidates are required to make comparisons within and between complex sources and draw valid conclusions from them, with justification by developed argument when required.

Answers may include:

The urban/rural divide in China compared with some of her neighbours

- Japan, has more than twice the urban (79% to 37%) and only one third of rural population compared to China (21% to 63%). It is the least like China of all the neighbouring countries.
- Nepal has less than one third of China's urban population (12% to 37%) but is the only country with a larger rural population than China (88% to 63%).
- India is most like China in terms of the urban/rural divide 28% and 72%.

The relationship between the urban/rural divide and employment in agriculture

- countries with large rural populations eg China, have a much larger agricultural workforce (63% rural and 50% in agriculture). The same is true for India, Vietnam and Nepal.
- countries with a large urban population have small agricultural sectors. Eg Japan has 79% urban and only 5% working in agriculture.
- the countries with the smallest rural populations have the smallest agricultural workforce. Japan has only 21% rural population and only 5% employed in agriculture ie a third of China's rural population but only a tenth of its agricultural workforce (5% compared to China's 50%).

The relationship between employment in services and their contribution to GDP

- Services provide more wealth than the proportion of the workforce would suggest in China and all of the neighbouring countries. eg China gets 32% of its wealth from 28% of its workers.
- Vietnam appears to have the most productive service industry - 14% of the workforce accounts for 38% of GDP. China's service sector is not as efficient, only contributing 32% of GDP from 28% of the workforce.
- Japan is the only service sector that adds less to GDP than China.

The importance of China to the economies of the neighbouring countries

- China buys a quarter of its imports from its neighbours. It is clearly important to them as their population is so large that this will be worth a lot of money.
- all of the neighbours buy and sell from China. Especially North Korea who buy almost 40% of their imports from China, and rely on China to buy 28.4% of their exports. This is much more than any of the other neighbours.
- China is comparatively less important to India and Nepal. India only buys 4.5% of its imports from China, 35.4% less than North Korea whilst Nepal only relies on China to buy 0.5% of its exports.

Syllabus Area 4 – International Relations

4. (*a*) The concept being assessed is Power. Candidates are required to use understanding of the concept to provide detailed explanations with relevant examples and appropriate generalisations.

Answers may include:

- the invasion of Iraq in 2003 by the US-led coalition forces happened because of intelligence reports which suggested that Iraq had Weapons of Mass Destruction (WMD).
- coalition forces launched the war on terror after 9/11. This took the form of getting rid of the Taliban government in Afghanistan and searching for Osama bin Laden.
- the bombings in Madrid and London ensured that the war on terror continued to be fought both within and outwith Europe.
- any other valid point.

(*b*) Candidates are required to provide evidence to support and oppose a personal point of view.

Answers may include:

Source 1

For (leaving):

- in UK 27% of the population would be happy if EU scrapped compared to only 16% unhappy. Similar figures in Finland.
- people don't view EU as relevant - less than 50% participated in the elections in 2004.

Against (ie staying in EU):

- clearly a popular union - 10 new members in 2004 and more set to join.
- in Ireland 44% would be sorry to leave EU.
- many countries receive a lot of funding eg Poland.

Source 2 and Source 3 NB Sources 2 and 3 cannot be used in isolation (unless discussing turnout)

For:
- dramatic rise of UKIP with 16% of the vote reflects desire to leave EU and opposition to the Euro.
- UKIP saw a dramatic increase in their vote and are only party advocating leaving.
- slump in vote for the mainstream parties who wish to stay in EU ie Labour fell from 28% to 21% and Conservatives from 36% to 28%.
- voter turnout in the UK is very low despite a 9% rise in 2004 which suggests that the people in the UK are still not sufficiently interested in the EU.

Against:
- low turnout reflects a lack of concern. Far higher turnout if voters wanted to leave EU.
- Labour and Conservatives polled far more than UKIP and they both want to stay in EU.
- Liberal Democrats only mainstream party to gain between 1999 and 2004 and they clearly wish to remain in.

Source 4
For:
- Since 1990 more people wish to leave EU.

Against:
- very unclear that UK people do want to leave as huge fluctuations according to pie charts.
- 49% currently wish to remain in compared to only 41% wishing to leave.

Overall, there is more evidence opposing the view of the UKIP voter. Eg only 41% of the UK electorate would vote to leave the EU. As far as the rest of Europe is concerned, twice as many would be unhappy if the EU was scrapped.

MODERN STUDIES GENERAL 2007

Syllabus Area 1 – Living In A Democracy

1. (*a*) The concept being assessed is Participation. Candidates are required to give detailed descriptions.
Answers may include:
- canvassing for support in the local area by going round all the houses in an area to speak to the public.
- putting leaflets containing information about the candidate through peoples' doors.
- phoning people at home to persuade them to support the candidate.
- putting posters up on lamp posts and in shop windows to advertise their candidate.
- mailing/posting campaign materials to voters in the area with information about the candidate.
- going around the area in a van/car with a loudspeaker encouraging people to vote for the candidate.
- using the electoral roll to check support for your candidate.
- organise/provide transport to the polling station for the elderly/disabled.
- any other valid point.

(*b*) Candidates are required to make comparisons within a source and draw valid conclusions.
The correct responses are:
- in 2001, the most popular activity was contacting a local council official with 64%. In 2005 this changed to signing a petition which 60% of people did.
- contacting your councillor has shown least change as it has fallen by only 3%.

(*c*) The concept being assessed is Representation. Candidates are required to provide detailed descriptions.
Answers may include:
Problems:
- no wage increase this year
- health and safety concerns
- canteen price rises
- concerns over paying for the creche
- any other valid point

The shop steward could help by:
- arranging a meeting/negotiating with the management to resolve the problem.
- contacting full-time union officials to ask for their help and advice.
- organise a ballot of members about industrial action.
- organise appropriate industrial action such as work-to-rule, overtime ban or strike action if negotiations are not successful.
- any other valid point

(*d*) Candidates are required to provide evidence to support a given point of view.
Answers may include:
- Salma Khan says that workers benefit from being members of a trade union. This view is supported from Source 2 by the fact that workers in a trade union enjoyed a higher rate of pay of £11.38 per hour, compared to only £9.72 for workers not in a trade union.
- Salma Khan also says that membership of trade unions continued to increase for some groups of workers. This is supported from Source 1 by the fact that the number of women members has increased from 3 210 000 in 2001 to 3 356 000 in 2005.

Syllabus Area 2 – Changing Society

2. (*a*) Candidates are required to express support for a personal point of view with valid reasons.
For House A – Ground floor flat
- A ground floor flat – Millie finds it more difficult to move about.
- A 2 bedroom flat – Millie was finding her 4 bedroom house too big.
- Elderly people live in the other 3 flats – Millie feels lonely.
- All residents share a conservatory which looks onto a colourful garden – Millie enjoys her garden.

For House B – Bungalow
- A one-storey house – Millie finds it more difficult to move about.
- A 2 bedroom house – Millie was finding her 4 bedroom house too big.
- There is a very pleasant summer-house for sitting in – Millie enjoys her garden.
- Fully double glazed throughout and with full gas central heating means the bungalow is cheap to heat in the winter – Millie is starting to feel the cold.

(*b*) The concept being assessed is Equality. Candidates are required to provide detailed explanations.
Answers may include:
- some elderly people have more money than others and so can afford private medical care and have their health problems attended to more quickly.
- some elderly people can afford adequate central heating in the winter whilst others have to choose between eating and heating.
- some elderly people choose to take regular exercise and stay fit whilst other elderly people suffer from obesity and heart disease.
- some elderly people take part in activities to stimulate their mind and so may enjoy better mental health than others.
- some elderly people have a wide social circle of friends and family and so are less likely to suffer from depression and loneliness.
- any other valid point

(*c*) The concept being assessed is Ideology. Candidates are required to provide detailed descriptions.
Answers may include:
- provides state old age pension, winter fuel payments and income support to provide for the financial needs of the elderly.
- provides free healthcare such as operations, GP consultations, eye examinations, prescriptions to meet the health needs of the elderly.
- provides for some social needs such as free TV licence for the over 75s.
- provides free personal care to meet the health needs.
- provides free bus travel throughout Scotland.
- any other valid point

(*d*) Candidates are required to detect exaggeration and provide explanations.
The correct responses are:
Statement 1
Sandy Brown said, 'Scottish men are the only men who work more than the EU weekly average.'
Reason 1
The statement is exaggerated because in Source 2 it shows that the EU Average is 41·3 hours, Scotland works 45·4 hours, Portugal 42·1 hours and Greece 41·7 hours per week'. They are all above the average.

Statement 2
Sandy Brown said, 'Very few Scottish workers fail to take all their annual holidays.'
Reason 2
The statement is exaggerated because in Source 1 it says 'About 73% of Scottish workers said they often failed to take all their annual holidays'. This is a lot, not very few.

Syllabus Area 3 –Ideologies

THE USA

3A. (*a*)The concept being assessed is Rights and Responsibilities. Candidates are required to provide detailed descriptions.
Answers may include:
Rights
- to stand for election in a Presidential or local election.
- to join a political party such as the Democrats or the Republicans.
- to vote for the candidate of their choice in election such as those for city mayor.
- to own a gun.
- to protest against a law passed by the Federal Government.
- to have free speech.
- to practise a religion of their choice.
- to have a fair trial.
- any other valid point

Responsibilities

- to use their vote in a considered way.
- to accept the result of the election.
- not to conceal their weapon or use it in an act of aggression.
- to accept the views of others.
- not to slander or libel someone.
- to tell the truth whilst under oath.
- any other valid point

(*b*) Candidates are required to support and oppose a given point of view.

Support the view:
Eva Kaye says 'It also showed greater participation in politics by voters in the USA'.

Evidence to support:
The percentage of voters turning out to vote was 49·0% in 1996 but had risen to 59·8% in 2004. This is greater participation in politics.

Oppose the view:
Eva Kaye says 'In the 2004 Presidential elections, the winner had a large majority'.

Evidence to oppose:
Bush only got 51% of the votes. This is not a large majority as he only won by 3% from Kerry.

(*c*) The concept being assessed is Ideology. Candidates are required to provide detailed explanations.

Answers may include:

- capitalism allows people to start up their own business such as Apple or Gap.
- the profit motive encourages people to work hard and to keep the profits from their business. Bill Gates of Microsoft is one example.
- competition between businesses such as Wal-mart and Target, keeps prices low and quality high.
- democracy allows American citizens to stand for election and challenge policies which they disagree with.
- affirmative action policies have helped many more women and ethnic minorities to become successful in education and employment.
- any other valid point

(*d*) Candidates are required to detect exaggeration and provide explanations.

The correct responses are:

Statement 1
Martin Baxter said 'The lowest level of support for President Bush has always been in his campaign against terrorism.'

Reason 1
The statement is exaggerated because in the table it shows that the level of support for his campaign against terrorism has always been the highest, in every year. This is not the lowest.

Statement 2
Martin Baxter said 'Support for his handling of the economy has steadily fallen each year.'

Reason 2
The statement is exaggerated because in the table it shows that his support for the economy actually increased by 4% between 2003 and 2004. This is not a fall.

RUSSIA

3B. (*a*) The concept being assessed is Rights and Responsibilities. Candidates are required to provide detailed descriptions.

Answers may include:

Rights

- to stand for election in a Presidential or local election.
- to join a political party such as United Russia, Yabloko or the Communist Party.
- to vote for the candidate of their choice in election such as those for the Duma.
- to own a gun.
- to protest against a law passed by the Government.
- to have free speech.
- to practise a religion of their choice.
- to have a fair trial.
- any other valid point

Responsibilities

- to use their vote in a considered way.
- to accept the result of the election.
- not to conceal their weapon or use it in an act of aggression.
- to accept the views of others.
- not to slander or libel someone.
- to tell the truth whilst under oath.
- any other valid point

(*b*) Candidates are required to support and oppose a given point of view.

Support the view:
Maria Chakvetadze says, 'In the 2004 Presidential election, the winner had a large majority.'

Evidence to support:
Putin won the election with 71% of the vote.
His nearest challenger only got 14% of the vote.
His winning margin was 57%, which is a large majority.

Oppose the view:
Maria Chakvetadze says, 'It also showed greater participation in politics by voters in Russia.'

Evidence to oppose:
Turnout at the election in 2004 was 64% which was 4% down on the turnout at the election in 2000 and 6% down on the election in 1996.

(*c*) The concept being assessed is Ideology. Candidates are required to provide detailed explanations.

Answers may include:

- the economic system in Russia allows people to start up their own business.

- the profit motive encourages people to work hard and to keep the profits from their business. Roman Abramovich is one example.
- competition between businesses can keep prices low and quality high.
- democracy allows Russian citizens to stand for election and challenge policies which they disagree with.
- any other valid point

(*d*) Candidates are required to detect exaggeration and provide explanations.

The correct responses are:

Statement 1

Alexia Gudrun said, 'More Russians thought Putin was 'doing a good job' in 2005 than in previous years.'

Reason 1

This statement is exaggerated because the table shows that 39% of the electorate thought he was doing a good job in 2005 but in 2003, the figure was higher at 42%.

Statement 2

Alexia Gudrun said, 'In 2003, most Russians thought Putin was 'doing a poor job'.'

Reason 2

This statement is exaggerated because the table shows that most Russians thought Putin was 'doing a good job' in 2003 with a 42% rating as opposed to 27% for 'doing a poor job'.

CHINA

3C. (*a*) The concept being assessed is Rights and Responsibilities. Candidates are required to provide detailed descriptions.

Answers may include:

- the right to elect village/local representatives/ deputies to Peoples' Congresses at city, provincial and national level. However, there is a responsibility for individuals themselves to take part in the running of villages, towns etc by voting or perhaps by becoming a candidate either for the Communist Party or for one of the approved opposition parties.
- the right to protest in pressure groups but the responsibility is to ensure that the authority of the Communist Party isn't challenged. Chinese people also have a responsibility to obey the law and to support the communist revolution by educating others and by reporting counter revolutionaries.
- the right to healthcare. Citizens often have to pay for treatments, drugs, etc.
- the right to an education. The responsibility is to send children to school in order to enhance the economy. Rural schools are often inadequate in terms of funding and staffing.
- the right to religion is written in to the Chinese constitution. Citizens can follow one of four recognized religions (Buddhism, Islam, Christianity and Taoism) but have the responsibility to only worship in 'patriotic' churches, temples, etc.
- the right to family life, within the limitations of the one child policy.
- any other valid point

(*b*) Candidates are required to support and oppose a given point of view.

Support the view:

Zi Yan says, 'It also showed greater participation in politics by voters in Duyun'.

Evidence to support:

This is true, as turnout figures have gone up from 85% in 1995 to 91% in 2005.

Oppose the view:

Zi Yan says, 'In the 2005 election, the winner had a large majority'.

Evidence to oppose:

This is not true as the winning candidate only had 46% of the vote ie less than half.

This is also not true as she only won by 6%.

(*c*) The concept being assessed is Ideology. Candidates are required to provide detailed explanations.

Answers may include:

- since the early eighties Chinese people have been allowed to start a business and keep the profit ie 'Socialist Market Economy'. Many millions of enterprises, of different sizes, are privately owned. Approximately 125 million Chinese work for small 'township enterprises'.
- many state owned enterprises have been forced to become more competitive, giving opportunities for bigger salaries in management etc. Some workers could buy shares in their factory etc.
- special Economic Zones have attracted a great deal of investment from foreign companies. Wages in these areas tend to be higher and unemployment lower. eg along the 'Coastal Strip'.
- China joined the World Trade Organisation, allowing greater freedom to business and hence greater affluence for some.
- Stock Market opened allowing individuals to invest in different companies. China now has many millionaires.
- Hong Kong returned to Chinese control bringing opportunities to Chinese citizens.
- agricultural reforms such as the responsibility system have brought wealth to some farmers.
- any other valid point

(*d*) Candidates are required to detect exaggeration and provide explanations.

The correct responses are:

Statement 1

Lye Zhang said 'The urban population of China will double between 1995 and 2010'.

Reason 1

This is exaggerated because the table shows that the

urban population will increase from 30% to 44%. This is an increase of slightly less than 50%.

Statement 2

Lye Zhang said 'The biggest rise in the total population came between 2000 and 2005'.

Reason 2

This is exaggerated because the table shows that the increase between 2000 and 2005 was only 0·01 billion. The biggest increase was between 1995 and 2000 at 0·08 billion.

Syllabus Area 4 – International Relations

4. (*a*) The concept being assessed is Need. Candidates are required to provide detailed descriptions.

Answers may include:

- UN tries to meet needs in Africa via agencies. UNICEF gives aid to mothers and children, such as supporting breastfeeding.
- countries can give bi-lateral aid eg Britain gave aid to Mozambique when a natural disaster occurred. The aid included tents, food and basic medicine.
- Oxfam or other aid agencies, acting as managing agents for either individual governments or for a UN specialised agency, give small scale aid to local people eg helping young men to learn a trade.
- any other valid point

(*b*) Candidates are required to make comparisons within sources and draw valid conclusions.

The correct responses are:

Difference 1

Source 1 says that 'They are being successful in making the lives of the people better' but Source 2 says that 'Afghanistan is now suffering from lawlessness, misery and starvation'.

Difference 2

Source 1 says that 'Some Afghans have had to flee from the fighting but they have been moved to clean, safe refugee camps' but Source 2 says that 'Many local people have been forced to flee to refugee camps where the conditions are dangerous and filthy'.

(*c*) Candidates are required to give relevant aims for an investigative topic.

The following receive no marks:

- to find out when the EU was set up.
- to find out who is in the EU.

The following receive one mark:

- to find out what Scotland gains from the EU.
- to find out how many MEPs Scotland has.
- any other valid aim

(*d*) Candidates are required to state and justify an appropriate method of enquiry.

Answers may include:

- quick method of contacting a person.
- people often respond quickly to an e-mail (compared to a letter).
- easy to find the address (Google/EU page).
- any other valid point

(*e*) Candidates are required to state and justify an appropriate method of enquiry.

The correct responses are:

- Services: you could see if there were any relevant statistics or opinion polls to answer the aims.
- 'In the Spotlight': the first topic, 'Crisis in Scotland', relates directly to Scotland and could have material for the investigation.
- Search facility: could be used to find information not already identified.
- Activities: 'What the EU does by subject'. 'Regional Policy' may have information about Scotland.
- any other valid point

MODERN STUDIES CREDIT 2007

Syllabus Area 1 - Living In A Democracy

1. (*a*) The concept being assessed is Rights.
Candidates are required to use understanding of the concept to provide detailed descriptions with relevant examples and appropriate generalisations.
Answers may include:
   - to demonstrate/protest outside public/ government buildings. This may attract media attention and get their arguments over to a wider audience.
   - to lobby their MP at the House of Commons. Constituents have the right to visit parliament and ask to speak to their MP.
   - to send letters/e-mails of protest to their MP, Minister in charge, or Prime Minister.
   - to set up a petition, perhaps on the Internet, which allows the public to express their concerns as well.
   - any other valid point

(*b*) The concept being assessed is Representation.
Candidates are required to use understanding of the concept to provide detailed explanations with relevant examples and appropriate generalisations.
Answers may include:
Advantages of Single Transferable Vote:
- no wasted votes. If a voter fails to get their first choice, it will be reallocated until it is counted.
- smaller parties have a better chance of getting a candidate elected. This means that one party is less likely to dominate.
- gives greater choice to voters as they could choose to vote for all the candidates in one party, or all women candidates, or all ethnic minority candidates. There are limitless variations as to how a particular person could vote.
- coalitions between parties are much more likely. This will encourage parties to work together more, and better reflect the way people have voted.
- any other valid point

Advantages of Additional Member System:
- the number of MSPs each party gains is much more proportional to the votes cast nationally. This better reflects the wishes of the people of Scotland.
- smaller parties have a better chance of gaining seats. The parties that do well on the first vote are penalised on the second vote. This has allowed MSPs to be elected from the Green Party, Scottish Socialists, Solidarity, and other smaller parties.
- fewer wasted votes, as in the second ballot, votes are redistributed. This gives a greater incentive to vote.
- From 1999–2007, Scotland has had a coalition government. This reflected the way people in Scotland had voted. Where one party did not get an overall majority of the seats, they decided not to form a minority government but to seek a coalition partner.
- any other valid point

Advantages of First Past the Post:
- it is fair as the candidate who gets most votes wins the constituency - more people voted for the winning party in a constituency.
- it is a simple system which is easy for voters to understand. One cross is placed against the name of a candidate. It delivers a quick and readily understandable result.
- each constituency has a personal link with a single MP who can keep in close contact with the people in the area.
- it usually provides a clear winner nationally, allowing one party to form a strong government without the need to form a coalition.
- any other valid point

(*c*) Candidates are required to detect and explain examples of lack of objectivity in complex sources, giving developed argument when required.
Answers may include:
'The Conservative Party did badly in all areas of the country.'
From Source 1:
- in Scotland they did very badly with only 16% of the vote and 2% of the seats. They came fourth behind Labour, Liberal Democrats and the SNP.
- in Wales they also did badly with only 8% of the seats, well behind Labour and the Liberal Democrats.
- in the UK as a whole they did better, coming within 3% of Labour in terms of % vote, but still well behind in number of MPs.
- in England they did well and actually got more votes than Labour. However, they got far fewer MPs.

Karen Mitchell is being slightly selective, as it was only in England that they did well, and only in % of votes, not in the number of MPs.

'The Liberal Democrats, on the other hand, are the only party whose support increased amongst different age ranges ... compared with other parties, between 1997 and 2005.'
From Source 3:
- the Liberal Democrats increased their support in all 4 age ranges shown.
- support for the Labour party fell in all 4 of the age ranges.
- the Conservative party had a decrease in 2 of the age ranges, but did better in both the 35-64 and the 65+ age ranges.

Karen is being slightly selective. She is correct in what she says with the exception of two age groups for the Conservative Party.

'The Liberal Democrats, on the other hand, are the only party whose support increased amongst different social classes ... compared with other parties, between 1997 and 2005.'
From Source 2:
- support for the Lib Dems increased in all 3 social classes shown.
- support for the Labour party decreased from both the Working Class (Skilled) and the Working Class (Unskilled), but increased from the Middle Class.
- the Conservative Party got less support from the Middle Class, but increased support from both the Skilled and Unskilled Working Class.

Karen is being slightly/quite selective because although the Liberal Democrats increased their support within all social classes, it is also true that both the Labour and Conservative parties did see some increased support from certain social class groups. Overall, Karen is being slightly/quite selective in the use of facts, as there is evidence to show that the Conservatives did not do badly in all areas of the country, and that other parties apart from the Liberal Democrats did get increased support from different groups in society.

Syllabus Area 2 – Changing Society

2. (*a*) The concept being assessed is Need. Candidates are required to use understanding of the concept to provide detailed explanations with relevant examples and appropriate generalisations.
Answers may include:
- some families are unemployed and survive on a low income and therefore cannot financially afford to buy a nutritionally balanced diet.
- some families are single parents who go out to work for long hours and so the emotional needs of the children are not being met.
- some parents may have a disability which means that they cannot meet the physical needs of their children.
- some parents do not have access to their children which prevents them from meeting the emotional needs of their children.
- some parents cannot meet the developmental needs of their children due to a lack of education.
- any other valid point

(*b*) Candidates are required to provide evidence to support and oppose a given point of view.
The correct responses are:
View of Tom Hicks
'In 1995, unemployment was a bigger problem in the North than it was in the South.'
Reason to support:
All 7 regions in the 'North' had higher unemployment than 4 out of the 5 regions of the 'South'. Therefore, it was a bigger problem.

View of Tom Hicks
'Ten years on, the situation was the complete opposite.'
Reason to oppose:
As all 7 regions in the 'North' still have higher unemployment than 4 out of the 5 regions of the 'South' it was not the complete opposite. It was still the same.

(*c*) Candidates are required to make comparisons within and between complex sources and draw valid conclusions from them, with justification using developed argument when required.
Answers may include:
Changes in marriage and divorce in Britain:
- Between 1970 and 2005 **marriages have decreased** by more than 50% from 400 000 to under 200 000.
- **Divorces have nearly trebled** over the same time from about 60 000 to just under 200 000.

The link between changes in marriages and changes in the 'traditional' family
- The 'traditional' family has always been seen as a **couple with dependent children**. The % of the **'traditional' family has fallen** from 52% of households in 1971 to 37% in 2004.
- Between 1970 and 2005, **marriages have decreased** by more than 50%. **Therefore, as the % of marriages fell, the % of the 'traditional' family also fell.**

The difference between the percentages of lone parent families in Britain and Scotland's four main cities
- The % of lone parent families in Britain was 12% in 2004. The % of lone parent families in Scotland's four main cities was over 22-26%, with 3 of them between 27 - 48%. **Therefore, the % was much higher in Scotland's four main cities.**

The main difference between ethnic minority families and white families
- 62% of white families are married couples while all 4 ethnic minority families are over 75% married couples. **Therefore, ethnic minority families are more likely to be married couples**.
- 25% of white families are lone parent families while all 4 ethnic minority families are under 20% lone parent families. **Therefore, ethnic minority families are less likely to be lone parent families**.
- 13% of white families are cohabiting couples while all 4 ethnic minority families are under 5% cohabiting couples. **Therefore, ethnic minority families are less likely to be cohabiting couples.**

Syllabus Area 3 – Ideologies

THE USA

3A. (*a*) The concept being assessed is Participation.
Candidates are required to use understanding of the concept to provide detailed explanations with relevant examples and appropriate generalisations.
Answers may include:
- increase in positive ethnic minority role models such as Condoleeza Rice, Colin Powell, Barack Obama and Ray Nagin.
- celebrity voting campaigns to encourage ethnic minorities to come out and vote. In 2004, P Diddy spearheaded the 'Vote or Die' campaign for the Presidential election.
- increase in the black middle class. More blacks are graduating college and are therefore more likely to register and vote in elections.
- concentration of ethnic minorities in a particular part of a city means that they are more likely to turn out to vote as they believe they have a better chance of getting an ethnic minority candidate elected.
- any other valid point

(*b*) Candidates are required to state a hypothesis relevant to the issue of 'Health care in the USA'.
For example:
The following receive no marks:
- film stars get the most plastic surgery done in the USA.
- health care is important.

The following receive one mark:
- *ER* is a real picture of health care in the USA today.
- health care costs a lot in the USA.

The following receive two marks:
- all races in the USA get similar health care.
- only the really rich in the US get good health care.
- any other valid hypothesis

(*c*) Candidates are required to state aims relevant to the issue.
For example:
Hypothesis:
'All races in the USA get similar health care'
Possible aims:
- to find out if health care in the USA is good for some and bad for others.
- to find out if blacks have the worst health care in the USA.
- to find out the reasons for poor health care amongst different ethnic groups.
- any other valid aim.

(*d*) Candidates are required to justify the use of a given method of enquiry relevant to the issue of 'Education in the USA'.
The following good points receive one mark:
- The e-mail content explains who the pupil is and what they are trying to do.
- The e-mail content explains that the pupil has tried to find information first by looking at the school website.
- The e-mail thanks the head teacher for their time and any help they give.

The following bad points receive one mark:
- The e-mail expects the head teacher to print out the questionnaires, hand them out and send them back.
- The pupil wants things done as quickly as possible.
- The e-mail has no name or address to send the 50 copies of the questions back to.

(*e*) Candidates are required to explain why investigation questions are wrong.
The correct responses are:
Question 3
Are your school meals good and do students get them free?
Reason to change
This is a double-barrelled question but you can only give one answer. You may think that the school meals are good but that students do not get them for free. However, there is no way in which you can say this.
Question 4
Why do Blacks and Hispanics not do well at your school?
Reason to change
This question presumes an answer 'that Blacks and Hispanics do not do well', without getting the facts beforehand.

RUSSIA

3B. (*a*) The concept being assessed is Particpation.
Candidates are required to use understanding of the concept to provide detailed explanations with relevant examples and appropriate generalisations.
Answers may include:
- it is the only way to peacefully change things within Russia.
- Russia has not been a democracy for very long so it is essential that people take part.
- the only way to get representatives from parties such as United Russia, Liberal Democratic Party of Russia or the Communist Party of Russia elected to the Duma is by voting for them or working on their behalf.
- any other valid point

(*b*) Candidates are required to state a hypothesis relevant to the issue of 'Health care in Russia'.
For example:
The following receive no marks:
- politicians get the most plastic surgery done in Russia.
- health care is important.

The following receive one mark:
- TV drama presents a real picture of health care in Russia today.
- health care costs a lot in Russia.

The following receive two marks:
- all nationalities in Russia get similar health care.

- only the really rich in Russia get good health care.
- any other valid hypothesis

(*c*) Candidates are required to state aims relevant to the issue.

For example:

Hypothesis:

'All nationalities in Russia get similar health care.'

Possible aims:

- to find out if health care in Russia is good for some and bad for others.
- to find out if Chechens have the worst health care in Russia.
- to find out the reasons for poor health care amongst different nationalities.
- any other valid aim

(*d*) Candidates are required to justify the use of a given method of enquiry relevant to the issue of 'Education in Russia'.

The following good points receive one mark:

- The e-mail content explains who the pupil is and what they are trying to do.
- The e-mail content explains that the pupil has tried to find information first by looking at the school website.
- The e-mail thanks the head teacher for their time and any help they give.

The following bad points receive one mark:

- The e-mail expects the head teacher to print out the questionnaires, hand them out and send them back.
- The pupil says they want things done as quickly as possible.
- The e-mail has no name or address to send the 50 copies of the questions back to.

(*e*) Candidates are required to explain why investigation questions are wrong.

The correct responses are:

Question 3

Are your school meals good and do students get them free?

Reason to change

This is a double-barrelled question but you can only give one answer. You may think that the school meals are good but that students do not get them for free. However, there is no way in which you can say this.

Question 4

Why is it that girls always do better than boys at your school?

Reason to change

This question presumes an answer 'that girls always do better than boys', without getting the facts beforehand.

CHINA

3C. (*a*) The concept being assessed is Participation. Candidates are required to use understanding of the concept to provide detailed explanations with relevant examples and appropriate generalisations.

Answers may include:

- **One-Party system:**
  Chinese Communist Party keeps strict control on politics at all levels and is given special protection by the constitution. Membership of the party is strictly controlled and is often essential for success in business.
- **Elections:**
  No free elections are held. Citizens can only vote at local level. Only candidates and parties sanctioned by the Communist Party are allowed to seek election. Eight other parties are legal but do not act as 'opposition' eg China Democratic League, Chinese Peasants' and Workers' Democratic Party.
- **Banned Opposition/dissent:**
  Several organisations that have opposed the Communist Party have been banned as dangerous and subversive, eg China Democracy Party, National Democratic Party of Tibet. Organisations like the Falun Gong and the independence movements for Taiwan and Tibet have also been banned and their members persecuted.
- **Arrest, imprisonment or exile:**
  The 'Laogai' system of 're-education through labour' still exists. Many dissidents have been in prison since Tiananmen Square and others have been exiled, eg Wei Jingshen.
- **Trade unions/pressure groups:**
  Independent trade unions are not permitted. The Federation of Trade Unions is linked to the Communist Party. Some pressure group activity is allowed but it cannot question the authority or legitimacy of the Communist Party. Environmental groups have grown in number, eg many campaigned against the building of the Three Gorges Dam.
- **Female Participation:**
  Discrimination stops many women taking part in politics. Attitudes have been slow to change and few women stand as candidates. The All-China Women's Federation (Linked to Communist Party) campaigns to promote equality.
- any other valid point

(*b*) Candidates are required to state a hypothesis relevant to the issue of 'Health care in China'.

For example:

The following receive no marks:

- politicians get the most plastic surgery done in China.
- health care is important.

The following receive one marks:

- TV drama presents a real picture of health care in China today.
- health care costs a lot in China.

The following receive two marks:

- all races in China get similar health care.
- only the really rich in China get good health care.
- any other valid hypothesis

(*c*) Candidates are required to state aims relevant to the issue.

For example:

Hypothesis:

'People living in cities in China have better health care than those living in the countryside.'

Possible aims:

- to find out if health care in China is good for some and bad for others.
- to find out if people living in Beijing have the best health care in China.
- to find out the reasons for the good health care they have.
- any other valid aim.

(*d*) Candidates are required to justify the use of a given method of enquiry relevant to the issue of 'Education in China.

The following good points receive one mark:

- The e-mail content explains who the pupil is and what they are trying to do.
- The e-mail content explains that the pupil has tried to find information first by looking at the school website.
- The e-mail thanks the head teacher for their time and any help they give.

The following bad points receive one mark:

- The e-mail expects the head teacher to print out the questionnaires, hand them out and send them back.
- The pupil says they want things done as quickly as possible.
- The e-mail has no name or address to send the 50 copies of the questions back to.

(*e*) Candidates are required to explain why investigation questions are wrong.

The correct responses are:

Question 3

Are your school meals good and do students get them free?

Reason to change

This is a double-barrelled question but you can only give one answer. You may think that the school meals are good but that students do not get them for free. However, there is no way in which you can say this.

Question 4

Why is it that children from rural areas always do worse at your school?

Reason to change

This question presumes an answer that 'children from rural areas always do worse' without getting the facts beforehand.

Syllabus Area 4 – International Relations

4. (*a*) The concept being assessed is Need.

Candidates are required to use their understanding of the concept to provide explanations in depth and detail.

Answers may include:

- **Euro**
  The policy on the Euro tries to meet the needs of Europeans by enabling businesses to deal with each other in the same currency. This saves time and money and encourages trade. Citizens are able to travel within the eurozone and not worry about changing money. A single currency makes Europe a strong partner to trade with and facilitates access to a genuine single market for foreign companies, who will benefit from lower costs of doing business in Europe.
- **Enlarged Membership**
  The policy on enlargement tries to meet the needs of Europeans by creating a larger market for products manufactured within the EU as there are few obstacles to trade. It allows workers to travel eg Polish workers to take up long-term vacancies in Scotland's less attractive jobs. All European citizens benefit from having neighbours that are stable democracies and prosperous market economies. Enlargement is a carefully managed process which helps the transformation of the countries involved, extending peace, stability, prosperity, democracy, human rights and the rule of law across Europe.
- **Common Fisheries Policy**
  The policy on fishing tries to meet the needs of Europeans by ensuring that there will be fish stocks in the future by using quotas and decommissioning vessels. This allows fish stocks to be conserved. This is important as many jobs in coastal areas of Europe are dependent on fishing and fish processing.
- **Aid to the regions**
  The policy on aid to the regions tries to meet the needs of Europeans by giving aid to poorer areas of the EU. The Highlands of Scotland have received money to improve transport links to try and improve employment in remote areas. This policy is now of great benefit to people in new EU countries which are poorer than older members.
- **European Defence Force**
  The policy on defence tries to meet the needs of Europeans by getting the members to work co-operatively to protect Europeans by providing manpower and equipment. In 2004 Eufor took over peace keeping in Bosnia-Herzegovina providing over 6 000 troops.
- **Common Agricultural Policy**
  The policy on agriculture tries to meet the needs of Europeans by supporting agriculture in the member states. It was reformed in 2004 as it was no longer meeting the needs of citizens as it was paying farmers to grow crops that weren't needed. Farmers mainly now receive money through The Single Farm Payment Scheme (SFPS). It also now tries to maintain the environment eg special payments for farmers who look after hedgerows etc.
- any other valid point on any of the policies

(*b*) Candidates are required to provide evidence to support and oppose a point of view.
Answers may include:
For Project One – Rose Energy
- Rose Energy want to develop large scale oil production and Focus on Chad supports this as many natural resources are underdeveloped.
- Rose Energy will build a city hospital near the oil development. This is needed as there is a lack of medical provision and health is the most important issue according to the pie chart at 27%.
- Drought is a problem and very little land is irrigated so building water pumps along the pipeline would be a positive development. This was a close third in the concerns with 23% and the introduction states 'lack of sanitation and clean water are major problems'.
- The project will raise much needed money for the government through tax which can be used to pay off some of the debt.

For Project Two – Helping Hands
- Chrissie is right, health care is the most important issue facing Chad (27%). Contraception is important as there's a much higher population growth than the UK and infant mortality is high at 94.
- Free health care is important as many live on a dollar or less a day and can't afford to pay doctors who need to be paid in advance. HIV/AIDS rate is high (5% compared to only 0·2% in UK).
- Chrissie says we must improve the income of farmers and 25% of people in Chad agreed that this was the most important issue. 80% of people rely on farming so this would improve the lives of many people.
- People have very few qualifications and are unable to get better paid jobs. Literacy is only 48% so community projects are needed to develop basic skills.

Against Project One – Rose Energy
- Only people in the south of the country will benefit from the oil development whereas Helping Hands will support people across the country.
- There has already been an oil development in the south of the country but people are still poor and the government is in debt.
- This is a company whose profits will go back to the parent company, not to the local community.

Against Project Two – Helping Hands
- People do not see education as a priority - only 15% see it as a concern compared to 27% for health.
- This project is only planning to invest $20 000 compared to Rose Energy's $1 billion.

MODERN STUDIES GENERAL 2008

Syllabus Area 1 – Living In A Democracy

1. (*a*) The concept being assessed is Rights and Responsibilities. Candidates are required to give detailed descriptions.
Answers may include:
Rights
- to organise a petition in which supporters can sign their name to express support for your cause. This can be delivered to the authority that you are trying to influence.
- to hold a protest march/demonstration in a busy public place. Supporters can carry banners and shout slogans to publicise your cause.
- publicity stunts to attract the attention of the media will get your message across to millions of people across the country.
- any other valid point.

Responsibilities
- to ensure that any protest/demonstration/stunt is peaceful and within the law.
- to ensure that all signatures in a petition are genuine.
- to support the group financially to help fund its activities.
- to tell the truth and not slander or libel someone.
- any other valid point.

(*b*) Candidates are required to make comparisons within sources and draw valid conclusions.
The correct responses are:
Difference 1:
Source 1 says 'We do not need special arrangements to attract more women into Parliament' but
Source 2 says, 'We must find new ways to encourage more women to become MPs.'

Difference 2:
Source 1 says 'that women are now well represented in the UK' but
Source 2 says 'women in the UK are still poorly represented when compared to other European countries.'

(*c*) Candidates are required to give relevant aims for an investigative topic.
The following receive one mark:
- to find out the main methods used by political parties when campaigning.
- to find out the laws/regulations that must be followed.
- to find out which methods are most effective
- any other valid aim.

(*d*) Candidates are required to state and justify an appropriate method of enquiry.

Answers may include:
- write a letter as this would allow detailed questions/questionnaire to be included.
- telephone them as this would be a very quick way of getting information.
- visit the local office as this would allow face to face contact.
- send an e-mail as this would allow detailed questions to be asked very quickly.
- any other valid point.

(*e*) Candidates are required to state and justify an appropriate method of enquiry.
Answers may include:
- lots of books, magazines and other publications which you can borrow and read to get information about your topic.
- expert advice from librarians who are trained to help you find information.
- most libraries offer free access to the Internet which you could use to search for information/ send e-mail.
- any other valid point.

Syllabus Area 2 – Changing Society

2. (*a*) The concept being assessed is Ideology. Candidates are required to provide detailed descriptions.
Answers may include:
- Jobcentreplus displays vacancies and can help people find jobs.
- computer courses and education for new skills.
- Modern Apprenticeships to help young school leavers get skilled jobs eg electrician.
- Government attracts foreign industry to Scotland with grants eg a Japanese computer factory.
- sign up for New Deal.
- getting a College course eg in plumbing skills.
- any other valid point.

(*b*) The concept being assessed is Need.
Candidates are required to provide detailed explanations.
Answers may include:
- Broadband gives very easy Internet access and easy communication.
- Web-cam means people can still communicate with their work.
- many people do their work on a computer which can be used just as easily at home.
- fax machine allows documents to be sent all over the world.
- any other valid point.

(*c*) Candidates are required to express support for a personal point of view with valid reasons.
The correct responses are:
For Scheme A – A Digital Community Centre
- It aims to give local unemployed people basic to advanced ICT skills – young people need help to improve their ICT skills.
- Help in completing application forms for anyone who feels that they need it – young people need help with completing job application forms.

For Scheme B – Personal Advisors
- It will concentrate on improving interview skills – young people need help to improve their interview skills.
- It will give advice on filling in application forms for new jobs – young people need help with completing job application forms.

(*d*) Candidates are required to disagree with a given point of view with valid reasons.
The correct responses are:
Disagree with the view:
Abigail Smith says 'Self-employment amongst Whites and Bangladeshis has grown every year.'
Evidence to prove:
Bangladeshi self-employment between 2001 and 2003 fell from 12·3% to 9·9% – this is a drop.

Disagree with the view:
Abigail Smith says 'Pakistanis had the largest decrease in self-employment between 2003 and 2005.'
Evidence to prove:
Pakistani self-employment between 2003 and 2005 fell from 22·5% to 21·0%, a drop of 1·5%. However, Chinese self-employment fell from 18·3% to 16·0%, a drop of 2·3% which is a bigger drop, as is Black Caribbean at 1·7%.

Syllabus Area 3 – Ideologies

THE USA

3A. (*a*) The concept being assessed is Ideology. Candidates are required to provide detailed descriptions.
Answers may include:
- Americans can work in an area they have dreamed about, fulfilling the American Dream.
- motive to work hard and make business successful.
- successful business people can keep a share of the profits from their company.
- higher income allows Americans to enjoy a higher standard of living.
- any other valid point.

(*b*) Candidates are required to provide evidence to support and oppose a given point of view.
Answers may include:
Support the view:
Kelly Halcomb says, 'The USA enrolls less of its children in primary school than most other major countries.'
Evidence to support:
America enrolls 92% of its children whereas the UK and Japan enrol 100% and China enrolls 99%. Only Russia enrolls fewer children than the USA.

Oppose the view:
Kelly Halcomb says, 'People in the USA have both the highest average income and live the longest.'

Evidence to oppose:
Whilst the USA is the richest country as their average income is the highest at $41 400, they are not the healthiest as their life expectancy is 78 which is lower than the UK and Japan.

(*c*) The concept being assessed is Equality. Candidates are required to provide detailed descriptions.
Answers may include:

Education
- attend ghetto schools which receive less funding than suburban schools.
- fewer staff per pupil in ghetto schools.
- some recent immigrants may struggle with English as the main language in school.
- some schools may have a gang/violence problem which limits ability to learn in school.
- any other valid point.

Housing
- some Americans may be homeless.
- some minority groups may have no choice but to live in poor quality housing such as the projects. (Robert Taylor homes)
- recent immigrants may not be able to afford good quality housing and live in overcrowded/ sub-standard houses.
- racial segregation still exists between mainly vanilla suburbs and minority ghettoes.
- any other valid point.

Health
- some Americans cannot afford private insurance such as Blue Cross or Blue Shield.
- elderly may have to rely on Medicare and poor on Medicaid if they have no private insurance.
- any other valid point.

(*d*) Candidates are required to detect exaggeration and provide explanations.
The correct responses are:

Statement 1
'the government was well equipped to respond to the disaster.'

Reason 1
From Source 1: it says that 'Americans were upset at the size of the disaster and how poorly prepared all levels of government were to deal with the problem.' The President himself recognised the government's slow response.

Statement 2
'The majority of people agree that the government is doing a good re-building job.'

Reason 2
From Source 2: it shows that only 30% think the government is doing an excellent/good job, whereas a majority, about 65%, think the government is doing a not so good/poor job.

RUSSIA

3B. (*a*) The concept being assessed is Ideology. Candidates are required to provide detailed descriptions.
Answers may include:
- Russians can work in an area they have dreamed about which helps them fulfil their hopes.
- motive to work hard and make business successful.
- successful business people can keep a share of the profits from their company.
- higher income allows Russians to enjoy a higher standard of living.
- higher incomes have given many Russian people the opportunity to travel both within and outside Russia.
- any other valid point.

(*b*) Candidates are required to provide evidence to support and oppose a given point of view.
Answers may include:

Support the view:
Georgi Safin says, 'Russia enrolls less of its children in primary school than most other major countries.'

Evidence to support:
Russia enrolls 90% of its children whereas the UK and Japan enrol 100% and China enrolls 99% whilst the USA enrols 92%. Russia enrolls the fewest.

Oppose the view:
Georgi Safin says, 'People in Russia have both the lowest average income and shortest life expectancy.'

Evidence to oppose:
Whilst Russia has the lowest life expectancy at 65 years, it does not have the lowest average income. Average income in Russia is $3 410 whilst in China it is lower at $1 290.

(*c*) The concept being assessed is Equality. Candidates are required to provide detailed descriptions.
Answers may include:

Education
- in Russia, education at all levels was free for anybody who could pass entrance exams.
- students were provided with small scholarships and free housing. This was considered crucial because it provided access to higher education to all skilled students, as opposed to only those who could afford it.
- expenditure on education has gone down over the years as the state could no longer afford it.
- schools and universities found themselves unable to provide adequate teachers' salaries, students' scholarships, and maintenance for their facilities.
- many private higher education institutions have now opened with students paying fees.
- latest figures show that 35% of students in Russia are now paying for their own education in state institutions and 20% are studying in private universities.
- any other valid point.

Housing

- under President Putin, affordable housing has been made one of Russia's four priority National Projects (along with healthcare, education and agriculture).
- the government is planning to invest on a large scale in upgrading Russia's run-down stock of municipal housing, while also promoting the growth of private housing.
- most Russians still live in apartment blocks which were built during the era of the Soviet Union. Many were poorly constructed.
- most Russians still rent their homes which are in poor condition.
- large private house-building projects have helped to provide more jobs in the construction industry.
- any other valid point.

Health

- basic medical care is available to most of the population free of cost, but its quality is extremely low by Western standards.
- significant increases in infant mortality and contagious diseases.
- the decline in health is due in part to environmental and social factors such as air and water pollution, contamination (largely from nuclear accidents or improper disposal of radioactive materials), overcrowded living conditions, inadequate nutrition, alcoholism and smoking.
- there is a lack of modern medical equipment and technology.
- any other valid point.

(*d*) Candidates are required to detect exaggeration and provide explanations.
The correct responses are:

Statement 1

'The majority of foreigners living in Moscow find the city expensive.'

Reason 1

Source 2 shows that only 15% of foreigners find the city very expensive whilst another 22% find it fairly expensive. Taken together, this is 37% which is not a majority.

Statement 2

'Shopping costs are similar both in the centre and in the outskirts of Moscow.'

Reason 2

Source 1 explains that shopping costs can be reduced by shopping in the outskirts of Moscow rather than in the city centre.

CHINA

3C. (*a*) The concept being assessed is Ideology. Candidates are required to provide detailed descriptions.
Answers may include:

- Chinese people are allowed to start a business and keep the profit ie 'Socialist Market Economy'. This has been especially common in the 'Special Economic Zones'.
- increased wealth can give access to better housing, education, health care etc. Many Chinese people now have access to consumer goods such as freezers, PCs etc. There has also been a boom in car ownership.
- small township enterprises have improved living conditions in rural areas.
- jobs are created by small businesses which spread wealth and create better living standards.
- higher incomes have given many Chinese people the opportunity to travel both within and outside China.
- any other valid point.

(*b*) Candidates are required to provide evidence to support and oppose a given point of view.
Answers may include:

Support the view:

An Qi says, 'China enrolls more of its children in primary school than most other major countries.'

Evidence to support:

This is true; Source 2 shows that only the UK enrolls more. China has a higher figure than India, Russia and the USA.

Oppose the view:

An Qi says, 'People in China also have both the second lowest average income and shortest life expectancy.'

Evidence to oppose:

This is not true; Source 1 shows that although China does have the second lowest average income, it does not have the shortest life expectancy. Both India and Russia have shorter life expectancies.

(*c*) The concept being assessed is Equality. Candidates are required to provide detailed explanations.
Answers may include:

Education

- cities and large towns have better quality schools, colleges and universities. Rural population has little choice and are often too poor to travel to towns for education. Rural lifestyle places low emphasis on formal education.
- many migrant workers who have gone from country to city have been denied access to education.
- some of the new business elite (of the cities) have access to foreign universities for their children.
- Communist party members still have greater choice and access to schools etc.

Housing

- rural housing is still very basic. Many still do not have running water and electricity. The major cities have a better choice of housing with access to electricity, running water etc. Many rural Chinese cannot afford such luxuries.

- migrant workers are often forced to live in very poor housing on the outskirts of the main towns. Conditions are as bad in some as the worst slums anywhere in the world.
- Communist party members tend to have better quality housing.
- although the one child policy was officially scrapped, some families are still disadvantaged.
- wages for skilled workers employed by foreign firms are higher than the average so better quality housing can be purchased.

Health
- towns and cities have more modern hospitals with more qualified doctors, nurses, specialist equipment etc. There is a shortage of medical staff in rural areas. People in these areas often rely on traditional methods.
- poor housing conditions and dangerous working conditions have damaged the health of many workers on the 'Coastal Strip' and in 'Special Economic Zones'. China is believed to have the world's worst figures for industrial injury and deaths. Official figures for this are impossible to find.
- air pollution in the largest cities is a serious problem. Rapid economic growth threatens air quality in many areas, including Beijing.
- levels of smoking have boomed in recent years. Experts from the WHO predict a crisis in future decades from cancer and other tobacco related illnesses.
- the new rich have more access to expensive treatments and to treatment abroad.
- any other valid point.

(*d*) Candidates are required to detect exaggeration and provide explanations.
The correct responses are:
Statement 1
'The majority of Chinese people are not pleased about the Olympics coming to their country.'
Reason 1
The statement is exaggerated because in Source 2 it shows that 20% are unhappy and 15% very unhappy. A total of only 35% which is not a majority.

Statement 2
'everyone in the country should benefit from the Games.'
Reason 2
The statement is exaggerated because in Source 1 it says that 'sixty-nine villages have been demolished to make way for the new Olympic facilities.' Clearly not 'everyone' is benefiting.

Syllabus Area 4 – International Relations

4. (*a*) The concept being assessed is Need. Candidates are required to provide detailed descriptions.
Answers may include:
- advice on farming methods.
- support to improve technology eg irrigation.
- campaign on children's rights.
- supporting mothers eg breastfeeding programmes.
- education – literacy programmes for adults and children.
- against child labour/child soldiers.
- immunisation programmes eg measles in Darfur/Sudan.
- training in basic medical skills – basic midwifery skills.
- any other valid point.

Good answers would identify specific agencies such as UNICEF, WHO, UNESCO, FAO. However, this is not essential for full credit.

(*b*) Candidates are required to make comparisons within a source and draw valid conclusions.
The correct responses are:
- the country with the biggest change in its armed forces is the USA. Its numbers fell by 689 000 compared to UK at only 92 000.
- as spending rises so does the size of a country's armed forces. Greece's armed forces went up by 8 000 and spending increased from \$500 pp to \$610 pp.

(*c*) The concept being assessed is Power. Candidates are required to provide detailed explanations.
Answers may include:
- cooperation between member states.
- regional aid eg Rosyth ferry.
- freedom of movement eg large numbers of Poles now working in UK.
- qualifications recognised so can work/study in 27 countries.
- larger market for products manufactured in their country ie improved trade.
- regional aid has raised living standards especially in poorer parts of Europe.
- opinion polls show that the majority of EU citizens are happy living in the EU.
- any other valid point.

(*d*) Candidates are required to detect exaggeration and provide explanations.
The correct responses are:
Statement 1
'No food aid was received by Niger.'
Reason 1
40 000 tonnes of energy biscuits received in August 2005.

Statement 2
'Debt is still a major problem.'
Reason 2
All debt cancelled at G8 summit in July 2005.

MODERN STUDIES CREDIT 2008

Syllabus Area 1 – Living In A Democracy

1. (*a*) The concept being assessed is Rights. Candidates are required to use understanding of the concept to provide detailed descriptions with relevant examples and appropriate generalisations.

Answers may include:

- to be represented by their shop steward or other union official who may try to negotiate a settlement to the dispute.
- to take industrial action to try to force their employer to settle the dispute. This may include a work-to-rule, overtime ban or strike action.
- to organise protest marches or demonstrations to gain publicity about the dispute, and try to gain the support of the public. This may attract the attention of the media and extend the coverage across the whole country.
- to lobby local and national politicians to try to gain their support, and perhaps put pressure on the employer to settle the dispute.
- any other valid point.

(*b*) The concept being assessed is Representation. Candidates are required to use understanding of the concept to provide detailed explanations with relevant examples and appropriate generalisations.

Answers may include:

- a major aim of the Scottish Parliament was to get more people involved in decision making and its working practices were therefore designed to get all groups, including women more involved.
- the working hours of the Scottish Parliament follow normal business hours, whereas Westminster works much later in the day, which may discourage women from taking part.
- holidays in the Scottish Parliament tend to be at the same time as Scottish school holidays.
- the Scottish Parliament has a creche to look after the young children of MSPs. This is not provided at Westminster.
- the AMS voting system has resulted in more women being voted in as MSPs.
- some political parties in Scotland have selected more women candidates to stand for election.
- any other valid point.

(*c*) Candidates are required to provide evidence to support and oppose a point of view. Answers must make explicit links between the background information about Gleninch Constituency **and** Sources 1 and 2.

Answers may include:

For Kirsty Reid

- the statistical profile of Gleninch shows school leavers with Highers is 13% above the Scottish average. Kirsty says that she will work to ensure that the excellent education in the area continues.
- she supports the new quarry because it will provide jobs to stop the decline of the local economy. The background information shows that 150 new jobs will be created in the quarry.
- there are a number of transport problems in the area such as poor public transport and high petrol prices. Kirsty says that she will make it a priority to improve transport links.

Against Kirsty Reid

- she says the wind farm will provide many local jobs and help the local environment. However, the information says that it will create only a few temporary jobs, and will impact on the scenery of the area.
- she says that she should be selected because she is a woman and that this issue is a major priority for local party members. This is untrue, as the survey shows that the issue was considered least important with 67% of members considering it either unimportant or not very important.

For Robbie McKay

- he opposes the wind farm because it will be a blot on the landscape, and deter tourists. Tourism is very important to the area as it employs a lot of people in hotels and restaurants. There will also be a 15 mile power line which will spoil the scenery.
- local party members are concerned about the issue of health, with 88% considering it either fairly or very important. Robbie says this will be one of his main concerns too.
- he will do all that he can to make people in the area better-off. This is important because average income is 14% below the Scottish average, and Income Support claimants are 22% above average.

Against Robbie McKay

- he says that as crime is among the worst in Scotland he will campaign to improve policing. However, the statistics show that crime in the area is quite low, with housebreaking 93% lower than the Scottish average, and assaults 73% lower.
- he opposes the new quarry because the local party are more concerned about the environment than jobs. However, this is not true. The survey shows that 52% think that jobs are very important, compared to only 30% for the environment.

Syllabus Area 2 – Changing Society

2. (*a*) The concept being assessed is Need. Candidates are required to use understanding of the concept to provide detailed explanations with relevant examples and appropriate generalisations.

Answers may include:

Community Care within their own home

- adaptations made to their own home to meet physical needs. For example stair lifts aid mobility and allow elderly people to move freely about their house.

- Need for security is met by intercoms allowing elderly to feel safe at home.
- Need for medical care can be addressed by personal care plans which build in visits from district nurses or GPs to take care of wound dressings, prescriptions etc.
- meals on wheels can be provided to ensure elderly receive adequate nutrition to stay healthy.
- the emotional needs of the elderly are met as the elderly continue to live in a familiar environment with their own possessions and family and friends nearby.
- any other valid point.

Sheltered Housing

- this meets the elderly need for independence. Elderly still have their own flat and can take their own furniture and possessions with them providing a familiar environment.
- a sense of security is provided as elderly know that there is a warden on call 24 hours a day in case of emergencies. This allows elderly to be independent, yet feel secure.
- the social needs of the elderly are met through the community which exists within the sheltered housing complex. They can meet with others in the communal lounge or else at one of the organised activities within the complex.
- the emotional needs of the elderly are met as the sheltered housing complex will often have rooms where relatives can come and stay for visits.
- any other valid point.

Residential Care Homes

- 24 hour trained nursing care can take care of physical needs of elderly such as assisting stroke victims with their personal care.
- meals are provided to ensure that elderly are receiving adequate nutrition, for example special meals can be prepared for diabetics.
- the social needs of the elderly are met via the common rooms in the nursing/residential homes allowing the elderly to have interaction with others.
- the homes are specially adapted with ramps to assist wheelchair users, bath hoists to assist stroke victims, etc.
- any other valid point.

(*b*) Candidates are required to state a hypothesis relevant to the issue of 'Help for families in the UK'.

For example:

The following receive one mark:

- the government gives a lot of help to families.
- different families get different help.

The following receive two marks:

- Child Care helps mothers get back to work.
- 'Child Benefit' should only be given to families in real need.
- any other valid hypothesis.

(*c*) Candidates are required to state aims relevant to their hypothesis.

For example:

Hypothesis:

'Child Benefit' should only be given to families in real need.

Potential aims:

- to find out if the value of Child Benefit has changed.
- to find out the ways in which Child Benefit helps different families.
- to find out if local people think that Child Benefit should be given to all families, no matter how well off they are.
- any other valid aim.

(*d*) Candidates are required to state relevant questions about the issue of 'Help for families in the UK'.

For example:

The following receive one mark:

- Do you help families?
- How much is Child Benefit today?

The following receive two marks:

- What kind of problems do families contact you with?
- What does Parliament do to help poor families throughout the UK?
- Do you think that the Child Support Agency does a good job?
- Any other valid question.

(*e*) Candidates are required to give a disadvantage and advantage of a method of enquiry.

Answers may include:

Disadvantage of buying from the website

- it costs £45 – this is very expensive for the school to buy for one investigation or pupil.
- it is out of stock – I need it right away so that I can finish my investigation on time.

Advantage of using Social Trends

- it is the 2008 edition – this is the latest edition which means that it will have very up to date statistics and tables.
- it is published by the Office for National Statistics using information from a range of government departments – so it will be very accurate and will be looking at statistics from all over the country.
- the data is presented in tables, figures and text – I can easily interpret them and use them in my investigation.
- any other valid point.

Syllabus Area 3 – Ideologies

THE USA

3A. (*a*) The concept being assessed is Participation. Candidates are required to use understanding of the concept to provide detailed descriptions with relevant examples and appropriate generalisations.

Answers may include:

- standing as a candidate in local, state or federal elections. For example McCain, Clinton and

Obama in 2008 Presidential election state primaries and Hillary Clinton for Senate in 2006.
- joining a political party such as the Republicans and voting at the national party convention.
- fundraising for the political party of their choice. Holding a house party for the Republicans.
- register as a voter and turn out to support a candidate in 2006 mid-term elections.
- door-to-door canvassing for the Democratic party.
- write to the editor of the Washington Post to express your opinion on the federal government policy on the War on Terror.
- protest with a demonstration against a bill being passed in Congress.
- joining an interest group, such as the NRA or Emily's List, and lobbying Congress about a bill.
- any other valid point.

(*b*) Candidates are required to provide evidence to support and oppose a given point of view.
The correct responses are:
View of Wall Street Economist
'The biggest increase in personal income between 2003 and 2005 has been in Connecticut.'
Reason to support:
Between 2003 and 2005 Connecticut income increased by $5 500, which is more than any other state.

View of Wall Street Economist
'The richest states in the US are **all** to be found in the Mid East of the country.'
Reason to oppose:
Some of the top 10 richest states are to be found in the Southeast, Mid West, Rocky Mountains and New England.

(*c*) Candidates are required to detect and explain examples of lack of objectivity in complex sources, giving developed argument when required.
Answers may include:
'The Red Pines gated development will cause many problems for our health.'
From Source 1:
- Red Pines, at the moment, is used for walking and exercise.
- Doctor Joan Quincy thinks Rockford residents need more exercise.
- the health statistics show that Rockford residents are more overweight and take less exercise than the American people as a whole.

From Source 2:
- the opinion poll suggests that 70% of Rockford residents think that the Red Pines area is Important or Very Important for exercise.

Therefore, Findlay Smith is **correct** when he says that The Red Pines gated development will cause many problems for health in Rockford as it will reduce the chances for exercise.

'The Red Pines gated development will change the ethnic mix in Rockford.'
From Source 1:
- gated communities are mostly white developments with affluent blacks being less likely to choose to live there.

From Source 2:
- the 10 000 homes in Rockford are 32% White, 31% Black, 29% Hispanic and 8% other. Therefore, the main ethnic groups in Rockford are roughly the same.
- the opinion poll suggests that keeping the racial mix as it is today is important with 65% of Rockford residents believing it to be important or very important.

From Source 3:
- the 500 families wanting to move into Red Pines are 50% white, 24% Black, 25% Hispanic and 1% other.

Therefore, Findlay Smith is **correct** when he says that The Red Pines gated development will change the ethnic mix in Rockford as it will add more whites to the ethnic mix.

'(The Red Pines gated development) ... will bring few benefits to the people of Rockford.'
From Source 1:
- a few short-term benefits but no long-term gain.
- building houses could cause problems for the residents of Rockford as it will lessen chances for exercise.

From Source 2:
- 60% of Rockford residents believe that jobs are a major issue. This is the majority of people in Rockford.

From Source 3:
- skilled workers needed in the building of the community.
- unskilled workers needed in the building of the community.
- unskilled jobs available later in servicing the community.
- more money spent in local shops providing more business from workers and then the residents.
- building companies increase trade.
- local shops can become suppliers.
- flood prevention measures will stop flooding.

Therefore, Findlay Smith is **wrong** when he says that The Red Pines gated development will bring few benefits as it will bring many benefits.

Overall conclusion on the extent of selectivity:
Findlay Smith is right in two statements and wrong in the other so he is slightly selective in the use of facts.

RUSSIA

3B. (*a*) The concept being assessed is Participation. Candidates are required to use understanding of the concept to provide detailed descriptions with relevant examples and appropriate generalisations.

Answers may include:

- standing as a candidate in local or national elections. Eg The Duma.
- fundraising for any of the national parties. Eg Yablonko.
- writing letters to local and national newspapers. Eg Pravda, Izvestia, Novosti Peterburga (St Petersburg) or the Moscow Times.
- many Russians use the Internet as a tool in the political process. It is here that many of the complaints about the clampdown on political expression are being made known.
- demonstrations are allowed but many are now more carefully controlled by the government.
- the Kremlin continues to separate Russia from Western democracies by tightening control over the media and harassing the already weak opposition. This has put a strain on people getting over their political point of view.
- any other valid point.

(*b*) Candidates are required to provide evidence to support and oppose a given point of view.

The correct responses are:

View of Russian Economist

'The amount spent on foodstuffs is the only one which has seen a rise between 2002 and 2005.'

Reason to support

Source 2 shows that although it dipped in 2003, foodstuffs overall have gone up by 3·5%. All the others have either stayed the same or gone down.

View of Russian Economist

'Both Industry and Agriculture have grown each year between 2002 and 2005.'

Reason to oppose

Source 1 shows that Industry has grown each year and whilst Agriculture has grown overall, in 2004, it went down from 309 to 302 before recovering to 625 in 2005. Therefore, both haven't grown each year.

(*c*) Candidates are required to detect and explain examples of lack of objectivity in complex sources, giving developed argument when required.

Answers may include:

'The Sosny Woods Gated Development will cause many problems for our health'

From Source 1:

- Sosny Woods, at the moment, is used for walking and exercise.
- Doctor Yuri Press thinks Vorkuta residents need more exercise.
- the health statistics show that Vorkuta residents are more overweight and take less exercise than the Russian people as a whole.

From Source 2:

- The opinion poll suggests that 70% of Vorkuta residents think that the Sosny Woods area is Important or Very Important for exercise.

Therefore, Dmitri Arshavin is **correct** when he says that The Sosny Woods Gated Development will cause many problems for health in Vorkuta as it will reduce the chances for exercise.

'The Sosny Woods Gated Development will allow outsiders to dominate Vorkuta.'

From Source 2:

- The opinion poll suggests that 65% of Vorkuta residents, which is the majority, believe that keeping in-comers to a minimum is important.

From Source 3:

- 90% of the new families coming into Vorkuta will be outsiders with 73% having no connection to the town whatsoever.
- however, the other 10% are already living in Vorkuta and as there will only be 500 new homes, this will cut the number of outsiders.

Therefore, Dmitri Arshavin is being **fairly selective** because the numbers involved do not mean that outsiders will dominate Vorkuta. They will change the balance somewhat but they will not be in the majority.

'It will bring few benefits to the people of Vorkuta.'

From Source 1:

- a few short-term benefits but no long-term gain.
- building houses could cause problems for the residents of Vorkuta as it will lessen chances for exercise.

From Source 2:

- 40% of Vorkuta residents believe that jobs are a major issue. This is a sizeable minority.

From Source 3:

- skilled workers needed in the building of the community.
- unskilled workers needed in the building of the community.
- unskilled jobs available later in servicing the community.
- more money spent in local shops providing more business from workers and then the residents.
- building companies increase trade.
- local shops can become suppliers.
- flood prevention measures will stop flooding.

Therefore, Dmitri Arshavin is **wrong** when he says that The Sosny Woods Gated Development will bring few benefits as it will bring a number of benefits. The jobs will be there for those who want or need them whilst the flood prevention measures will help the whole town.

Overall conclusion on the extent of selectivity:

Dmitri Arshavin is right in one statement and wrong in the other two so he is very selective in the use of facts.

CHINA

3C. (*a*) The concept being assessed is Participation. Candidates are required to use understanding of the concept to provide detailed descriptions with relevant examples and appropriate generalisations.

Answers may include:

Party Membership

Membership of the party is strictly controlled and is often essential for success in business. Ordinary citizens can be invited to join. Eight other parties are legal but do not act as 'opposition' eg China Democratic League, Chinese Peasants' and Workers' Democratic Party.

Elections
Elections are held regularly but are not 'free' in the western sense. Citizens can vote at local level for village congresses or councils. Only candidates and parties sanctioned by the Communist Party are allowed to seek election. Peoples' Congress elections are held at city, province and national levels.

Banned Opposition/dissent
Several banned organisations offer the chance to participate but these carry the risk of arrest and imprisonment. Eg China Democracy Party, National Democratic Party of Tibet. Independence movements for Taiwan and Tibet have been banned and their members persecuted.

Trade union/pressure groups
Independent trade unions are not permitted. The Federation of Trade Unions is linked to the Communist Party and offers some opportunities to participate. Some pressure group activity is allowed but it cannot question the authority or legitimacy of the Communist Party. Environmental groups have grown in number eg many campaigned against the building of the Three Gorges Dam.

Peasants' revolts/demonstrations
In rural areas peasants have been involved in demonstrations against local party leaders. Many are being forced from their land to make way for factories. The government recorded 87 000 protests against forced relocation in 2005 alone. Some have been violent.

Female Participation
The All-China Women's Federation (linked to Communist Party) campaigns to promote equality. Small success in recent years – small increase in female candidates.

Any other valid point.

(*b*) Candidates are required to provide evidence to support and oppose a given point of view.
The correct responses are:
View of Chinese Economist
'The greatest increase in personal income has been experienced by those living in Shanghai.'
Reason to support
Source 1 shows that this is true, as Shanghai's average personal income has grown by 10 000 Yuan between 2003 and 2005. This is bigger than any other region.
View of Chinese Economist
'However, the wealthiest regions are evenly distributed throughout China.'
Reason to oppose
Source 2 shows that this is not the case. The ten wealthiest regions are concentrated on the eastern coast of the country.

(*c*) Candidates are required to detect and explain examples of lack of objectivity in complex sources, giving developed argument when required.
Answers may include:
Pu Wei – 'The Riverside Gated Development will improve the health of people living in Hankou.'
This is correct because:
- new sports facilities will be built (Source 1 column 1).
- sports facilities were very poor before (Source 1 'The Riverside area before').
- opinion of Doctor Pu Zihao – local residents aren't good at exercise and new facilities are needed to improve health.
- Doctor's opinion is backed by four statistics in Source 1 – ie Higher than national average overweight, fewer cyclists, fewer walkers, fewer golfers and tennis players.

Conclusion: In this part of the view, Pu Wei is not selective as all the evidence supports him.

Pu Wei – 'It will bring much needed benefits to the people of Hankou.'
This is correct because:
- the area is depressed. Wages are lower than the national average (Source 1) so new jobs are needed and many are low skilled. Source 3 highlights the impact that the development will have whilst Source 2 shows that jobs are important because according to it, 54% of people agree that this is very important (The sample for the survey was large at 8 900).
- 300 well paid jobs will be created. As well as improving average wages this will bring extra business to local shops.
- 81% in the survey say that attracting new business is either 'Important' or 'Very Important'. Source 1 states that many of the people attracted to the area will be business people and that new business will be set up. Source 2 states that existing businesses will become suppliers to the new restaurants.
- affordable sports facilities will be created which will benefit a lot of the people.

This is not entirely correct as:
- a few fishermen have lost their jobs including Li Jie and six others. However, 65% of those who responded in Source 2 didn't think this was important.
- according to Li Jie the benefits to the people of Hankou will not be that great as the residents will not shop in the town. They will stay in the complex or drive to the city.

Conclusion: in this part of the view, Pu Wei is being selective to a very small extent as jobs, wages, business and sports facilities will improve. The only opposition seems to come from one person ie Li Jie.

Pu Wei – 'Everyone living in Hankou is excited by the opening of Riverside Garden.'
This is not entirely correct as:

- Li Jie and his six friends who lost their jobs are not happy about it. He claims that all the fishermen are against the development. Although this is a small number out of a 50 000 population, it is clear that not 'everyone' is excited.
- 35% of people thought that protecting farmers and fishermen was important or very important. Although this isn't a majority there is some opposition to the plan.

Conclusion: in his third sentence, Pu Wei is being quite selective. Most people seem to favour the development, but it is not **all**.

Overall conclusion on the extent of selectivity
Overall, Pu Wei is being only **slightly** selective in his use of the facts.

Syllabus Area 4 – International Relations

4. (*a*) The concept being assessed is Need. Candidates are required to use their understanding of the concept to provide explanations in depth and detail.
Answers may include:

Civil War
Environment not safe for civilians, roads mined or prone to ambush. Money spent on arms not services (over $9 billion pa). Wars in Somalia and Angola worsening.

Trade
Terms of trade mean that cash crops don't generate sufficient income eg coffee/cotton/sugar.

HIV
Life expectancy decreasing after improvements in 1990s, working population becoming ill eg nearly 40% of pop in Swaziland HIV positive. Millions of AIDS orphans.

Any other valid point.

(*b*) The concept being assessed is Power. Candidates are required to use their understanding of the concept to provide explanations in depth and detail.
Answers may include:

- airport security – reduction in hand luggage, stricter security checks, armed police, new 'Borders Agency'.
- counter-terrorism Bill, length of detention.
- heightened security in UK generally eg Houses of Parliament.
- MI5 has doubled in size since 2000.
- removal of easy targets eg litter bins in tube stations.
- architects encouraged to think of security eg Emirates Stadium and Scottish Parliament building.
- any other valid point

(*c*) Candidates are expected to make comparisons within and between complex sources and draw valid conclusions from them with justification using developed argument when required.
Answers may include:

Progress towards MDG 1 – reduce child mortality

- Source 3 shows that there has not been an increase in child mortality for any of the countries shown. Burundi's rate has stayed the same but the others have all improved eg Malawi down by 41 to 175.

This shows progress.

Progress towards all of MDG 3 – remove extreme poverty and hunger

- According to Source 1, the third MDG is to eradicate extreme poverty and hunger. Source 3 shows that in the world's four poorest countries, Tanzania and Malawi have reduced the % of people who are undernourished. In Malawi, it is down from 50% in 1996 to 34% in 2006.
- Source 3 also shows that in the world's four poorest countries, Sierra Leone and Burundi have seen an increase in the % of people who are undernourished. In Sierra Leone, it has gone up by 6% whilst in Burundi, it has gone up by 4%

This would suggest some progress towards Goal 3 in some places but not in others.

- The bar graph in Source 1 shows how many people live on less than a dollar a day and **this shows a lack of progress** towards the MDG 3 as the figure has increased between 1995 and 2001 and it is over double the target figure or goal of 22%.

The commitment of More Developed Countries to meeting the UN aid recommendation

- Source 1 states that UN recommends 0·7% of GNI to be spent as aid. Source 2 shows that in 2004, only Portugal was close at 0·63%.
- By 2010, 3 out of the 4 countries shown were close eg UK at 0·59% but Portugal's aid has decreased and the USA still only gives 0·18%.

This shows a slight overall improvement but not a strong commitment to meeting the UN recommendations.

The commitment of Donor Countries to the world's four poorest nations

- Source 1 shows that the four poorest nations are Sierra Leone, Tanzania, Burundi and Malawi.
- Source 2 shows where the selected donor countries send their aid. Only Tanzania receives any aid ($265 million from UK).

This shows an almost complete lack of commitment to the world's four poorest nations.

MODERN STUDIES GENERAL 2009

Syllabus Area 1 – Living In A Democracy

1. (*a*) The concept being assessed is Representation. Candidates are required to provide detailed description.

Answers may include:

- an MSP represents his/her constituents by listening to what they say. They do this by having a surgery or reading letters sent to them. This means the MSP knows what people want
- asking questions about the things that matter to local people. The MSP can do this at First Minister's questions on a Thursday or during a debate at the parliament. They could also raise local matters in committee
- MSPs go on local visits eg to schools and factories. This allows them to discuss local issues with people and might highlight things they weren't aware of. They can decide how to use this information
- MSPs can represent constituents by writing letters/talking to other representatives eg councillors as MSPs are more influential than individuals.

(*b*) Candidates are required to both support and oppose a point of view with evidence.

Two pieces of evidence are required for full marks.

Support the view

- Holly Kerr says, "Edinburgh and Glasgow have the highest percentage of spoilt ballot papers".

Evidence for this:

- This is correct as both Glasgow and Edinburgh are in the two regions with the highest numbers of spoilt papers.

Oppose the view

- Holly Kerr says, "The number of spoilt ballot papers did not affect the result in any of the selected constituencies".

Evidence for this:

- This statement is incorrect as in one of the constituencies the spoilt papers is greater than the majority so this could have affected the result. Airdrie and Shotts were affected in this way.

(*c*) The concept being assessed is Rights and Responsibilities. Candidates are required to provide detailed descriptions.

Answers may include:

- a right TU members have is to be safe at their work
- they might work with dangerous machinery so the boss needs to give them goggles and a hard hat
- another right TU members have is to get the right pay
- the union might help them get pay when they are pregnant or off sick
- members of a trade union have the right to elect a representative/shop steward
- this person will take their views to management during a dispute eg local council workers
- trade union members have the right to take industrial action
- if they feel their rights are being ignored eg postal workers went on a go slow and then on strike over pay and conditions.

(*d*) Candidates are required to make comparisons between sources and draw conclusions.

Answers may include:

- the main cause for industrial disputes in 2006 was Pay. It was 73%, with the next biggest being Redundancy at only 22%
- the year which was the furthest from the average for working days lost was 2002. It was approximately 0·7 or 700000 away from the average, with the next closest being 2004 at approximately 0·4 or 400000.

Syllabus Area 2 – Changing Society

2. (*a*) The concept is Need. Candidates are required to provide detailed descriptions.

Two ways are required for full marks.

Answers may include:

- a Warden to look out for any problems will make them feel secure
- a communal lounge area to meet friends to stop them feeling lonely
- a spare room for family to stay when visiting allows them to keep in touch
- ramped access to make moving about easy for those in wheelchairs
- a garden where they can enjoy good weather and mix with others.

(*b*) Candidates are required to detect exaggeration and provide explanations.

The correct responses are:

Statement 1

"The percentage of male workers has increased much more than the percentage of female workers."

Reason 1

Source 1 shows that the increase of male workers was only 5·6% compared to 11·2% for women.

Statement 2

"Total unemployment has fallen every year since 2000."

Reason 2

Source 2 shows that in 2006 total unemployment rose from 3·2% to 3·3%.

(*c*) The concept is Equality. Candidates are required to provide detailed explanations.

Answers may include:
- some may have private or occupational pensions as well as a state pension
- some may not get the state pension and depend on other benefits
- some may have had a good job and have savings, but others may have been unemployed
- financial help from family members for some but not for others.

(*d*) Candidates are required to make comparisons within sources and draw valid conclusions.

Two differences are required for full marks.

The correct responses are:

Difference 1
Source 1 says that JSA is just enough to meet the needs of the unemployed, but Source 2 says it is not enough for them to live on.

Difference 2
Source 1 says that JSA aims to get unemployed people into a job that best suits their qualifications, but Source 2 says that it pushes them into any low paid job that is available.

Syllabus Area 3 – Ideologies

THE USA

3A. (*a*) The concept being assessed is Participation. Candidates are required to provide detailed descriptions.

Two ways are required for full marks.

Answers may include:
- Americans can register to vote in elections
- They can then use their vote in elections, eg greater numbers of Black Americans voting for Barack Obama for President in 2008
- Americans can stand for election eg to be Mayor of Rockford City or President
- Americans can join an Interest Group eg The American Association of Retired Persons or Rock the Vote.

(*b*) Candidates are required to provide evidence to support and oppose a given point of view.

Two pieces of evidence are required for full marks.

Answers may include:

Support the view
Ann Struther says, "The group with the lowest unemployment in 2006 has seen the greatest increase in home ownership".

Evidence to support
From Source 1 the group with the lowest unemployment in 2006 was Asian at 3·0%.

From Source 2 Asians had the biggest increase in home ownership at 8%, much greater than any other group.

Oppose the view
Ann Struther says, "In 2006, unemployment was at its lowest for all ethnic minority groups".

Evidence to oppose
Source 1 shows that 2000 was the lowest unemployment for blacks at 7·6%, not 2006.

(*c*) Candidates are required to give **relevant** aims for an investigative topic.

Two aims must be given for full marks.
- to find out if blacks commit more crime than whites
- to find out if crime rates are the same all over US
- to find out about the Death Penalty
- any other valid aim.

(*d*) Candidates are required to state and justify an appropriate method of enquiry.

Two methods must be addressed for full marks.

Answers may include:
- can plan questions in advance
- should be knowledgeable about situation in their own city
- can ask supplementary questions
- relaxed, informal interview with someone you know
- first hand information
- can record answers and refer to them later.

(*e*) Candidates are required to state and justify an appropriate method of enquiry.

Two methods must be addressed for full marks.

Answers may include:
- can use the statistics which give 'Violent crime figures'
- these show how states differ and will make a good graph to use in the investigation
- can read and use the 'Crime in the USA – Special Report' on pages 10 and 11
- might have more statistics, information and figures for the investigation
- can sign up for a weekly e-mail on youth crime
- will be kept up to date and get very recent figures to use in the investigation.

CHINA

3B. (*a*) The concept being assessed is Participation. Candidates are required to provide detailed descriptions.

Two ways are required for full marks.

Answers may include:
- polling clerk helping to count vote in village/township elections
- becoming a member of the Communist Party
- voting at the Communist Party Congress
- taking part in a protest march/demonstration, eg residents of the eastern Chinese city of Xiamen have blocked construction of a chemical plant with a text message campaign.

(*b*) Candidates are required to provide evidence to support and oppose a given point of view.

Two pieces of evidence are required for full marks.

Answers may include:

Support the view
- Kathy Lou says, "Unemployment has increased in all selected regions".

Evidence to support
- Unemployment in Beijing has increased from 0·8% to 2·5%, in Guangdong from 3·0% to 3·7% and in Henan from 3·0% to 4·8%.

Oppose the view
- Kathy Lou says, "The region with lowest rate of unemployment in 2006 has the highest average monthly income".

Evidence to oppose
- Beijing has lowest unemployment with 2·5% yet Guangdong's average wage is $11 higher.

(*c*) Candidates are required to give relevant aims for the investigative topic.

Two aims must be given for full marks.
- to find out if the crime rates are the same in all regions of China
- to find out whether youth crime is a problem in China
- to find out what types of crime are most common in China
- to find out about the Death Penalty
- any other valid aim.

(*d*) Candidates are required to state and justify an appropriate method of enquiry.

Two advantages must be given for full marks.

Answers may include:
- can plan questions in advance
- should be knowledgeable about situation in their own city
- can ask supplementary questions
- relaxed, informal interview with someone you know
- first hand information
- can record answers and refer to them later.

(*e*) Candidates are required to state and justify an appropriate method of enquiry.

Two methods must be addressed for full marks.

Answers may include:
- can use the statistics which give 'Violent crime figures'
- these show how parts of China differ and will make a good graph to use in the investigation
- can read and use the 'Crime in China' – special report on pages 10 and 11
- might have more statistics, information and figures for the investigation
- can sign up for weekly e-mail on youth crime
- will be kept up-to-date and get very recent figures to use in the investigation.

Syllabus Area 4 – International Relations

4. (*a*) The concept being assessed is Need. Candidates are required to provide detailed descriptions.

Answers may include:

War/Conflict
- Health care unable to cope with casualties/civilian casualties
- Increased numbers of orphaned children
- No foreign investment
- No agricultural produce
- Refugees

Debt
- Unable to invest in schools, hospitals etc
- Obligation to richer countries
- Dependency on Aid

HIV/AIDS
- Strain on health services
- Orphans
- Falling population affects economy

Unsafe water
- Disease
- Strain on medical services
- Low incomes.

(*b*) Candidates are required to detect exaggeration and provide explanations.

The correct responses are:

Statement 1
"A large percentage of the UK's population are undecided about the Treaty."

Reason 1
It is not a 'large' percentage. 'Don't know' is not only the smallest of the three responses to Question 1 in Source 2, but it is only 9%

Statement 2
"Most people agree with the UK government about a referendum on the Treaty."

Reason 2
In Source 1 it states the government doesn't think a referendum is necessary but the majority appear to disagree in Source 2, Question 2. Almost 75% answered 'Yes'.

(*c*) The concept being assessed is Power. Candidates are required to provide detailed explanations.

Answers may include:
- co-operation between member states eg 2008 banking crisis
- Regional Aid bringing investment and jobs eg Rosyth ferry, infrastructure in the Highlands and Islands
- freedom of movement eg large numbers of Poles now working in UK to fill the 'skills gap'
- qualifications recognised so can work/study in 27 countries
- larger market for products manufactured in their country ie improved trade

- Regional Aid has raised living standards especially in poorer parts of Europe
- opinion polls show that the majority of EU citizens are happy living in the EU.

(*d*) Candidates are required to express support for a personal point of view with valid reasons.

Two pieces of evidence are required for full marks.

The correct responses are:

For Project A – New Factories
- Wages are $1000 for permanent workers which is twice the town's average income.
- Jobs are low skilled and require little education, which is good as only 58% of the town is literate.
- Wages are $1000 for permanent workers whilst at the moment, half of the people in the town live on less than $1 per day.

For Project B – Schools
- 2000 children will get the chance to go to school; this is good as only 58% are literate.
- 100 teachers will earn $1200, which is more than double the town's average.
- 100 teachers will earn $1200, whilst, at the moment, half of the people in the town live on less than $1 per day.

MODERN STUDIES CREDIT 2009

Syllabus Area 1 – Living In A Democracy

1. (*a*) The concept being assessed is Participation. Candidates are required to use their understanding of the concept to provide explanations in depth and detail.

Answers may include:
- joining a political party eg Liberal Democrats and actively supporting them
- attending political meetings
- watching Party Election Broadcasts, reading election literature
- helping a candidate during the campaign eg putting up posters, handing out leaflets
- canvassing with a candidate in the local area
- contributing financially to an election campaign.

(*b*) The concept being assessed is Responsibilities. Candidates are required to use their understanding of the concept to provide explanations in depth and detail.

Answers may include:
- inform the police before a demonstration
  - enables the police to plan and have enough officers available, close routes
  - people might get hurt, chaos can ensue if police not informed
- keep protests within the law
  - the law is designed to protect citizens
  - group might lose respect or political support
- represent members' views
  - people joined in good faith, let down if their views are ignored
  - membership would fall if group seen as irresponsible
- only use accurate information during campaigns
  - group could be prosecuted if they make false claims.

(*c*) Candidates are required to detect and explain examples of lack of objectivity in complex sources, giving developed argument when required.

For full marks, all three sources must be used.

Answers may include:

In 2007 there were more MSPs in favour of independence then ever before.

Source 1

The SNP and the Green Party are in favour of independence. The overall numbers in favour of independence increased from 34 out of 129 MSPs in 2003 to 49 MSPs in 2007. This shows that Callum is correct.

The West of Scotland Region had the largest increase in voter turnout.
Source 2
The turnout did increase in the West (by 3·2%). However, in Lothian Region it increased by 3·5%. Therefore, Callum is incorrect.

...since the establishment of the Scottish Parliament people feel more Scottish.
Source 3
In 1999 25% of people said they felt more Scottish than British. This increased to 32% in 2006. Therefore, Callum is correct.
Overall, Callum was correct in two statements and incorrect in one.

The conclusion as to the degree of selectivity is that overall, he was being **slightly** selective.

Syllabus Area 2 – Changing Society

2. (*a*) The concept being assessed is Ideology. Candidates are required to use understanding of the concept to provide detailed descriptions with relevant examples and appropriate generalisations.

Candidates are required to describe two policies.

Answers may include:

Educational Maintenance Allowance
- A weekly payment of between £10 – 30 paid directly to young people from low-income families who continue to attend full time education in school or college.
- This may then improve their qualifications and therefore job prospects when they eventually leave.
- Bonuses are awarded if attendance and attainment targets are achieved, thus motivating pupils from poorer families.

New Deal
- Helps unemployed people to find a job as part of the governments "Welfare to Work" strategy.
- Gives the unemployed new opportunities to gain new skills and work experience, and makes them more employable. A personal adviser will provide support until they are ready for work.
- Gives subsidies and training grants to employers to take on unemployed people. The unemployed can claim benefits and help with transport costs.

Child Benefit
- A regular payment for each child under the age of 16, or up to 19 if in full time education or training.
- It is not means tested and is available to all parents to help pay the cost of bringing up children.
- In 2009, parents received £20 per week for the eldest child and £13·10 for each additional child.

Child Tax Credits
- A regular payment from the government to help with the everyday cost of caring for children.
- It is means tested, but 9 out of 10 families with children get it. The amount received varies depending on income, so poor families get more.
- It is paid directly to the main carer to make sure it is more likely to benefit the children.

Sure Start
- A government initiative to provide the best start in life for every child, especially in the early years (0-3).
- It encourages close cooperation between education, social work, health services and voluntary groups to meet the needs of families with young children.
- Help is to be targeted to the poorest and most deprived areas of the country.

Child Trust Fund
- A tax-free savings account set up by the government for each child born on or after 1 September 2002. Any money put into this cannot be taken out until the child reaches 18.
- The government puts £250 into the account to start it off, with a further £250 on each child's seventh birthday. Children from poorer families receive more than this.
- Parents and family can put money into this account for the children as well.

(*b*) Candidates are required to provide evidence to support and oppose a given point of view.

The correct responses are:

View of Asif Iqbal
"Pakistani households have had a bigger fall in poverty than all other ethnic groups."

Reason to support:
Source 1 shows that they have fallen by 15% from 70% in 2000 to 55% in 2005. All other groups fell less than this, with Bangladeshis being closest at 13%.

View of Asif Iqbal
"The group with the smallest increase in hourly pay had the smallest drop in poverty."

Reason to oppose:
Source 2 shows that Blacks had the lowest pay increase of only £0·29 and Source 1 shows that White households had the smallest fall in poverty from 22% down to 18% – a fall of only 4% compared to a fall of 7% for the black group.

(*c*) Candidates are expected to make comparisons within and between complex sources and draw valid conclusions from them with justification using developed argument when required.

The correct answers are:

The relationship between education and unemployment.
Using Source 3 and Source 4, it is clear that those boroughs with the best education tend to have lower

unemployment. For example, Sutton has the highest % of pupils with 5 or more exam passes (70·8%) and it also has the lowest unemployment rate (4·9%)

The relationship between total crime and income.
Using Source 2 and Source 4, it is clear that the boroughs with the lowest income tend to have higher total crime. For example, Newham, Brent and Barking and Dagenham had the highest total crime. They are also the 3 with the lowest income.

The borough whose ethnic mix is most like that of London as a whole.
Using "Focus on London" and Source 1, it is clear that Kensington and Chelsea is most like London as a whole. It is closest to the London % for 4 groups (White, Black, Bangladeshi and Chinese), second closest for 2 others (Pakistani and Others), and third closest for Indian.

The borough that would be the most desirable to live in.
Sutton would be most desirable because it has the highest % of pupils attaining 5 or more exam passes, the lowest crime rate, the lowest unemployment rate and the second highest average income.
OR
Kensington and Chelsea would be most desirable as Source 4 shows that it has by far the highest weekly income of £818·40 which is £312 higher than Sutton.

Syllabus Area 3 – Ideologies

THE USA

3A. (*a*) The concept being assessed is Equality. Candidates are required to use understanding of the concept to provide detailed descriptions followed by detailed explanations with relevant examples and appropriate generalisations.

Answers that do not mention detailed American examples should be awarded a maximum of 5 marks.

Answers may include:

Education
- The inequality is that lower attainment leads to poor employment prospects for some groups.
- Some Americans attend and stay on at excellent schools, others do not and may drop out early.
- Asians and Whites are most likely to complete education, followed by Black Americans with Hispanics the least likely.

Health
- The inequality is that there is poorer health for some minority groups.
- Black Americans having the highest death rates.
- Some Americans can afford private health, others may have to rely on Medicare and Medicaid.
- Whites are most likely and Hispanics least likely to have private health insurance.
- Asians/Hispanics can have much lower death rates.

Employment/Unemployment
- The inequality is that some groups have poorer incomes.
- Most Americans are in work but some cannot find work due to poorer qualifications.
- Asians/Whites are the ethnic groups most likely to be employed, Blacks/Hispanics the least.
- The recent economic changes have hit some groups more than others.

Wealth/Poverty
- Asians/Whites are the ethnic groups with the highest incomes followed by Hispanics and Black Americans.
- Many Americans have a wealthy lifestyle due to a good job and pay – The American Dream.
- Some Americans have a very low income due to unemployment or low pay.
- American government welfare payments are low.
- This leads to poverty for some groups.

Prejudice and Discrimination
- Inequality in all of the above can be the result of discrimination on the basis of race, gender, religion and nationality.

(*b*) Candidates are required to provide evidence to support and oppose a point of view.

Answers must make explicit links between the background information about The Illegal Immigration Debate and Sources 1 and 2.

Answers may include:

For Corrine Padilla
- Corrine says, "I, like many Californians, feel that illegal immigrants in California are exploited. My first priority will be to improve their pay and working conditions." This is **true** as 'Many Californians are concerned that illegal immigrants often live and work as 'modern-day slaves' because they work for low wages.
- Corrine says, "… many Californians are not in favour of a high-tech fence". This is **true** as the statistics show that 59% of Californians say no to a high-tech fence', which is many.
- Corrine says, 'California needs workers to come and help our farmers pick their crops'. This is **true** as 53% of farming workers and 90% of crop pickers in California are illegal immigrants.

Against Corrine Padilla
- Corrine says, "I am not concerned about illegal immigration as the numbers entering the US are not rising steeply". This is **wrong** as the USA Illegal Immigration graph shows they are rising steeply, from 0·1 million in 1990 to 0·9 million in 2005.
- Corrine says, "We do not need to increase the number of Border guards and most Californians agree with me". This is **wrong** as the statistics show that 71% of Californians say yes to increasing the number of border guards.

For Peter Head

- Peter says, "Illegal immigrants already in California cost a lot of money. Because of this they should become legal citizens so that they pay their taxes". This is **true** as illegal immigrants cost $650 million healthcare, $2·2 billion education and $5 billion overall which is a lot of money.
- Peter says, "The high-tech fence should not be built as it will not protect all of the California/Mexico border". This is **true** as the map shows the border is 140 miles long and the high-tech fence is in two parts only 67 miles long.
- Peter says, "The money saved by not having the high-tech fence would be better spent on more guards patrolling the border, which is what Californians want." This is **true** as the statistics show that 71% of Californians say yes to more border guards.

Against Peter Head

- Peter says, "California only has a very small percentage of all US illegal immigrants." This is **wrong** as California has one-third of the US total, which is 33% and so not a very small %.
- Peter says, "I, like most Californians, believe that illegal immigrants take the jobs that Californians want". This is **wrong** as 70% of Californians think that illegal immigrants are doing jobs that others do not want.

CHINA

3B. (*a*) The concept being assessed is Equality. Candidates are required to use understanding of the concept to provide detailed descriptions followed by detailed explanations with relevant examples and appropriate generalisations.

Candidates must link the description of the inequality which exists with the reasons why it exists.

Answers may include:

Rural/Urban

- Economic inequalities exist between rural and urban Chinese. Chinese in urban areas earn up to 3 times that of rural Chinese. Lack of industry and a reliance on farming mean income is low in the countryside.
- Those Chinese who live in "Special Economic Zones" are allowed to start up their own business and keep the profit through the "Socialist Market Economy". These Chinese are wealthier than others living outwith these zones.
- Increased wealth has given some Chinese access to better housing, education and the opportunity to buy consumer goods. Many more Chinese in urban areas now own freezers, PC's, televisions and cars compared to those in rural areas.

Housing/Education

- Within the urban areas, inequality exists between rich and poor. Migrant workers live in slum conditions on the outskirts of cities whereas those skilled workers who are employed by foreign companies based in China earn higher wages and can afford better quality housing.
- Members of the Communist party have access to better housing and education than those who are not members of the party.
- Poor levels of education in the countryside mean that many Chinese are only educated to primary level and therefore have to rely on low paid jobs. Few make it to university from the countryside.

Gender

- There continues to be gender inequality within the Communist Party. Although there has been some success in recent years there are still fewer women candidates than men.

Health

- The standard of healthcare is lower in the countryside than in urban areas as there are fewer hospitals and a shortage of medical staff; people in these areas rely on traditional Chinese medicine.
- The new rich in China may also be able to afford to travel abroad to access medical treatments there.

(*b*) Candidates are required to provide evidence to support and oppose a point of view.

Answers must make explicit links between the background information about the Migration Debate and Sources 1 and 2.

Answers may include:

For Liu Wang

- Liu says, "I want to see temporary migrant workers being made permanent residents to stop them being exploited". It is **true** that many are exploited as they often have their wages withheld by their employer and many (74%) Beijing residents agree with Liu and would like them to become permanent.
- President Hu Jintao has promised greater spending on health and education in rural areas to reduce the differences which exist between there and the cities. Liu believes that something must be done to raise the standard of living in the countryside. Therefore, the evidence supports Liu Wang.
- 62% say 'No' to additional taxes being imposed on people moving to the city. This is **true** as it agrees with Liu's opinion when he says that it is no good punishing workers who move to the city with additional taxes and that most people agree with him.

Against Liu Wang

- Liu says many migrants are college educated or better. This is **wrong** as in the information it shows us the educational background and only a very small % are college/university educated, most are educated to junior high school level or less.
- Liu Wang believes that Chinese citizens think they should look after themselves. This is **wrong** because over half of Beijing residents believe that foreign firms ought to invest in rural development when they locate in China.

For Cho Yuen

- Cho believes that the income which migrant workers send home to the countryside is vital to the rural economy and that it should continue. This is **true** as urban workers can earn three times that of rural workers and the money they send home helps to look after aging parents and pay for siblings to study.
- China has become the 'workshop of the world' and Cho says that she is not alone in thinking that foreign firms should invest in rural China. This is **true** as 52% of Beijing residents believe that foreign firms ought to invest in rural China's development.
- Until education in the countryside improves, Cho wants to work to allow migrants to come to Beijing to gain basic schooling. This is a reason to **support** Cho as few (1%) have college/university education, only 4% have completed high school and 2% have no education. This accentuates the wealth gap.

Against Cho Yuen

- Cho thinks that the numbers moving to the cities are small and are not rising steeply. This is **wrong**. Between 1990 and 2005, the urban population will have increased by 200 million and by 2020, 60% of China's population will live in towns and cities.
- Cho's first priority is to encourage further migration as migrants fit in well and make Beijing a better place to live. **This is not a priority that people would support** as many feel that the cities cannot cope with the growing number of migrants as there is a shortage of housing, hospitals, power and transport. It is also claimed that migrants are responsible for 70% of crime.

Syllabus Area 4 – International Relations

4. (*a*) The concept being assessed is Power. Candidates are required to use their understanding of the concept to provide descriptions in depth and detail.

Answers may include:

Threats – International Terrorism

- 9/11 attacks, London underground bombings, Madrid bombings, Bali bombings, Glasgow airport attack.

Responses

- Airport security – reduction in hand luggage, stricter security checks, armed police, increased use of 'Sky marshals' by some airlines, new 'Borders Agency'.
- Counter-terrorism Bill, length of detention.
- Heightened security in UK generally eg Houses of Parliament.
- MI5 has doubled in size since 2000.
- Removal of easy targets eg litter bins in tube stations.
- Architects encouraged to think of security eg Emirates Stadium and Scottish Parliament building.
- Introduction of ID cards.
- Invasion of Afghanistan and Iraq as part of the 'War on Terror'.

Threats – Nuclear proliferation

- Attempts by some countries to build nuclear weapons eg, North Korea, Iran.

Responses

- Sanctions placed on trade etc through the UN Security Council.
- Diplomatic discussions.
- Aid used as bargaining tool.
- US missile defence system built across Europe.

Threats – Russian Aggression

- Russian aircraft straying into foreign airspace eg UK, Georgia, Ukraine.
- Russian military action against neighbours eg in Georgia.
- Use of Oil reserves to force cooperation from the west and some neighbours, eg Ukraine.
- Alexander Litvinenko affair.

Responses

- UK aircraft scrambled to intercept Russian planes.
- Protests to UN and direct to Russian government.
- Georgian army opposed Russian invasion but to little effect.
- 'Tit for tat' diplomatic expulsions between UK and Russia.
- US missile defence system and willingness of states like Georgia to join NATO.

(*b*) Candidates are required to state a hypothesis relevant to the issue of 'HIV/Aids in Africa'.

The following receive 1 mark:

- HIV/Aids causes serious problems in Africa.
- A lot of aid is given to help with HIV/Aids in Africa.

The following receive 2 marks

- Better education would help with the problems caused by HIV/Aids in Africa.
- Botswana cannot afford to feed and educate the numbers of 'Aids orphans' it has.

(*c*) Candidates are required to state aims relevant to their hypothesis.

For example:

Hypothesis: "Botswana cannot afford to feed and educate the numbers of 'Aids orphans' it has."

- To find out what has happened to the numbers of orphans in recent years.
- To find out the specific health problems facing orphans.
- To find out how UK aid is helping in Botswana.
- To find out what action Botswana's government is taking to tackle the problems.

(*d*) Candidates are required to describe the factors which determine the validity of a method of enquiry.

Answers may include:

- sample size, eg 10 – 1000. It makes a difference
- type of sample eg random or stratified
- type of questions eg open or closed
- phone, postal, face to face
- time of day
- location.

(*e*) Candidates are required to demonstrate an awareness of the benefits or limitations of a method for the collection of information relevant to a topic.

The correct answer is:

- "EU expansion or EU growth – The benefits explained"

This is the only result that deals with "benefits" and it is the most up to date result. (ie 9/5/2009)

Hey! I've done it

BrightRED PUBLISHING

Published by Bright Red Publishing Ltd, 6 Stafford Street, Edinburgh, EH3 7AU
Tel: 0131 220 5804, Fax: 0131 220 6710, enquiries: sales@brightredpublishing.co.uk,
www.brightredpublishing.co.uk

Official SQA answers to 978-1-84948-022-2
2006-2009

[BLANK PAGE]

Acknowledgements

Permission has been sought from all relevant copyright holders and Bright Red Publishing is grateful for the use of the following:
The UNICEF logo © UNICEF (2006 General page 15);
The FAO logo © Food and Agriculture Organization of the United Nations (2006 General page 15);
The WHO logo, reproduced with permission of WHO (2006 General page 15);
The Europa webpage © European Communities (2007) (2006 General page 19);
A table from the Home Office Citizenship Survey (Statistics Directorate), September 2004 © Crown Copyright. Reproduced under the terms of the Click-Use Licence (2006 Credit page 3);
Logos for New Deal and EMA © Crown Copyright. Reproduced under the terms of the Click-Use Licence (2006 Credit page 4);
The logos for Skillseekers and Modern Apprenticeships are the property of Scottish Enterprise and Skills Development Scotland. Reproduced with permission (2006 Credit page 4);
The logo for the UK Independence Party (2006 Credit page 23);
The Liberal Democrats logo (2006 Credit page 23);
The logo for the Labour Party (2006 Credit page 23);
The logo for the Conservative Party (2006 Credit page 23);
The UNICEF flag © UNICEF (2007 General page 16);
A drawing containing The United Nations flag © The United Nations (2007 General page 16);
The logo for the SNP (2008 General page 3);
The logo for the Conservative Party (2008 General page 3);
The logo for the Labour Party (2008 General page 3);
The Liberal Democrats logo (2008 General page 3);
Logo for EMA © Crown Copyright. Reproduced under the terms of the Click-Use Licence (2009 page 6);
Logo for Sure Start © Crown Copyright. Reproduced under the terms of the Click-Use Licence (2009 page 6);
Logo for Child Trust Fund © Crown Copyright. Reproduced under the terms of the Click-Use Licence (2009 page 6);
The logo for The Organisation of American States © The Organisation of American States (2009 page 12).